ॐ

TECHNOLOGY FOR REVOLUTION

TECHNOLOGY FOR REVOLUTION

OPPORTUNITY
FOR

A NEW RELIGION
AND
A NEW SOCIETY

by

Mithilesh Kumar Jha

Technology for Revolution
Opportunity for A New Religion and A New Society

Author : **Mithilesh Kumar Jha**
Phone : +91-9818935615
Email : mithilesh.jha@kaizenprofessional.com

First Edition   :   16 March 2014
फाल्गुन शुक्ल पुर्णिमा

Price   : US$ 9.95
                   : US Dollar Nine and Ninety Five Cents

ISBN   13   : 978-14-99341-63-8
ISBN 10   : 14-99341-63-6

Publisher   : **Nayee Kitab**
                   1/11829, 1st Floor, Panchsheel Garden
                   Naveen Shahdara, Delhi-110032
                   Phone : +91 11 22825606
                   e-mail : nayeekitab@gmail.com

Soft copy of this work can be obtained by sending an email to the author or can be downloaded from http://tinyurl.com/l9rqvjt.

Printed at   : AARVEE Printers Private Limited,
                   B-235, Naraina Industrial Area Ph-I,
                   New Delhi-110028
                   Phone – 91-11-41410627/28

Cover Design   : Maheshwar

THIS WORK IS DEDICATED

TO

**GOD
ALMIGHTY**

IT IS YOUR CREATION.

You
as the mind
that is identified with my name
thought of it.

You typed it
using the body that is identified with my name.

It is your work and it is being presented to you
In your form as all the human beings on this planet

त्वदीयं वस्तु गोविन्द तुभ्यमेव समर्पये

CONTENTS

THINK OF A PLANET IX

ACKNOWLEDGEMENTS XI

ABOUT THE AUTHOR XIII

FOREWORD XV

PREFACE XIX

INTRODUCTION 1

MOMENTS OF TRUTH 9

FROM DARKNESS TO LIGHT 17

THE BUSINESS OF RELIGION 33

MY INDIA 71

POLITICS IN INDIA 103

UNIVERSAL AND GLOBAL MANIFESTO 125

THE ROAD MAP 167

APPENDIX 191

ABOUT THE BOOK 215

THINK OF A PLANET

THINK OF A PLANET

Where people voluntarily do only what is right

Where countries do not fight

Where no firearm is in sight

Where every face is shining bright

Where the path of humanity is guided by divine light

Where the universal humanism is stronger than animal might

THINK OF A PLANET

Where everyone gets what they need

And there is no place for greed

Where anger, envy and hatred are nowhere to be found

Where love, compassion and kindness are all around

Where peace and prosperity abound

Where true paradise is experienced by all on the ground

THINK OF A PLANET

Where the mind is at peace and the soul is in bliss

Where everyone is free to focus his mind

Where no one feels to have been left behind

Where everything is seen as divine

Where we and us replaces I, me and mine

Where Ganga and Yamuna is as clean as Thames and Rhine

THINK OF A PLANET

Where art and science complement each other

Where people treat people as their own brother

Where opposite views are heard with respect and tolerance

Where there is no place for rape, arson or violence

Where everyone does his best to help and care for the rest

Where all are happy, healthy, creative & constructive at their best

THINK OF A PLANET

Where all thoughts are progressive

Where technology is not used for anything destructive

Where there is unity in diversity

Where the whole society is a divine university

Where Buddha, Jesus, Mohammad and Krishna dance together

Where they sing, "we are brothers and sons of same father"

THINK OF A PLANET

Where everyone is treated with dignity and respect

Where nature and environment do not have to face neglect

Where constructive thoughts and creativity are at its best

Where peace and progress spans north to south and east to west

Where mind is without fear, relaxed and at rest

Where everyone is filled with happiness, health and zest

ACKNOWLEDGEMENTS

First and foremost, I would like to express my gratitude to God, Almighty who chose the entity identified with my name as the medium to bring this work before all. It is His grace which annihilated the ego that I used to identify myself with. Had the ego remained in the form "I", this work would not have been possible.

I am thankful to my grandparents who sowed the seeds in me for this work. It is because of the environment, love and care that I received under them while I was still in my formative years that I could develop a particular way of thinking. This work is a result of the thought process that they nurtured in a highly impressionable young child.

I am indebted to my parents and the members of my family, particularly my wife Shwetika and my children Aakriti and Aakarsh who have supported me through this work.

I would like to express my deep sense of gratitude to all the teachers who transformed a raw animal into someone capable of producing this work. The teachers in Netarhat School have made a significant contribution in shaping my beliefs in me and about my potential.

One of the important persons behind this work has been my senior in school, Prof. Manindra Nath Thakur of Jawaharlal Nehru University, Delhi, who continuously encouraged me to focus on it until this task came to an end.

I am thankful to my friends, colleagues and other co-workers who helped me with their valuable inputs and comments on the various ideas presented in this work. I am grateful to Kishan Kaljayee - the editor of Sablog, Anupal Kalia and Sanghamitra Choudhury for their special support and help in finishing this work.

Last but not the least: I beg forgiveness of all those who have been supporting me over the course of the years and whose names I have failed to mention here.

Mithilesh Kr Jha
March 2014, New Delhi.

ABOUT THE AUTHOR

Name – Mithilesh Kumar Jha

Education.-
PGDFM (IGNOU, New Delhi)
B. Tech. (Civil Engg., IIT Delhi)
I. Sc. – Science College, Patna
Schooling- Netarhat School, Jharkhand and
Primary & Middle School, Rahua Sangram, Bihar

Place of Birth - Patna (Bihar)

Mithilesh has been an engineer and business manager with 25+ years of professional experience. He has worked with some of the globally reputed large business organizations in the areas of engineering, construction and project management, corporate real estate, IT infrastructure services and related fields. He has held senior corporate leadership positions for more than a decade.

Besides the numerous professional and corporate training seminars and conferences, Mithilesh has attended a number of other personal effectiveness and empowerment programs. He has attended a number of courses on NLP, Hypnosis, Pranic Healing, Yoga, Zen and Holistic Healing. He has attended a ten day Vippassana meditation course. Additionally, he has also attended the Forum and Advanced Course of the Landmark Education and the Basic Course of the Art of Living. Besides, he has attended a number of other spiritual retreats and camps. He considers himself to be the richest person in the world defining the richest as the one who needs the least and not the one who has accumulated the most. He also claims to be spiritually enlightened.

Mithilesh believes in the unlimited potential of the human mind. He has been helping people through his self designed personal empowerment seminars wherein he helps people realize why they do what they do and how to move away from "as is" to the desired states of physical, social and professional environment.

FOREWORD

Humanity is passing through difficult times. The trust deficit, fear, anger and constant provocation of animal instincts have become the order of the day. The knowledge of the nature that we have developed over the centuries is being directed towards the destruction of the nature itself. The famous physicist, Stephen Hawking, explaining about the motivating factor behind his 'Zero Gravity Flight', that is, being in the space where the gravitational force is zero said that he wanted to experience the future habitation of human beings, as there was a real danger that the earth would become unlivable in the course of time due to natural disasters and nuclear wars but more so due to the new weapons of mass destruction that are in the offing. His apprehensions appear to be scary.

Perhaps we need to ask ourselves as to why humanity has reached to this situation; why the human mind is producing inhuman thinking. The idea of enlightenment promised us a better world, a world with an organizing principle based on the concepts of 'LIBERTY, EQUALITY AND FRATERNITY'. It promised us, an 'age of reason', democracy and justice. However, one would agree, that the world that we are living in, is hardly representing the promises of the enlightenment.

Human beings have tremendous ability to diagnose the problems that they face and also to innovate solutions thereof by using their unique capacity of creative thinking. The journey of human beings' social and political organizations is witness to this as every time they were unhappy with the state of affairs, they worked hard to change them refusing to live with the frozen circumstances.

We are living in a special moment. On the one hand, there is a real danger of destruction of the human species, as Hawking feels, due to growing distrust and proliferation of instruments of mass destruction; on the other hand, it is a time of upsurge in creative thinking. Globally speaking, there are numerous people's movements to save humanity, save nature and to transform the social and political systems. The dominant framework of defining human beings' relation with nature, with the self and with the other human beings based on the philosophy of Enlightenment is being questioned. The fundamental principles governing the production and distribution of resources and the political and social intuitions are under scrutiny. The anti-graft movements, Occupy Wall Street or Arab Spring are only symptoms of dissatisfaction of the human beings with the existing state of affairs.

Ours is the time of churning for new set of philosophies, institutions and imaginations. It is time to think beyond the boundaries set by the project of Enlightenment; perhaps, it is time for new Enlightenment. It is with this backdrop that we need to look at the book written by Mithilesh K. Jha. As he keeps saying, this is not an end product but an invitation for a democratic dialogue with one goal in mind that the humanity has to survive this crisis and if the needs arise, we have to rethink religion, culture, nation, politics etc. This book opens up so many issues for rigorous debates and provokes one to think. The first issue is that of religion and he proposes that there are no religions but one Religion, which is not about rituals but about spirituality. The idea of separation of religion and politics does not arise if one takes this seriously as he proposes a model of spiritual politics or politics as a profession in the service of humanity. This calls for an ethical training of the people interested in politics. He argues that a politician without spiritual bent of mind and without proper ethical training will distort any constitution whatsoever it may be. The best of the constitutions would produce worst of the result if the politics is defined as pursuit of the self interest. Therefore, religion for him is the resource of spirituality and it is true of all the so called religions. This reminds one of Gandhi, Ambedkar and Tagore as they have also proposed similar understanding of religion. Vaishnawism for Gandhi, Buddha for Ambedkar and Baul for Tagore provided similar inspiration for the politics of unconditional love. It is interesting to note that Mithilesh, without being a formal student of philosophy or politics, has arrived on the same conclusion that is being endorsed by many of the contemporary philosophers.

The framework of politics has many more complex layers to offer. He thinks that one should decide to enter into the formal arena of politics only if one has completed one's duty as householder so that one can have feeling of devotion towards the well being of the human race as a whole; one can think beyond the boundaries of caste, community or nation. There are series of institutional reforms he has to offer. Many of them depend on the assumption that in future, the technology would help us resolve issues that seem to be complicated at the moment. For instance, he thinks that the model of representation available in the democratic system of today is highly limited. The timeframe for representation normally is five years. Now, in the age of fast communication, such an idea of representation is not only obsolete and outdated but self defeating. The recent movements in the different part of the world have raised this issue. He suggests that the available technology provides an opportunity to collect public opinion on every issue without much expenditure. Therefore, there should be change in the models of representation too. In fact, these proposals may sound too Utopian and technology dependent however, one would agree that they are worth considering.

This text has many more ideas to offer and in the age of intellectual churning, many of them are merely implicit instead of being explicit. The idea that our education system should be drastically reformed is one of them. The huge structure of university systems, according to the text, needs major transformation. The traditional class room teaching system should be replaced by availability of technology based resources. The knowledge seeking individuals should be able to acquire information as much as possible. This does not mean that human interaction in education is not needed. In fact, he suggests that there should be qualitative interaction instead of unnecessary and unfruitful engagements.

In short, the text is a vision document with the signature of time on it. The author is transparent and modest. He has nothing to hide and expects the reader to be equally transparent in order to initiate a live dialogue for the future of humanity. The canvas is huge as it covers the project of universal human liberation. I am sure thinking with Mithilesh will give sleepless nights to many of us and that should be considered as signs of success as the text aims at provoking us to commit to an idea, which is crucial for the survival of the humanity.

Prof. Manindra Nath Thakur
Centre for Political Studies
Jawaharlal Nehru University
New Delhi 110067

PREFACE

1.   "हरि ॐ तत् सत्". This is the beginning and the end of my understanding and all that I want to say through this work. This is so because if someone has truly understood the meaning behind this four syllable phrase, he or she need not read this or any other book. Any other book or any other attempt to transmit this understanding through words would be limited to the capacity of the linguistic abilities and vocabulary of the person trying to transmit the essence of this understanding. That would have the limitation that is always there in an attempt to describe the whole with part and the unknown with the known. The words carrying the message would be limited to their meaning and would not be able to convey the whole truth that is intended to be transmitted through this phrase or mantra. This is my humble attempt to dwell on this subject with my very limited English language vocabulary. This is my attempt to convey that God, irrespective of the name by which we are trained to perceive and conceive Him, viz. ईश्वर, अल्लाह, ख़ुदा, ब्राह्मण, परमात्मा, परमपिता, रहमान, रहीम etc. is the only truth. I believe an attempt to utter the sound (if that sound could be uttered) associated with ॐ would have been sufficient to convey the message to those who already know the truth. This work is to help those seekers who are yet to have achieved the state of full understanding of the truth but are on the path and sooner or later would have achieved the truth on their own without any external help or support from me or someone else. This work might help such seekers accelerate their pace to reach their ultimate goal.

2.   In the previous paragraph as well as here and in many subsequent paragraphs to come, "I" have used the phrase "I, me, my, mine etc." at many places. This phrase would be used to dwell upon and explain some particular and specific concept or meaning as the context may necessitate, however it is being clarified here that this work is purely the result of a totally detached action. These words have been dictated to or typed through the physical body that is being carried out and used in my name without "I" having to do anything with this work. I believe there is no trace of "I", the ego or the belief in an individual and distinct identity, left anymore in my case. I know the whole universe is my home and all humanity is my family. This work is based on certain assumptions and one of the

core assumption is that all of us are entwined with each other because of we all sharing a common origin and root. Any attempt to make a change in an individual would not be complete until all of us are part of that change and that change is applied to the root.

3.   I am aware of the intrinsic and natural thrust and hunger in the consciousness of every individual for the realization and understanding of the ultimate truth and the purpose of their existence. I am also aware of the hindrances and other road blocks being faced by each and every individual in their conscious and unconscious efforts to realize and understand this ultimate truth. This work is an attempt to help people understand why they are where they are and what has been preventing them from reaching where they actually have been attempting to go. Substantial part of this work would focus on what went wrong where and why. It would also attempt to suggest the solutions and ways to correct the course.

4.   There have been many attempts in past to dwell upon this and related subjects by many people like Maharshi Ved Vyas, Kapil, Gautam, Kanad, Jaimini, Patanjali, Siddharth Gautam, Vardhman Mahaveer, Lao Tsu, Moses, Socrates, Jesus Christ, Prophet Mohammad, Karl Marx, Friedrich Engels, Martin Luther King, M K Gandhi, Nelson Mandela and many others. However, despite their best efforts and intentions, the combined consciousness of the world has taken a direction that has led to where it is today. This work is another attempt to relook at those same issues and questions that these people have already looked upon. This is an attempt to take note of the advancement in science and technology and the advent of internet, Google, Youtube, facebook, Twitter, Iphone, android etc. to present this subject once more before the humanity using these technology tools. This is an attempt to imagine and say what these people would have said if they had the luxury of sharing their thoughts with people across the world and then receiving the feedback on the meaning of their communication. Had these people known that their message and communication to the people would be interpreted in such a way that it would lead to the formation of distinct identity groups always eager to fight and finish each other; they would have definitely rephrased their messages and communication. Had they known that a time would come when some people, in the name of their messages, would be instigating

people to hurt others and their messages could be a possible reason for violence, corruption, misery and a cause for deviation from the actual path they intended to show, they would have packaged their messages and communication in a totally different way so that there were no scope for corruption, misery and grief to engulf the world. They intended to show a path which could lead to a happy and healthy world. They wanted an absolutely perfect physical body and eternal mental bliss for all. This work is an attempt to rediscover a path out of misery and sorrow to a state of happiness and bliss. The need and importance of a fresh packaging as per the specific requirements of the present day time and space to deliver the same old message was conveyed by Lord Krishna in Geeta when he said,

"यदा यदा हि धर्मस्य ग्लानिर्भवति भारत । अभ्युत्थानमधर्मस्य तदात्मानं सृजाम्यहम् ।।
परित्राणाय साधूनां विनाशाय च दुष्कृताम् । धर्मसंस्थापनार्थाय सम्भवामि युगे युगे ।।"

"yada yada hi dharmasya glanir bhavati bharat.
abhyutthanam adharmasya tadatmanam srijamyaham .
paritranaya sadhoonam vinashaya cha dushkritam
dharma-sansthapanaarthaya sambhavaami yuge yuge "

"Whenever and wherever there is decline in dharma and a predominant rise of adharma, I manifest myself time and again in every era to re-establish the principles of Dharma."

5.   The background to this work has been the socio-political issues being faced by the people that live within a geo-political boundary that is called India, however its application is intended to be applicable to the whole world. India is home to some 1.2 billion people, more than one sixth of the total number of approximately 7.1 billion people that live on this planet. India is, at present, the second most populous country in the world after China. It shares the same basic system of governance, viz. democracy that is followed in the United States of America which is often referred to as the most advanced, developed and strongest country on this planet. India's population comprises of more than two thousand ethnic groups and almost every major religion and language of the world is represented here. Its linguistic, cultural, geographical and ethnic diversity gives it a unique position in the world. This special position of India in the world provides a good opportunity to study the socio-political issues in India and then extrapolate the studies and findings

to the whole world. Secondly, since I was born and brought up in India and have lived here most of my life, it is easier for me to take references from the Indian society. I have been mentally active in the age when internet and information technology revolution has taken the world under its grip and the whole world has turned into a small village as far as the spreading of ideas and beliefs are concerned. The geo-political boundaries of the twentieth century world have absolutely no meaning today when it comes to the mental interaction between the people on this planet. The physical distance has lost its significance in the technology enabled virtual world that we are living in. Additionally, I have had the opportunity to travel to places like USA, UK, France, Germany, UAE, Saudi Arabia, Malaysia and China and interact with the local population in these countries. I have also had the opportunity to work together and have extensive interaction with colleagues from many more countries as part of my professional assignments with some of the large multi-national corporations. These colleagues helped me understand the issues being faced by the people from across the globe as well as their expectations and aspirations. This has facilitated me to understand the issues being faced by the humanity as a whole, even though most of the references and examples that would be used in this work would be mainly from the Indian perspective.

6.   There may be apparent contradictions in some of the thoughts and ideas being presented through this work. I am aware of this limitation, specifically, when I have taken upon me this daunting task of expressing in language what I myself feel is impossible to bind in words. A rational and analytical mind might come across many such points which may initially appear to be contradicting each other. However, once someone has gone through the entire text, preferably more than once, and the essence of what is intended to be presented through this work starts sinking in into his or her mind, there is a high probability that the questions related to those apparent contradictions would vanish on their own. Yet, I would request and appreciate an honest feedback on this work from the intelligent readers so that any query or issue which appears to have been left without an answer in this edition is further clarified in the subsequent editions.

7.   My way of thinking would appear to be influenced by and somewhere in between the thought process of Osho Rajneesh and Karl Marx. This is so because I have had the opportunity to study their thoughts. I consider them to be amongst the very few people in history who have had the opportunity to lead the minds of people and still they remained honest about what they said or did, particularly in terms of their genuine concern for the humanity. They said what they believed to be true without adding any personal and selfish interest or motive into it. On this consideration, my yardstick is Siddharth Gautam - the Buddha. These two great thinkers named above, measure very close to my expectations in terms of what they genuinely believed and what they said. Sant Kabir also meets my expectations on this measuring scale. While I have a lot of respect for many other spiritual and socio-political leaders including but not limited to the people like Swami Vivekanand, Swami Dayanand, Mahatma Gandhi, Nelson Mandela or Martin Luther King, I wish I could say the same for these people also what I have said for Marx, Osho, Kabir or Buddha. This does not mean that their contribution to the humanity is not significant. My certificate to them for what they did is not important and does not mean anything at this stage as I have no way to fully understand the circumstances under which they functioned specifically in terms of their space, time and the collective consciousness of the people around them. I also consider myself closer to the thought process of Charu Mazumdar, one of the founders of the CPI (M-L), with a difference that I am proposing the use of information and communication technology in the place of gun and bullet to achieve the same objectives that he wanted to achieve. At this stage, I am consciously aware that my refusal to accept something unless I am personally convinced about it may appear to be one of the limitations of this work. So be it.

My personal experiences of having grown up in a farmer family with mid size land holdings in a small village with modest means and my schooling in a highly subsidized government residential school with rich scholastic and cultural traditions may also become apparent at places in this work. The thought process associated with the philosophical traditions of Nyayashastra of Gautama, Mimamsa of Jaimini and Vedanta or Uttara Mimamsa of Ved Vyasa may also be visible at places in this work as the beliefs associated with these philosophical traditions were deeply rooted in the culture and traditions of the Mithila region of Bihar where I spent my formative years as a child under the care of my grandparents. I still remember the discussions and debates between the pundits and philosophers in the forecourt of my ancestral house with active participation of my grandfather in these discussions while I just listened, memorized and sometimes internalized what they uttered during the course of their chat. Many of the Sanskrit shlokas and their literal as well as contextual meaning that I remember till date was learned through this process and not by reading any text at a later stage.

8.   I was born in a so called Hindu Brahman family. Since childhood, I have been taught directly or indirectly, tacitly or openly that I am a Hindu, a Brahman, an Indian and so many other things through which I could put a label of distinct identity on my persona. All these teachings have also subtly implied that since I am distinct from other human beings, there exists a big difference between me and the people who do not belong to the same distinct identity group. I have been taught that because of these differences, I am better than the others. As a result of all these teachings, I am supposed to think that Hindus are better than Muslims, Brahmans are better than Chamaars, Indians are better than Pakistanis and so on. I have come to realise and understand that all these distinctions have been created by the vested interests to keep the general mass of the populace sedated with their perceived belief of superiority/inferiority with respect to others so that these vested interests could carry on with their agenda of perpetuating their rule and exploitation. I have been thinking and analyzing as to why this has happened. I have discovered that it has been a vicious cycle. The process of this cycle is very simple. It is very easy to create a dislike for whatever is different because most humans are normally born with this tendency as a result of their trainings and experiences during their previous births. All that it needs, then, is to make people believe that they are different and therefore superior to whoever is not like them. This helps the vested interests create the pressure groups or groups with aspirations and interests in direct conflict with the aspirations and interests of the other groups. This clash of interest results in physical violence and wastage of valuable resources which otherwise could have been used productively and in a positive manner. However, these clashes give an opportunity to the vested interests to carry on with their rule, exploitation and extortion. This

motivates others to join this elite group of exploiters and the cycle has been continuing ever since the beginning of history.

I would like to add that I am not a patriot as I believe that any artificial distinction between the human beings in the name of religion, caste, language, country or any other man made attribute which makes them feel that they belong to a particular and specific group is perpetrated by the vested interests in the general language and ignorant idiots in my own understanding. I would like to clarify that I not being a patriot does not mean that I am a traitor or a turncoat. I would rather be happy if my body gets an opportunity to repay its debt by serving the soil that has nourished it. However, when Allama Iqbal wrote "Sare Jehan Se Achchha Hindostan Hamara" in 1904, he would not have realized that this would someday be sung to generate hatred against the country that he would be a citizen of. I have been taught since my infancy that I am an Indian and therefore I am not a Pakistani or Chinese or Bangladeshi or American. I have been taught that I as an Indian is different from being a Pakistani and since we are different, my values as an Indian is better than the values of a Pakistani, Chinese or American. Since all the different groups with specific identities consider themselves to be better than the rest of others, this leads to a conflict between Indians and Pakistanis or Hindus and Muslims or speakers of Hindi and Tamil or black and white. This concept of "I am I and you are you and therefore, I and you are different and since we are different, I am better than you" is the root cause of all the evil encountered by the humanity in its true spiritual development and in this sense, I am not able to call myself a patriot because I cannot hate my brother from across an artificial and imaginary line drawn on the surface of mother earth. I am not able to identify myself with any particular caste or religion in the way I have been taught about these concepts since my childhood and yet I would like to call myself a religious person and a Brahman. As per my definition, a Brahman is the one who has awakened to the absolute truth. As per this definition, Kabir, Raidas, Nanak, Buddha, Jesus, Muhammad, Socrates, Gurdjieff, Lao Tzu, Ved Vyas, Patanjali, Osho, Krishnamurti, Raman, Telang Swami are all Brahmans and so am I and many others. When I call myself religious, I do not mean to say that I am "Hindu" in the sense the word is being used by the politicians these days. Being Hindu for me does not mean being the one who goes to a temple and worships idols or listens to Ram Katha or Shrimad Bhagwat or Geeta. For me, the word "Hindu" means the religious way of life that has evolved since the Indus Valley Civilization and which has been clearly visible in the way of life practiced by Buddha, Mahavir, Kabir, Nanak, Mother Teresa, Khwaja Moinuddin Chisti, Nizamuddin Auliya and many others who have carried their body in this part of the globe.

9.   I am able to visualize a spiritual model of governance and administration wherein there is no exploitation, there is no military or army and there is no undue restriction on free movement of men on this planet. I see a world order where everyone is happy, healthy and smiling. I see a world where there is no hunger, no enmity, no jealousy and no need for army and weapons of mass destruction. I have a very very strong belief that such a world order is possible despite the views of many others that this appears to be too idealistic, too optimistic and too romantic to be true. Some of the early indicators of this vision are already visible to all. The technology has already broken almost all the barriers of communication between the minds of people on this planet. The world is increasingly becoming smaller and smaller as far as the spreading of ideas and beliefs are concerned. The model of globalization has already brought all the economies of the world to be in sync with each other. All that we need now is to have a perfect sociopolitical model for governance and administration which could not only meet the physical and economic needs of the people but also their universal spiritual needs. The moment such an experiment takes place in a country, it would spread like a wild fire to the whole world. The whole planet would adopt that sociopolitical model of governance and administration. No government or vested interest group would be able to stop it. No opium of caste, creed, religion, nationalism or any other divide and rule formula would be able to stop this model from being adopted across the globe.

10.   I am aware that people like me have taken a lot from the society. The education that I received in the public funded residential school and in IIT Delhi has helped me reach in life where I am today. This education has had major positive impact in nurturing my mental growth and thinking process. The cost of this education was funded mostly by the tax payers in the society. Only a small part of expenses on this formal education was paid for by my guardians. After the studies, till date, I have been interested only in accumulating more

and more for "I, me and mine". All that I have done so far is for my own body and ego, my family, my relatives and my friends. I feel that I have taken so much from the society and have given so little in return that the balance of account is greatly against the interest of the society. Having realised that I am almost past the middle point of my life span, I decided that I am no longer interested in continuing with the same practice of accumulating whatever I can for "I, me and mine". I have decided that I would try to do whatever I can for those from whom I have been taking so far. I feel that I have already given at least, if not more, fifty percent of all that I could to my family and for my very personal and selfish interests and therefore would like to devote hundred percent of whatever is left of me for the society and the humanity as a whole to pay part of my debt. This work is a part of this effort.

11.	There may be questions related to my personal life. I believe that I lived a life like that of Lord Krishna. I thoroughly enjoyed my childhood and did all the nasty things I could indulge in under the loving care of my grandparents. I received the best of the education that anybody could have got in India. I have also worked in some of the best companies of the world. I can claim that I have directly experienced the extremes that life can teach. I have had the opportunity to study till class six in a school in my village wherein the thatched roof of the classrooms leaked during the monsoons drenching the bare earth floor and the sacks or mats on which we used to sit in the classrooms. As a result, we were forced to stand up, with our books in hand, to continue with our studies. This school had no toilet for the students or teachers. In contrast, I did the four year B.Tech. course in Civil Engineering from IIT Delhi which is probably considered to be the best engineering college in India. In between, I studied at Netarhat School, which I believe was the best residential school in India at that time. During my early days, I spent a lot of time in my mango orchards and in my small farms looking after and directly being associated with the agriculture and farming activities that my family was engaged in. I have had the happy opportunities to take my cattle out for grazing in the fields along with my uncle. I spent most of the days during my formative years in my village being engaged in the activities like fishing, farming and loitering around in the village and fields. However, this did not mean that we could skip the regular studies with a fixed routine under the supervision of the family elders. At the other extreme, I have stayed in almost all the luxury hotels in the major cities of India during the course of my business and personal travels.

I have worked as an engineer and business manager for many reputed companies. On many occasions, I have had differences of opinion with my managers; however none of my managers ever questioned my technical capability, will and dedication to my job.

12.	I claim that I am enlightened. I claim to have awakened to the absolute truth. I am अनंत (Anant – the one who has no beginning or end). I am सच्चिदानन्द (Satchidanand -the one in eternal bliss). I am ब्रह्म (Brahman). الحق أنا *Ana al-Haqq,* अहं ब्रह्मास्मि , तत्त्वमसि, सोहं, तदहं. I am aware of the consequences of these claims. I know what Socrates, Mahaveer, Jesus Christ, Meera or Mansur al-Hallaj had to endure. If I too have to go through something similar, it would be considered as His divine grace which would be accepted with a smile.

INTRODUCTION

Let us open any newspaper today and what we would come across are the stories of violence, rape, cheating, corruption, inefficiency, hunger, adultery and so on and so forth. At the same time, we would also come across examples of exemplary sacrifice, service, honesty, integrity, camaraderie, loyalty, efficiency, achievements and many other such stories. These stories would not be limited to any particular area of life. They would encompass all areas of political, social and economic environment. Watch any television channel and we would come across some news, story, advertisement, debate, discussion, message or something else which we would either like or dislike. Any event or incident that would occur is expected to trigger either a like or dislike, if I am allowed to use the terminology used by the developers of facebook. Thinking of facebook, I was wondering whether one should like or dislike a posting when someone posts the news of some sad event, e.g. death of a close relative. Without going into the semantics of the pages on facebook, what I intend to submit here is that we are programmed to think, like a robot, in a particular fashion in response to every event or incident. The moment our sense organ receives a signal from the environment in the form of some audio visual or kinesthetic input, a program is triggered in our mind. This program governs as to how we are going to respond to the inputs from the environment. Most of the typical responses triggered in the mind as a result of this programming are binary in nature, e.g. good or bad, applicable or not applicable to me, like or dislike, friend or foe, match or mismatch, move towards or run away from etc.

In the binary thinking process, there is no scope for anything in between the two extremes of good and bad, black and white and light and dark. The reality is limited between the two extremes of duality, opposing and contrasting in nature. This has become part of our day to day life. This was typically demonstrated when after reading one of my satirical letters to the leaders of Aam Aadmi Party, one of my classmate questioned, "It is not clear if you are trying to tear into AAP or support AAP?"

The binary programming of the mind limits it to perceive the world limited between the two extreme and discrete ends of good and bad, honest and dishonest, efficient and inefficient, intelligent and dull and this and that. This process of binary thinking is very useful in the context of engineering and technology, computer programming and where some very critical instant decision may be required particularly related to the physical, material or technical issues. However, when it comes to contextual thinking and perception, we have to understand that the picture of the reality that we have in our mind is only a picture and not the reality in itself. Using the terminology that the exponents of Neuro Linguistic Programming (NLP) use, it is only a map of the territory and map is not the territory. The way we perceive the reality and construct our map of it is a function of the environment that we have been experiencing since our childhood. It is a function of what we have learnt and stored in our mind from our interactions with our parents, siblings and other family members, spouse, relatives, friends, teachers, colleagues and everything and everybody around us in the environment and society like the sweepers, cleaners, shopkeepers, postman, electrician, labourer, taxi driver, the bureaucrats, the political leaders, the pet animals, the plants and trees, the river, the mountain, the type of soil, the weather and the climate and so on and so forth. Becoming aware of the way we think and then taking conscious actions and decisions, individually as well as collectively, to influence our process of thinking is the way out of violence, rape, cheating, corruption, inefficiency, hunger and adultery to sacrifice, service, honesty, integrity, camaraderie, loyalty, efficiency and achievements. This understanding provides a direction and tool to move away from continuing to live a life by default which is full of misery, sorrow, grief, hatred, greed, envy, anger, fear, helplessness, scarcity, and predicament. This also provides an opportunity of moving towards living a life by design full of happiness, satisfaction, fulfillment, pleasure, love, passion, enthusiasm, excitement, abundance and freedom. Quoting Elbert Einstein,

> "If we don't change our way of thinking, we will not be able to solve the problems that we create ourselves with our current ways of thinking"

There have been significant contributions from the greatest masters the mankind has ever had in terms of making people aware of how to live a life by design in contrast to living a life by default. During the life time of these masters, there appeared to be a direction for the mankind under their direct supervision and guidance. In their mission of salvation, they taught people how to think in a particular way which would lead to a life of liberation or freedom. I am aware that all the true religious and spiritual masters have said the same thing because I know that when they were speaking of "THE TRUTH", they could not be talking about different things. It is so because THE TRUTH is not relative or contextual. It is absolute. By definition, THE TRUTH is what does not change over time. THE TRUTH remains THE TRUTH and would reveal itself to anyone who would be serious and deserving. The apparent difference in what the masters have spoken about THE TRUTH is mainly because of their attempt to bind THE TRUTH in the language, in words, in traditions, and in stories. This apparent difference about THE TRUTH which has flourished in the form and name of creed and sects like Christianity, Islam, Hinduism, Buddhism, Jainism, Sikhism, Zoroastrianism etc. is because of the attempts of the masters to use the references from their immediate environments and the people around them. During their life time, the masters were around to correct the course of the people in the society if the stories and pictures to illustrate THE TRUTH appeared to be becoming more important than THE TRUTH itself. However, with the passage of time and with the masters not being around, THE TRUTH became obscured and the stories and the pictures to illustrate and explain THE TRUTH have become more important. The only test of THE TRUTH being prevalent in a society is whether the people in the society are happy, healthy, peaceful, progressive, prosperous, creative and constructive or not. In a spiritual and religious order, the people would be happy and in a state of bliss. The whole society would be in a state of joy and enthusiasm and beaming with a sense of fulfillment and abundance. There would be no place for hunger, predicament, violence, envy and cheating in such a society. In such a society, all human efforts would be focused towards creative and constructive works and all endeavours intended to enrich the lives of not only the humans but all the animate and inanimate creatures and objects on the planet.

Applying this test, can we say that we have truth around us in the society? Is the society in a state of bliss? What does our focused attention to enrich our military and weapons of mass destructions signify? What message is emanating from numerous political and social unrests across the world? Is THE TRUTH as being derived and preached by the so called religious leaders in the name of Bible, Quran, Vedas, Upanishads, Puranas, Guru Granth Sahib or Zend Avesta leading to a world order that can signify the presence of THE

TRUTH? If the answers to all these queries clearly indicate that our sociopolitical order of the day is devoid of truth, it ought to be a natural corollary to stop, look back and make efforts to re-establish THE TRUTH. Using the test parameters of truth as enshrined in the Buddhist literature, the truth ought to be

1. Svakkhato or Svakhyata i.e. "well proclaimed". It means that it need not be speculative but an exposition of the Universal Law of Nature based on a causal analysis of natural phenomena. It should be possible to test the principles associated with the truth in the same way as any other universal physical law.

2. Sanditthiko or Samdrustika i.e. "able to be examined". It means that it is open to scientific and other types of scrutiny and is not based on faith. It can be tested by personal practice by anyone and the one, who follows it, will see the result for oneself by means of one's own experience.

3. Akaliko or Akalika i.e."timeless, immediate".
   The truth does not change over time and it is not relative to time.

4. Ehipassiko or Ehipasyika i.e. "which you can come and see" — the truth invites all to put it to the test.

5. Opanayiko or Avapranayika i.e. "leading one close to". This can be understood with an analogy as follows. If one says a ripe mango tastes delicious, and if several people listen and come to believe it, they would imagine the taste of the mango according to their previous experiences of other delicious mangoes. Yet, they will still not really know exactly how this mango tastes. Also, if there is a person who has never tasted a ripe mango before, that person has no way of knowing exactly for himself how it tastes. So, the only way to know the exact taste is to experience it. In the same way, truth is said to be Opanayiko which means that a person needs to experience it within to see exactly what it is.

6. Paccattam veditabbo vinnuhi or Pratyatmam veditavyo vijnaih i.e. "To be personally known by the wise". No one else can "enlighten" another person. Each intelligent person has to attain and experience the truth for themselves. As an analogy, no one can simply make another

4

know how to swim. Each person individually has to learn how to swim.

Having accepted the above parameters of testing the truth, I would also like to apply the "The Triple Filters Test" that is attributed to Socrates. This is in the form of a story which goes like as below.

"One day an acquaintance met Socrates and said, "Do you know what I just heard about your friend?"

"Hold on a minute," Socrates replied. "Before telling me anything, I'd like you to pass a little test. It's called the Triple Filter Test."

"Triple filter?"

"That's right," Socrates continued. "Before you talk to me about my friend, it might be a good idea to take a moment and filter what you're going to say. That's why I call it the triple filter test.

The first filter is TRUTH. Have you made absolutely sure that what you are about to tell me is true?"

"No," the man said, "actually I just heard about it and…"

"All right," said Socrates. "So you don't really know if it's true or not. Now let's try the second filter, the filter of GOODNESS. Is what you are about to tell me about my friend something good?"

"No, on the contrary…"

"So," Socrates continued, "you want to tell me something bad about him, but you're not certain it's true. You may still pass the test though, because there's one filter left: the filter of USEFULNESS. Is what you want to tell me about my friend going to be useful to me?"

"No, not really."

"Well," concluded Socrates, "if what you want to tell me is neither true nor good nor even useful, why tell it to me at all?"

The Truth that I am about to talk about in this work would meet the test parameters of Svakhyata, Samdrustika, Akalik, Ehipasyika, Avapranayika and Pratyatmam Veditavyo Vijnaih. I also declare that what I am going to talk about is not only true but also highly useful for the mankind as a whole and it is intended to be good and well meaning information for the human society. This work is intended to be a guide for a new way of sociopolitical thinking and to work as a catalyst for a revolution to usher in a holistic and spiritual model of governance and administration. It is intended to delve deeper into the issues being faced by the society and mankind as a whole and then devise meaningful and relevant solutions to establish a new sociopolitical order which would reflect the presence of truth in the form of a happy, healthy, creative, blissful and fulfilled human society and a very healthy, meaningful, constructive and positive relation between the man and his environment.

What I am going to talk about in this work is something similar to the concepts of Ram Rajya that Mahatma Gandhi had envisioned. The twin principle of his Ram Rajya was "Right Means and Right Ends". Using the quotes of Gandhi from some of the Gandhian literature, I would like to present what Gandhi meant by Ram Rajya.

> By Ramarajya, I do not mean Hindu Raj. I mean by Ramarajya Divine Raj, the Kingdom of God. For me Rama and Rahim are one and the same deity. I acknowledge no other God but the one God of truth and righteousness.

> Whether Rama of my imagination ever lived or not on this earth, the ancient ideal of Ramarajya is undoubtedly one of true democracy in which the meanest citizen could be sure of swift justice without an elaborate and costly procedure. Even the dog is described by the poet to have received justice under Ramarajya.

> Ramarajya of my dream ensures equal rights alike of prince and pauper.

> My conception of Ramarajya excludes the replacement of the British army by a national army of occupation. A country that is governed by even its national army can never be morally free and, therefore, its so-called weakest member can never rise to his fullest moral height.

> There can be no Ramarajya in the present state of iniquitous inequalities in which a few roll in riches and the masses do not get even enough to eat ... my opposition to the Socialists and others consists in attacking violence as a means of effecting any lasting reform.

Despite the passage of more than six decades when Gandhi shared his vision of "Ram Rajya" or an "India of My Dreams" and despite the country having been mostly under the rule of the party, of which Gandhi is still considered to be the most important leader ever in its history, his vision has almost lost its significance in the current day political setup. While this work is not advocating the exact concept of 'Ramrajya' of Gandhi, it would definitely delve into many issues which were considered in Gandhian model of governance. We would also look into the issues that prevented the Gandhian model of governance from being adopted and implemented in India. It would be very easy to say that the degeneration of the moral and ethical values of the people who inherited the legacy of Gandhi have been the main reason for obscuring his vision of governance. However, this simplistic statement or explanation would not give any clue as to what would have been the origin of the degeneration of moral and ethical values that led our society to where we are today. Why is it that Gandhi has lost all relevance in politics and governance today beyond just being remembered on his birth and death anniversaries and being used for some political mileage? We would also need to look into why the ordinary and common citizens of India seemed to have lost all interest in politics until the AAP under the leadership of Arvind Kejriwal emerged as a ray of hope. Why is it that people had become so cynical about the polity of the country that their interest got limited only to guard their very own personal selfish interest and they were ready to ignore everything else as long as they were not directly and immediately being affected? We would need to look into the root cause and not only the superficial reasons of all the sociopolitical and economic issues being faced by the society. We would also look into what opportunity do we have, at this stage, to correct the course of the history and bring the society back on track. There are realms of knowledge about which people are consciously aware or unaware of or the realm of consciously known or unknown. However, there is a vast ocean of knowledge beyond this conscious realm and we would also try to get into this realm to find out if this could help our society.

Before we look into the issues that have been mentioned above, we would need to go through the basic elements of spirituality or the core of all religious belief systems. What is it that was supposed to be the core of the guiding principles of social life? What have been the common elements in the messages from all the masters which passes the tests and filters as mentioned above? What are those basic human values or belief that would lead to a social order wherein every citizen is happy and excited about his life and does not have to live in an environment of constant fear and apprehensions? Let us examine those elements which could create a social order capable of providing an opportunity to every soul to aspire to achieve the highest level of evolution.

MOMENTS OF TRUTH

THE TRUTH WILL SET YOU FREE

There are five pillars on which the growth of human soul and progress of a harmonious and prosperous society rests. These five pillars have been listed by almost all the religious and spiritual traditions of the world. The "Ten Commandments", which plays a fundamental role in Judaism and Christianity and which is said to have been given by God to Moses, a religious leader and prophet as per Bible and Quran, lists, inter-alia, the following as the basic code of conduct in social life.

- Thou shalt not kill
- Thou shalt not commit adultery
- Thou shalt not steal
- Thou shalt not bear false witness against thy neighbour
- Thou shalt not covet

The five precepts or "Panchasheela" as per Buddhist traditions which were formulated to be undertaken voluntarily by everyone to facilitate the practice of Dhamma were commitments to abstain from

- Harming living beings,
- Stealing,
- Sexual misconduct,
- Lying and
- Intoxication

In the Hindu tradition, the Yoga Sutra of Maharshi Patanjali lists the five don'ts or ethical rules as part of Yama which is prescribed as the first step in his Ashtangik (Eightfold) Raj Yoga. Yama prescribes the social behavior or how one ought to treat others and the world around them. These are the moral principles for the society. These same five principles are prescribed in Jainism as vows for self control. These five Yamas are:

- **Nonviolence (Ahimsa)-** Do no harm to any creature in thought or deed. It involves minimizing intentional and unintentional harm to other living creatures.

- **Truth and honesty (Satya)-** This means "Always speak the truth". Tell no lies.
- **Non-stealing (Asteya)-** Do not steal material objects and do not accept anything that is not voluntarily offered by the legitimate owner. Attempting to extort material wealth from others or to exploit the weak is considered theft.
- **Non-lust (Brahmacharya)-** spiritual advancement by education and training. It also means avoidance of adultery and meaningless sexual misconduct
- **Non-possessiveness (Aparigraha)-** Free yourself from greed, hoarding, and collecting.

A lot of research material is available in the print form and on the internet on these codes of ethics that have been prescribed by the authorities in almost all the religious traditions. I do not intend to discuss here the details of these concepts. The only purpose of mentioning these codes of conduct here was to assert that I am not trying to reinvent the wheel. These codes of ethics are well known to the humanity as a whole and they have been considered important steps in leading the humanity towards a happy, healthy, peaceful, progressive, harmonious and prosperous society. The point that I am trying to establish is whether despite being aware of these prescriptions, is the humanity on course? Let us examine.

The first concept that we would examine is truth. Satyameva Jayate (सत्यमेव जयते) or "The Truth Alone Triumphs" is a mantra from the ancient Indian scripture. Upon independence of India, it was adopted as the national motto of India. It is inscribed at the base of the national emblem of this country. The emblem and the words "Satyameva Jayate" are inscribed on one side of all Indian currency. The origin of the motto is a mantra from the Mundaka Upanishad. The mantra is as follows:

सत्यमेव जयते नानृतं
सत्येन पन्था विततो देवयानः |
येनाक्रमन्त्यृषयो ह्याप्तकामा
यत्र तत् सत्यस्य परमं निधानम् ||

satyameva jayate nanrutam
satyena pantha vitato devayanah
yenakramantyrshayo hyaptakama
yatra tat satyasya paramam nidhanam

Translated in English, it is:
Truth alone triumphs; not falsehood.
Through truth the divine path is spread out by which the sages, whose desires have been completely fulfilled, reach where that supreme treasure of Truth resides.

Almost all the people, who have grown up in India, have heard the legendary story of King Harishchandra. The story goes like this.

It is said that the great sage Vishwamitra, once approached Harishchandra and informed him of a promise made by the king during the sage's dream to donate his entire kingdom. Harishchandra was so virtuous, that he immediately made good his word and donated his entire kingdom to the sage and walked away with his wife and son.

Since, the entire world was under the sage after he donated his kingdom; the king had to go to Varanasi, a holy town dedicated to Lord Shiva. This was now the only place outside the influence of the sage. But the sage proclaimed that for an act of donation to be completed, an additional amount as Dakshina (honorarium) had to be paid. Harishchandra, with no money in his hands, had to sell his wife and son to a Brahman to pay for the Dakshina. When the money collected still did not suffice for the purpose, he sold himself to a guard at the cremation ground, who was in charge of collecting taxes for the bodies to be cremated.

The king, his wife and son had to sustain tremendous hardships doing their respective chores. The king helped the guard cremate the dead bodies, while his wife and son were used as household helpers at the house of the Brahman. Once, while the son had been to the garden to pluck flowers for his master's prayer, he was bitten by a snake and he died instantly. His mother, having nobody to sympathize with her, carried his body to the cremation grounds. In acute penury, she could not even pay the taxes needed to cremate him. Harishchandra did not recognise his wife and son. He asked the lady to sell her golden mangalasutra (the symbol of her being married and loyal to her husband) and pay the tax. It is at this instance that the wife recognizes the man as her husband as she had a boon that her husband only could see her mangalasutra. Harishchandra then came to her and recognized her as his wife and was stung by pangs of agony.

But, Harishchandra was duty bound by his job to perform the cremation only after the acceptance of the tax. So, he asked his wife, if she was willing to undergo further hardships and stand by him in this hour of calamity. The faithful wife readily gave assent. She had in her possession only a saree, a part of which was used to cover the dead body of her son. She offers half of her lone dress as the tax, which Harishchandra could accept and perform the last rites of his son. When she proceeded to remove her dress, miracles happened.

Lord Vishnu, Indra, all Devas and sage Vishwamitra himself manifested themselves on the scene and praised Harishchandra for his perseverance and steadfastness. They brought his son back to life. They also offered the king and his wife, instant places in heaven. Harishchandra refused, stating that he was bound to his master, the guard. The gods then revealed that the guard was none other than Yama. He refused again saying that according to his Kshatriya Dharma, he cannot leave behind his subjects. He asked for a place in heaven for all his subjects. But the gods refused, explaining that the subjects had their own Karma and they have to undergo them. The king was then ready to forego all his virtues and religiousness for his people, so that they could ascend to heaven leaving him behind. The gods, now immensely pleased with the unassailable character of the great king, offered heavenly abode to the king, the queen and all their subjects. The sage Vishwamitra helped to populate the kingdom again and installed Harishchandra's son as the king. Rohitashwa was the son of Harishchandra. People with family name as Rohtagi, Rastogi, and Rustagi are considered to be descendants of Rohitashwa.

Despite having got such an important place in Indian traditions, let us now look at what the actual condition of truth in the present day society is. To consider this question, I would like to take help from a reality TV show "Sach Ka Saamna" (सच का सामना) which means facing the truth. The first season of this show was telecast on STAR Plus TV channel in the year 2009 and the second season on STAR TV in 2011. In this show, prior to appearing on the actual show, contestants were asked 50 questions while being hooked up to a polygraph machine. The biological indicators of the contestant, such as pulse rate, blood pressure, etc. were measured and used by the polygraph to decide whether the answer was true or not. The contestant was not aware of the results of the polygraph for his or her answers.

During the actual show, the contestant was to be asked 21 of the same questions again. If the contestant answered honestly, he or she moved on to the next question; however, should a contestant lie in his or her answer, or simply refuse to answer a question after it has been asked, the game ended and the contestant lost all his prize money.

There were six levels of prize money in the game. The first level consisted of six questions, and answering all of them truthfully would win the contestant ₹1,00,000 of prize money. The next level had five questions and the prize money went up to ₹5,00,000. The third, fourth and fifth levels consisted of four, three and two questions respectively, with the prize money being ₹10,00,000, ₹25,00,000 and ₹50,00,000 respectively. The final level had only one question, with the truthful answer fetching the maximum prize money of ₹ 1,00,00,000.

The questions became increasingly personal and potentially embarrassing in nature as the stakes got higher. The contestants were usually accompanied by close family members or friends, who were seated beside them and the host. Several of the questions tended to be related to the relationship between them and their acquaintances present there. Next to the guests was a buzzer, which they could use to override a question which they felt was better left unanswered. In that case, the contestant would be asked an alternate question which may be easier or tougher than the question it replaced. The buzzer could only be used once during the game. The first season of the show had 48 episodes while the second season had 58. The important fact about this show was that nobody could win the prize money of rupees one crore whereas the buzzers were pressed several time during the show. In a country, where the monthly salary of the President of the country is ₹1,50,000, a prize money of ₹1,00,00,000 would have been too big an incentive for anybody to speak the truth and yet nobody could win this prize. Nobody in this whole country of 1.2 billion people, who have grown up hearing the story of Harishchandra, had the courage to speak the truth at the cost of revealing something which they had kept as a closely guarded personal secret even when the incentive was in the form of such a high cash prize. The hypocrisy of our so called spiritual and religious society stands totally exposed before the world through this reality TV show.

What I wanted to illustrate through this example is that truth is definitely no longer a cherished value in our society and this shift in value is well accepted by all. I do not intend to find fault with or curse the society and start preaching people, like most of the present day religious and political leaders do at every opportunity even while they themselves would not let go of any opportunity to lie if that suits their personal interest. I see nothing wrong in them doing so, since for them, personal comfort is more important than speaking the truth and truth only. They have adopted it in their value system in the process of learning from their environment and no discourse or preaching can upset this value system.

In fact, the social position about truth gradually shifted towards the need and convenience and is epitomized in the Sanskrit shloka

सत्यं ब्रूयात्प्रियं ब्रूयान्न ब्रूयात्सत्यमप्रियम् ।
प्रियं च नानृतं ब्रूयादेष धर्म सनातनः ॥

satyam bruyat priyam bruyat na bruyat satyam apriyam
priyam cha nanrutam bruyat esha dharma sanatanah

Speak truth in such a way that it should be pleasing to others. Never speak truth, which is unpleasant to others. Speak untruth, which might be pleasant. This is the path of eternal morality, the Sanatana Dharma.

Here, we see that conditions are being attached to the truth and it is being diluted for the convenience. This is what I would call adultery with truth. We learn to lie and be at peace with it in the day to day events and incidents in our routine life. Some of the examples are

The landline telephone in the house rings. A child goes to pick up the phone. While the child is still about to pick the phone, the father calls from behind and says "if someone asks for me, tell him I am not home". The child complies and in the process learns that speaking lies like this is no big deal. The father has taught the son how to tell a lie comfortably without giving any thought to it.

A child absents himself from school due to family reasons and misses his class exam. He goes to the teacher the next day to request for a compensatory exam. The teacher advises him to submit a medical certificate justifying his absence on health ground. The parents go to a doctor and get a fake medical certificate which the child submits to the teacher. Everybody is happy about it.

These trivial and seemingly innocent incidents prepare the family to accept lies as a part of their life. It prepares the daughter to say that she is going for a group study with her friends while she is actually going for a movie or on a date with a boyfriend. It prepares the husband to say that he was in the office while he had actually been flirting with a lady. It prepares the son to steal the money while buying the vegetables for the family and then claiming that the rates have gone up. It prepares the lady of the house to proclaim that she got a precious gift from her parents whereas she actually purchased it from her own savings.

These are all very very innocent lies. Apparently, there does not seem to be any serious problem or harm to the family or the society with such kind of lies. However, what we need to notice here is that all these lies are arising out of a need to meet ones very personal aspirations and desires and yet continue to look good in the eyes of the others. This need to look good in the eyes of others slowly programs the thought process of a person in such a way that they lose their freedom to do openly and explicitly what their natural tendency to do is and they feel constrained to start living a life of deceit and pretense. People would start wearing a social mask by which they would like to be recognized by others while they themselves would know that they are not what they are thought to be. Some of the examples of this phenomenon are visible when we see people spending more than they could actually afford. This makes the whole society gradually move towards becoming a puppet and giving their control into the hands of others. They would try to meet the expectations of others from them and would continue to look for opportunity to look good. Children, from the very beginning, start living a life of meeting the expectations of their parents. Students don't mind letting go of their natural talents in their zeal to meet the expectations of their teachers and friends. Adults kill the actual person that they are and just try to live up to the expectations of their spouse, their boss and their colleagues. Parents forget that they have a life of their own and just try to live up to the expectations of their children. People build an image of themselves in the eyes of the society and then put all their efforts and energy to save that image rather than being what they are. The image becomes more important than the actual. This game of social compulsion to forget who you actually are and living up to the expectations of others continues till one realizes that he is leaving his body but by that time it is too late a realization to do anything.

What we have discovered here is that one of the major determinants of human beings as a social animal, individually as well as collectively, is to look good in the eyes of others. This insight provides us an opportunity to influence the individual and social behaviour. We would also explore the status and influence of the other core codes of conduct that we listed earlier in this discussion and would attempt to discover further insight into how we can influence the social behaviour.

FROM DARKNESS TO LIGHT

ॐ असतो मा सद्गमय ।	Om asato ma sadgamaya |
तमसो मा ज्योतिर्गमय ।	Tamaso ma jyotirgamaya |
मृत्योर्मामृतंगमय ।।	Mrityor ma amritangamaya |
ॐ शान्तिः शान्तिः शान्तिः ।।	Om Shantih Shantih Shantih
बृहदारण्यक उपनिषद् 1.3.28.	Brihadaranyak Upanishad 1.3.28

Lead Us From the Unreal To the Real,
Lead Us From Darkness To Light,
Lead Us From Death To Immortality,
Let There Be Peace Peace Peace. – Brihadaranyaka Upanishad

Everybody wants to be in peace. All actions and efforts that one undertakes are motivated from achieving a state of mental peace. So, why is it that despite their best efforts, there is no peace in the life of people? What is it that has taken the peace away from the life of people on this planet? Ask someone and he would say that he would be at peace once he achieves a particular state of health, wealth, relation, status, position, power or something else. If someone has got health, he is craving for wealth. If someone has got relation, he is craving for position. If one has got power, he is dying to get recognized for his status. No one seems to be happy or at peace. If someone has got all that is mentioned above, he would find himself desirous of something else which would not let him live a life of peace and happiness. This is quite surprising. Let us explore the root cause of this perennial craving and desire which keeps people deprived of peace and bliss.

Can health, any other physical possession, relation or material success bring peace and bliss? A healthy person having an absolutely perfect physical health would probably not have any physical pain in the body. His body may be full of energy and muscle power. However, once someone has achieved this state of perfect physical health, he would be constrained to maintain it and might be burdened with a thought to preserve this state of perfect physical health forever. He might even stop attaching any value to a state of a healthy body and may stop caring for it. He may not be ready to accept it as a divine gift and grace and would not understand how and what goes through the mind of those who are weak, sick and diseased. He would probably forget that time would change the state of his perfect physical body like it does to everything else. As long as the body is healthy and as long as death is not imminent (like in the age of youth), people tend to just forget about it. I remember one story that I had once read somewhere. It goes like this,

There was a rich merchant who had four wives.

He loved the fourth wife the most. He adorned her with rich robes and treated her to delicacies. He took great care of her and gave her nothing but the best.

He also loved the third wife very much. He was very proud of her and always wanted to show her off to his friends. However, the merchant was always in great fear that she might run away with some other men.

He loved his second wife as well. She was a very considerate lady. She was always patient and in fact was the merchant's confidante. Whenever the merchant faced some problems, he always turned to his second wife and she would always help him out and tide him through difficult times.

Now, the merchant's first wife was a very loyal partner and had made great contributions in maintaining his wealth and business as well as taking care of the household. However, the merchant did not love the first wife and although she loved him deeply, he hardly took notice of her.

One day, the merchant fell ill. Before long, he knew that he was going to die soon. He thought of his luxurious life and told himself, "Now I have four wives with me. But when I die, I'll be alone. How lonely I'll be!"

Thus, he asked the fourth wife, "I loved you most, endowed you with the finest clothing and showered great care over you. Now that I'm dying, will you follow me and keep me company?"

"No way!" replied the fourth and the youngest wife and she walked away without another word. The answer cut like a sharp knife right into the merchant's heart.

The sad merchant then asked the third wife, "I have loved you so much for all my life. Now that I am dying, will you follow me and keep me company?"

"No!" replied the 3rd wife in a terse voice. "Life is so good over here! I am going to remarry when you die!" The merchant's heart sank and turned cold.

He then asked the second wife, "I always turned to you for help and you have always helped me out. Now I need your help again. When I die, will you follow me and keep me company?"

"I am sorry, I can't help you out this time!" replied the second wife.

"At the very most, I can only send you to your grave. I will also ensure that all your after death rituals are properly conducted."

The answer came like a bolt of thunder and the merchant was devastated. Then a voice called out: "I will live with you. I will follow you no matter where you go." The merchant looked up and there was his first wife. She was so skinny, almost like she suffered from malnutrition. Greatly grieved, the merchant said, "I should have taken much better care of you while I could have!"

This story reminds us that actually we all have four wives in our lives. The fourth and the youngest wife is our body. No matter how much time and effort we lavish in making it look good, it will leave us when we die. Our third wife is our possessions, status and wealth. When we die, they all go to others. The wealth and other material possessions are always owned by someone and no one is able to continue his ownership on these items beyond the life time of his physical body. The second wife is our family, friends and relatives. No matter how close they had been there for us when we are alive, the furthest they can stay by us is up to the grave and conducting the after death rituals.

The first wife is, in fact, our soul. Often neglected in our pursuit of material wealth, health and sensual pleasure, we tend to forget about this beloved lady that has been with us forever. It is actually the only thing that follows us wherever we go. Why do we wait to think of and care for this most essential part of us during our lifetime until we're on our deathbed to lament? This question has been answered by Ved Vyas in Shreemadbhagvatam through Yudhishthira. The legend in the epic Mahabharata has it as below.

The righteous prince Yudhishthira is confronted by a fearsome demon, Yaksha-the God of Dharma, guarding a lake in Dvaitavana, a forest where Pandavas were staying after they had lost the game of dice to Kauravas. The other Pandavas, while searching for the arni (an implement for making sacrificial fire) of a Brahman, could not answer the questions of the Yaksha and still drank waters of the lake and died instantly as a result of this defiance. One of the questions of the Yaksha was:

"Kim Aashcharyam (किमाश्चर्यम्)?" (What is a great surprise?)

To this question, Yudhishthira' s reply is very profound. He says

अहन्यहनि भूतानि गच्छन्ति यमालयम् ।
शेषाः स्थावरमिच्छन्ति किमाश्चर्यमतः परम् ॥

"Everyday day we witness death all around us. It strikes everyone, the high and mighty and the lowly. However, the biggest surprise is that those alive are rarely perturbed on witnessing death and strangely, most people cannot relate it to their own impending mortality and carry on with their lives unruffled. What is more surprising than this?"

In reply to another question, Yudhishthira says that Time (as Kala) is cooking jivas in a vessel, called attachment (Maha Moha), stirring them with tools such as months and seasons, with days and nights as fuel and the mighty sun as fire. This is the great news of earth.

In another story from Shreemadbhagvatam, king Dhritarashtra was worried about the outcome of the inevitable war and the possibility of the death of his sons at the hands of Pandavas. Vidura told him that the sage Sanatsujata holds the view that there was no death in reality. When Vidura was asked to clarify his statement, he invoked the presence of the great sage. The great sage materialized in their presence. Dhritarashtra asked him, "You are said to hold the view that there is no death. Please teach me the underlying secret." Sanatsujata then expounds his teaching. He says that,

"Death is apparent only because of the ignorance or the lack of true knowledge. The question of bondage arises because of this ignorance. Another name for this ignorance is Moha (attachment). If the true nature of soul is known, then there is no death. This death is personified by the divine being Yama. Yama is also part of the ultimate reality. Yama, therefore, is truth and death is an illusion caused by the ignorance of the true knowledge. Yama is part of soul. For jivas who have true knowledge, Yama is Guru, part of the Almighty, and the custodian of the true knowledge regarding death. Jivas steeped in ignorance are afraid of him."

The same understanding about the immortality and continuity of the soul is established in Shreemad Bhagvatgeeta. In chapter two of this epic, which deals with the basic concepts of Sankhya Yoga, Lord Krishna, in his discourse to his disciple Arjuna, to help him overcome the ignorance and understand the truth, repeatedly establishes the eternity of the soul through the verses like

अंतवन्त इमे देहा नित्यस्तोक्ताः शरीरिणः |
अनाशिनोप्रमेयस्य तस्माद् युद्ध्यस्व भारत||

Antavanta ime deha, nityasyoktah sharirinah |
Anashino aprameyasya tasmad yudhyasva bharata | | 2.18

The material body of the indestructible, immeasurable and eternal living entity is sure to come to an end; therefore, fight, O descendant of Bharata.

न जायते म्रियते वा कदाचिन्नायं भूत्वा भविता वा न भूयः |
अजो नित्यः शाश्वतोयं पुराणो न हन्यते हन्यमाने शरीरे || 2.20

Na jayate mriyate va kadachinnayam
bhutva bhavita va na bhuyah
Ajo nityah shashvatoyam purano,
na hanyate hanyamane sharire

The soul is never born nor dies at any time. Soul has not come into being, does not come into being, and will not come into being. Soul is unborn, eternal, ever-existing and primeval. Soul is not slain when the body is slain.

वासांसि जीर्णानि यथा विहाय नवानि गृह्णाति नरोऽपराणि।
तथा शरीराणि विहाय जीर्णाणि अन्यानि संयाति नवानि देही||(2.22)

Vasamsi jirnani yatha vihaya navani grihnati naro 'parani |
Tatha sharirani vihaya jirnani anyani samyati navani dehi| |

Just as a man casts off worn-out clothes and puts on new ones, so also the embodied Self casts off worn-out bodies and enters others that are new.

नैनं छिन्दन्ति शस्त्राणि नैनं दहति पावकः |
न चैनं क्लेदयन्त्यापो न शोषयति मारुतः || 2.23

Nainam chhindanti shastrani nainam dahati pavakah |
Na chainam kledayantyapo na shoshayati marutah | |

The Soul can never be cut by weapons, fire burns it not,
water wets it not, and the wind dries it not.

अच्छेद्योयं अदाह्योयं अक्लेद्यो अशोष्य एव च |
नित्यः सर्व गतः स्थाणुरचलोयम सनातनः || 2.24

Achchhedyoyam adahyoyam akledyo ashoshya eva cha |
Nityah sarva-gatah sthanur achaloyam sanatanah ||

This imperishable Self cannot be cut, burnt, wetted nor
dried up. It is eternal, all-pervading, stable, ancient and
immovable.

We do not need to use a heavy dose of quotes and excerpts from
scriptures and epics to establish what I intend to establish. In very
simple terms, it is our ignorance or un-mindfulness of WHO we
actually are, that prevents us from practicing non-violence (ahimsa),
asteya (not-stealing), aparigraha (non-possessiveness) and
brahmacharya (non lust or detached action). It is only because of
ignorance that we get induced to indulge in violence, stealing,
possessiveness and other such activities which keep us away from
awakening and realizing the truth. It is ignorance which is the main
cause of misery and grief in our lives. But the question still persists,
why do we continue to remain in ignorance and why don't we
awaken and realize the truth about who we actually are?
I have been pondering over this question and the answer that I have
is not very pleasing for the religious and political leaders of our
society. However, before I get into the arena of current day religious
and political life, I would like to dwell upon the subject of written
material on truth. The life on this planet, as per Sankhya philosophy,
is an interplay between the Purush or the pure, absolute and
independent cosmic consciousness, Prakriti or nature in all its
physical and material and energy form, buddhi or intellect, mind, ego
and five sense organs (eyes, ear, nose, tongue and skin), five action
organs (limbs and mouth), five subtle elements of Sound (Shabda),
Touch (Sparsha), Form (Rupa), Taste (Rasa), Smell (Gandha) and
five gross elements of Sky (Akash), Air (Vayu), Fire (Agni), Water
(Jala) and Earth (Prithvi). All physical events are considered to be
manifestations of the evolution of Prakriti from which all physical

bodies are derived. Each sentient being or Jiva is a fusion of Purusha and Prakriti, whose soul/Purusha is limitless and unrestricted by its physical body. Samsara or bondage arises when the Purusha does not have the discriminate knowledge and so is misled as to its own identity, confusing itself with the Ego/ahamkara, which is actually an attribute of Prakriti. The spirit is liberated when the discriminate knowledge of the difference between conscious Purusha and unconscious Prakriti is realized by the Purusha. The intellect, after receiving cognitive structures from the mind and illumination from pure consciousness, creates thought structures that appear to be conscious. Ahamkara, the ego or the phenomenal self, appropriates all mental experiences to itself and thus, personalizes the objective activities of mind and intellect by assuming possession of them. However, the consciousness itself is independent of the thought structures it illuminates. Purusha, the eternal pure consciousness, due to ignorance, gets identified with products of Prakriti such as intellect (buddhi) and ego (ahamkara). This results in endless transmigration and suffering. However, once the realization arises that Purusha is distinct from Prakriti, the Self is no longer subject to transmigration and absolute freedom arises. This simple explanation, as espoused in Sankhya of Kapil, has been discussed, deliberated and presented in the various forms by people who have actually realised the absolute truth. These various forms of presenting the truth have had various names such as Nyaya, Vaisheshika, Mimamsa, Yoga, Vedanta, Upanishads, Bhagvad Geeta, Yoga Vashishtha, Ashtavakra Samhita, Brahmans, Aranyaks, Tripitaka, Agams, Guru Granth Sahib etc.. Outside India, these have been known by the names like Zen, Zind Avesta, Holy Bible, Holy Quran and many other names. The people responsible for the origin of these texts always wanted to say exactly the same thing. And they did say exactly the same thing. However, in their efforts to communicate their understanding of TRUTH to others, they used the language and references from the space and time where they themselves and the people they wanted to convey the message to lived. This message was captured in words and language and that has been one of the root causes of corruption in what was intended to be said and what is being inferred out of what has been said. It is simply not possible to capture and bind the TRUTH in words and language. It can only be felt and experienced but not understood by reading a text or listening to a discourse. Understanding of TRUTH by someone by reading a book or listening to a discourse is analogous to a man who tries to learn how to swim or how to ride a bicycle by reading a book or listening to a discourse and then thinks that he has learnt how to swim or ride a bike. Here, this person has an opportunity to test his knowledge of swimming or riding by actually plunging into a pool or going out with a bike. Similarly, the test of having understood the truth is very simple. The one who has actually understood the truth would instantly and spontaneously get detached from all his actions or reach to a state which Rishi Ashtavkra calls a state of Sakshi (detached observer). He would perennially and eternally be in bliss irrespective of the external events, incidents and circumstances in his life. This would not mean that he would not have any issue or affliction with his physical body or social status. It also does not mean that people around him would start treating him in a different way. However, his responses and reactions would no longer be a function of what others want but of his own choice. He would have absolutely no trace of ego left in him. He would be able to see the presence of same essential element in everything around him. He would transcend all kinds of fear. No matter what happens to his finance, his health, his social status, his relations, his livelihood or anything else that is generally identified with his body or ego, he would be in a state of perennial mental equanimity.

The understanding of truth leads to an instant and spontaneous state of unconditional devotion or Bhakti. In this state, the person is able to visualize everything, physical, mental or spiritual as divine. Everything he does appears to be a manifestation of unconditional love for the divinity. The food he consumes, the music he listens to or the pains he bears – all appear to be a form of worship to him. A devout is a person who is not away from god even for a fraction of a second. He would also completely stop asking for any personal favour from the supreme consciousness who may be known to him by various names such as God, Allah, Raheem, Rehmaan, Ishwar, Paramatma, Rama, Krishna, Shiva, Vishnu, Durga, Laxmi, Ahura Mazda or even as the one without a name or form. He would not be able to see anything else but God in everything and everywhere. All actions, events and incidents in the social sphere, irrespective of how the society at large may look at it, would appear to a part of divine cosmic grace to him and he would accept everything with grace and love. He would look at all these events as if it is simply a game being played by the divine design and would never ever again get perturbed by anything whatsoever. He would be at absolute peace and would enjoy every moment of "HERE and NOW" as a present or gift from the almighty without having any fear or worry for imagined problems and pains in future. He would become a true devout person similar to the Kings friend whose story goes like as below.

An African king had a close friend who had the habit of remarking "this is good" about every occurrence in life no matter what it was.

One day the king and his friend were out hunting. The king's friend loaded a gun and handed it to the king, but alas he loaded it wrong and when the king fired it, his thumb was blown off.

"This is good!" exclaimed his friend.

The horrified and bleeding king was furious. "How can you say this is good? This is obviously horrible!" he shouted.

The king put his friend in jail.

About a year later the king went hunting by himself. Cannibals captured him and took him to their village. They tied his hands, stacked some wood, set up a stake and bound him to it. As they came near to set fire to the wood, they noticed that the king was missing a thumb. Being superstitious, they never ate anyone who was less than whole. They untied the king and sent him on his way.

Full of remorse the king rushed to the prison to release his friend.

"You were right, it was good" the king said.

The king told his friend how the missing thumb saved his life and added, "I feel so sad that I locked you in jail. That was such a bad thing to do"

"NO! This is good!" responded his delighted friend.

"Oh, how could that be good my friend, I did a terrible thing to you while I owe you my life".

"It is good" said his friend, "because if I wasn't in jail I would have been hunting with you and they would have killed me."

Another story of a true devout farmer goes like below.

This farmer had only one horse, and one day his only horse ran away. The neighbors came to condole over his terrible loss. The farmer said, "Well, that is what the divine will is" A few days later, the horse returned back, this time bringing with her two beautiful wild horses. The neighbors became excited at the farmer's good fortune and exclaimed, "Such lovely strong horses"!
The farmer said, "Well, that is what the divine will is"
Next day, the farmer's son went riding a new horse. He was thrown off from the back of the wild horse and in this process, he broke his leg. All the neighbors came and consoled him, "what a bad luck"!
The farmer said, "Well, that is what the divine will is"
Next week, a war broke out with the mighty neighboring kingdom and every able-bodied man was conscripted and sent into battle to fight the ferocious and strong enemy army. Only the farmer's son, because he had a broken leg, was left behind in the village. The neighbors congratulated the farmer and the farmer said, "Well, that is what the divine will is"

Devotion does not mean chanting some name, offering some flowers and other gifts to the deity, lighting a lamp in the temple or singing hymns in the praise of god while the mind is focused on something else. If there is absolutely even an iota of a desire or expectation in mind to receive any favour from the deity in response to the apparent devotional activity, then it is simply an effort to indulge in a business of trade. It may be anything else but definitely not devotion. A true devout, who is enlightened, would not even have a thought of indulging in any kind of commercial agreement or trade with the deity. He would not even have a thought of bribing the deity to obtain some undeserved favour as for him anything that happens in his life is a divine gift which he would gracefully accept with a sense of gratitude.

Simultaneously with devotion, one would also instantly and spontaneously get into a state of renunciation (Vairagya). Renunciation would not mean that one would leave his home and family and would start living in a forest or an ashram. It would also not mean getting one's head shaved or start wearing clothes of different kind to distinguish him from the rest of the society. A true renunciate is the one who does not feel the need to leave his home or change his clothes and appearance or his life style. Renunciation is simply a state of mind wherein despite doing everything in the same manner like anyone else in the society, a renunciate would feel completely detached from not only the results of his actions but also from whatever one does. Since in this state, there is absolutely no trace of ego left in the person, he completely lets go of the sense of being a doer. He is able to see things happening through his body as if he is a third person watching him doing things that he does from a distance without being a party to it.

Unless someone has simultaneously all the characteristics of a Gyani (someone who has acquired the knowledge of TRUTH), a devout with unconditional love for God and graceful acceptance of all the events and incidents in his life as divine gift irrespective of whether they appear to be good or bad and also that of a true renunciate who is completely detached from all his actions, he is simply talking about these qualities without actually having experienced it. A pundit or a Gyani who does not display the characteristics of a devout and renunciate is like a parrot who has memorized some epics, some scriptures and some theories and keeps repeating them without actually having understood the true meaning of what he is talking about. A very interesting story in the folklore attributed to Ramkrishna Paramhans exemplifies such kind of characters.

There was once a pundit who lived on the bank of a river. So learned was he that other pundits came from far and near to consult with him. They showered him with appreciation and praise.

On the other side of the bank lived a milkmaid, called Lakshmi, who sold milk to the pundit. Hers was a busy day. She woke up early in the morning, bathed her cows, milked them, then cooked a meal for her old father and then set out to deliver the milk. She had to cross the river on a boat.

One day the pundit was waiting for her for a long time. When she finally arrived, the pundit said, "Ah, Lakshmi you have come at last. I was waiting for you since early morning. From tomorrow, I want the milk before sunrise."

The next morning, Lakshmi rushed to the riverbank at the crack of dawn but the boatman did not show up until late morning. Hurry, hurry, Lakshmi urged the boatman, knowing that the pundit would be waiting for the milk.

The pundit complained, "You are late again, what happened?"
The pundit was in a bad mood that day. "Don't give me excuses"! He shouted.
"How dare you disregard my wishes? Don't you know who I am?"
Lakshmi began to cry.
But the pundit continued to boast, "Do you know how learned I am? You are just a simple milkmaid. I know so many things. That river is like the river of life. People safely cross the river of life by invoking the name of Hari, another name for Vishnu".
Lakshmi took the pundit's words very seriously and happily departed, saying to herself, "I wish punditji had told me this earlier"
The next day Lakshmi arrived at the pundit's house before sunrise. The Pundit was surprised to see her as he could not see the boatman. "How did you cross the river", he inquired.
Lakshmi smiled and said, You taught me to cross the river by chanting the name of Hari and I did.
"That is impossible", the pundit shouted and ordered her to cross the river again.
Lakshmi crossed the river again without any difficulty, chanting the name of Hari as she did so. She stayed completely dry.
The pundit tried to do the same chanting the name of Hari. But as he tried to protect his clothes from getting wet, he fell into the river. Lakshmi was astonished. "Oh Punditji, she said, You were not thinking of Hari at all. You were busy thinking about your dhoti. That is why it did not work".
Now we should not try to research for history in such stories. Any logical mind would know that this is simply a story to prove a point. The intention of the story- teller here is to establish the point that knowledge without devotion is meaningless. Memorizing such knowledge by rote like parrots would not help anybody. Similarly, devotion without knowledge and renunciation is simply an act of devotion but not devotion. We need to distinguish the difference between devotion and the acting of devotion. We can chant the names, offer services and conduct devotional rites and rituals as

instructed by the pundits but that does not make us a devout. Chanting of scriptures and devotional songs has no meaning unless the true devotion emerges in the heart simultaneously with knowledge and renunciation. This is demonstrated by the story of the parrots and the hunter.

Once a saint had domesticated some parrots in his hut and for their security, he had taught them a song, "Shikari aayega, jaal bichhayega, lobh se usame phansana mat", meaning that the hunter will come, lay his trap, but don't get trapped due to greed. One day, the saint went to a nearby village to seek alms. In the meantime, a hunter came and saw several parrots sitting on the branch of a tree. He felt greedy upon seeing so many parrots and started making plans to trap them; just then the parrots started singing the taught slogan, "Shikari aayega, jaal bichhayega, lobh se usame phansana mat". When the hunter heard this, he was left surprised!! He had never seen such wise parrots and thought that it would be impossible to catch them, as they appeared to be trained parrots. The hunter was feeling sleepy, so he put some pieces of guava inside the trap and went off to sleep, thinking that may be one or two greedy, or stupid parrots might fall into the trap. After an hour, when he got up from his sleep, he saw all the parrots singing the same slogan "Shikari aayega, jaal bichhayega, lobh se usame phansana mat". But where were they singing it – inside the net of the trap!! Seeing the condition of the parrots, the hunter laughed and trapped all the parrots and carried them off!

Today, the condition of the so called devouts is similar to that of these singing by-rote parrots, as everyday in the Aarati, they sing "Tan, man, dhan sab hai tera, tera tujhko arpan, kya lagey mera", meaning my body, mind and wealth are all yours and I offer it to you however, in reality while singing this, they actually have a lot of desire and expectations from God in return for these services and offerings. This is no devotion. This is sycophancy. Sycophancy works with the humans but not with God.

The apparent renunciation without knowledge and devotion is simply cowardice. People get distressed with their household problems and finding no other way; they run away to become a sannyasi. This does not lead them to anywhere. They may run away from one set of problems but then they will have to face another new set of problems. A true renunciate need not leave his home as his knowledge leads him to understand the truth and gives rise to devotion in him.

Knowledge, devotion and renunciation cannot be separated. Charlatans running their business in the name of religion and spirituality talk of different paths of Gyan, Bhakti and Vairagya. It is simply cheating the people in the name of religion. Anybody talking on these lines would not be able to demonstrate the characteristic of an enlightened person, i.e. to remain in a state of perennial bliss. Enlightened people, out of compassion for other humans, to help them reach the state of getting the TRUTH and to help them achieve the ultimate state of supreme consciousness where they can say "Aham Brahmasmi" or "Ana al-Haqq", tried to put their own experiences in words. They tried to make people understand the truth with the use of some imagined stories, some anecdotes and some fabricated events and incidents. Their intention, while they did this, was very pious and positive but that also created the foundation for corruption in religion.

Cunning people have converted religion into a commercial organisation and have used all their best efforts and talents to maximize the material profit out of their shops. They have used all the tools described in the books of marketing to maximize the top line and bottom line of their business. They have effectively used the tools of manipulation to exploit the emotional states and vulnerability of the people in the society. It has become a common characteristics of all the current day religious traditions. As a result of this, the religions, as they are being practiced today, have led to a state where most people in the society are in a state of misery and grief. The corruption of religion has led to the corruption and degeneration of the politics and administration. The tools that have been used most commonly to manipulate the people by the charlatans in the name of religion are the emotions of fear, guilt, insecurity, sense of obligation, withholding, question, double bind, prescriptions of the sages or learned people etc. We will explore how these manipulations, to expand their business, by the people who are supposed to be religious leaders and torch bearers, have almost completely eradicated the true religious traditions from this planet. We would also explore how it has affected the social and political order wherein almost every thinking mind is compelled to exclaim "religion is the most lucrative and risk free business".

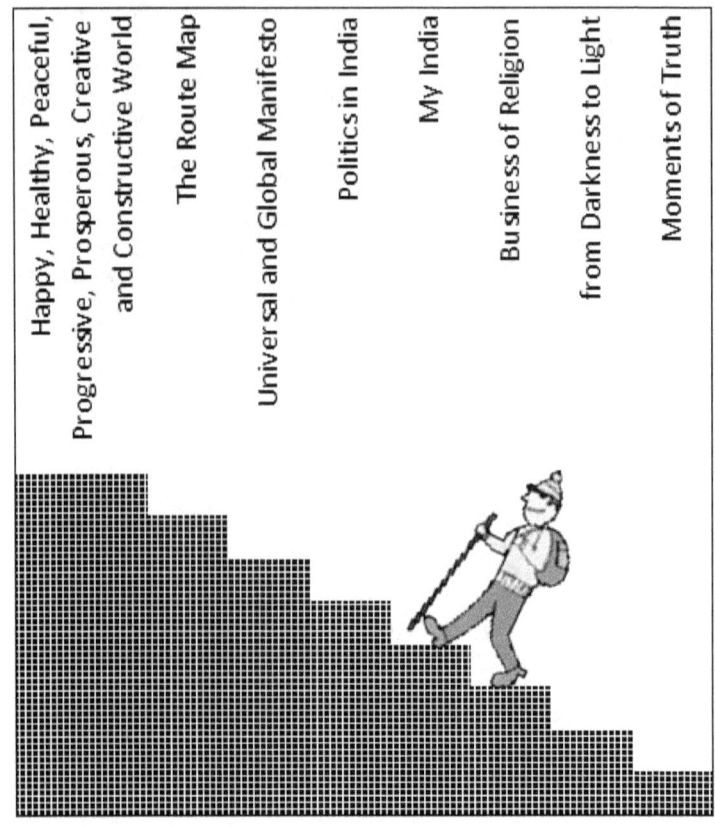

THE BUSINESS OF RELIGION

The tendency to claim God as an ally for our partisan value and ends is the source of all religious fanaticism. - Reinhold Niebuhr

The essence of religion, related to the social life, can be summarized as

अष्टादश पुराणेषु व्यासस्य वचनद्वयम् ।
परोपकारः पुण्याय पापाय पड़पीडनम् ॥

Ashtadash Puraneshu, Vyasasya Vachanadwayam
Paropakarah Punyay, Paapaay Parpeedanam
In all the 18 puranas sage Vyas says only 2 things, doing good to others is virtue (punya) and troubling others is sin (paap).

सर्वे भवन्तु सुखिनः, सर्वे सन्तु निरामयाः ।
सर्वे भद्राणि पश्यन्तु, मा कश्चिद्दुःखभाग्भवेत् ।

Sarve Bhavantu Sukhinah,
Sarve Santu Nir-aamayaah
Sarve Bhadraani Pashyantu,
Maa Kashcid-Duhkha-Bhaag-Bhavet

May All become Happy, May All be Free from Illness. May All See what is Auspicious, May no one Suffer.

न त्वहं कामये राज्यं न स्वर्गं नापुनर्भवम् ।
कामये दुःखतप्तानां प्राणिनाम् आर्तिनाशनम् ॥

Na Twaham Kamaye Rajyam
Na Swargam Na-apunarbhavam.
Kaamaye Dukha-Taptanam
Praninamaarti Naashanam.

I do not want any Kingdom, nor heavenly pleasure nor even escape from rebirth. But I do want that the affliction of all beings tormented by the miseries of life may cease."

परहित सरिस धरम नहि भाई । पर पीड़ा सम नहि अधमाई ॥
Parhit saris dharam nahi bhai, Par peeda sam nahi adhmai

Serving others is the best religion; causing pain to others is the biggest sin.

All the people who have awakened to the TRUTH have tried their best to share this divine knowledge and understanding with the people in their immediate environment. Out of compassion for their fellow humans, they felt a need to share their wisdom and knowledge. Those who reached the shores of Truth, they longed to convey the joy of their experience to those they loved; so that those who could not come that far may also get a glimpse of that wonderful experience. In their attempt to share this divine wisdom and knowledge, they used the vocabulary and language to the best of their linguistic abilities. In this process, The Geeta, The Bible, the Quran reached us. They used the stories, anecdotes and references from their time and environment to pass on the essence of TRUTH to their followers. During their own lifetime, if they found that the stories or references they used to present a point was being misinterpreted, they intervened and helped people correct their course and stay on the path of TRUTH. However, after these people left their body, there was no one to guide the followers. The stories and references became more important than the true essence of the message that was intended to be conveyed.

The TRUTH does not change over time and space. It is absolute. It is not dependent on any reference. Since all the enlightened people tried to convey the TRUTH, they conveyed exactly and absolutely the same thing without any mismatch of understanding between all of them since the truth does not change over time. I often wonder if people like Kapil Muni, Gautam, Kanad, Jaimini, Patanjali, Ved Vyas, Balmiki, Vashishtha, Vishwamitra, Bhardwaj, Jamadagni, Atri, Agastya, Kashyap, Siddharth Gautam, Vardhaman Mahaveer, Zoroaster, Moses, Socrates, Jesus Christ, Mohammad, Lao Tsu, Kabir, Nanak, Tulsidas, Surdas, Meerabai, Ramkrishna, Telang Swami, Raman Maharshi, Krishnamurti, Osho and other such people ever assembled for a get together, how would they converse amongst themselves. I feel that they would simply sing and dance since they all would find the TRUTH all around them. There would be absolutely no discussion in language between them since they would be able to feel and sense the TRUTH around them. They would find themselves amongst the people that they would have dreamt of while thinking of conveying the TRUTH to the society.

However, today the religion has reached to such a stage that all these people, if they could somehow sense what is being interpreted out of what they said or conveyed, they would simply faint. A story from Fyodor Dostoyevsky in the novel "The Brothers Karamazov" illustrates this. In this story, Dostoyevsky imagines the return of Jesus to earth. In "Book Five: Pro and Contra", in the chapter "Grand Inquisitor", the author says that after eighteen hundred years since his death, Jesus thought that the time was ripe for him to re-visit the earth.

So one Sunday, Jesus descended into a village and stood under a tree. People were returning from the village church; the morning mass was over. They were surprised to see a Christ-like figure standing under the tree. Who is this man dressed like Jesus? He must be an actor, they thought.

They gathered around him, full of curiosity and began to question him: "Your acting is perfect. You look exactly like Christ."

"But I AM Christ," said Jesus. They laughed aloud; one threw a stone, another a slipper and they all danced round him, calling him insane. One, out of pity, told him to go before the priest caught him.

"Your priest? He is my priest. Don't you recognize me? I am the one to whom you pray every morning."

"We shall worship you as you deserve, if you do not make yourself scarce quickly!" they told him.

Jesus, in his compassion, forgave them; perhaps they really did not recognize him. However, the priest was bound to, for he sang his praises all day. Then along came the priest. The noisy crowd became silent as he approached. Then, one by one, they touched his feet (such is the world, it will stone God but it will prostrate before those who make business out of Him).

"This is blasphemy!" exclaimed Jesus.

"Keep quiet," people said. "If the priest hears you, he will feel insulted." This drew the priest's attention.

"Who is this rascal?" he asked, "Bring him to me."

"You too do not recognize me?" Jesus asked the priest, "And you wear my cross around your neck!"

Jesus overlooked the fact that the cross he was hung on was made of wood, while the cross that hung round the priest's neck, was made of gold. (Was ever a cross to hang a man by made of gold? And it is the man who is hung on to the cross and not the cross on the man!)

"This man looks like Satan himself!" proclaimed the priest, "Our Jesus came to earth but once. There is no need for him to come again. Now we are here to look after his work." So Jesus was locked up in the attic of the church. He was shocked! This was the same kind of treatment he had received eighteen hundred years ago. "Will I be crucified again?" He wondered.

The priest came to visit him in the middle of the night. He fell at his feet and begged forgiveness. "I recognized you alright, Oh Glorious One! But we are constrained to deny you in the market-place.

You need not take the trouble of coming again. We are carrying out your work with all sincerity.

Business is good, and if you come, there is bound to be confusion. We have barely got things going smoothly and you come again! Please understand, we cannot acknowledge you in public. Not only that, we might have to resort to the same tactics to disown you, as we did eighteen hundred years ago. Please forgive us; we are helpless."

This outlines how the religion has turned into a roaring commercial business of perennial nature. The business has become more important than the truth. The charlatans have used (or rather misused) the religions to perpetrate the exploitation of the masses. They have gathered people around them and enslaved them mentally using the manipulative handles of fear, guilt, sense of obligation, question, double bind, prescriptions of the sages etc. This has happened in all the religions and religious traditions across the world without even a single exception. This has got so deeply programmed in the minds of people that it has become a Herculean task to undo it and bring the humanity back onto the religious and spiritual path or the path of truth. People have been manipulated, by misinterpretation of the stories and references that were used to present the truth or by concocting new stories, traditions, rites and ritual in the name of religion. The self-styled fake religious leaders have never been interested in helping people and masses get rid of misery and sorrow. All, that they have been interested in, is their own personal interest and benefits. Their interest is limited to acquire immense wealth and luxury for their very personal use and to have a position of power by virtue of commanding control over a large number of people in the name of religion. By definition, these self styled godmen known by the names like swami, baba, mahant, mahatma, maulvi, imam, father, pastor etc. are diagonally opposite to what a religious leader is supposed to be. We will look into some of the stories that are in use to cheat masses to induce them to let go of their rational thinking and to create a belief system which is based on illogical faith. Once people are driven out of the realm of reason and logic, it becomes easy for these fake religious leaders to control their mind and belief system and enslave them for their very own vested interest. These vested interests have corrupted our religious and spiritual traditions which in turn have created a corrupt and crooked society with myriad sociopolitical and economic problems. Let us examine the current state of all the religions and religious traditions.

We will start with Hinduism. Let us go through the story of Ramayana wherein Lord Rama is supposed to have been depicted as the most ideal personality amongst all the humans. This most ideal person is born as a result of a Putrakaam Yajna. I wonder why this Putrakaam Yajna is not prescribed in Ayurved for all the infertility treatments! Lord Rama is ordered by his father to leave his house without any wrong doing on his part and despite all his best efforts to meet the expectations of his father in the past. He does not question his father in terms of why should he be made to suffer for something for which he is absolutely not responsible at all. Where does Lord Rama get an authority from, to let his newly married wife and younger brother share and suffer the pains that he voluntarily accepts to go through? What should be done to a man who mistreats and causes the severance of the nose of a lady through his younger brother just because she fell in love with him at first sight and proposed marriage? Was it justified for Lord Rama to take side of Sugreeva in his fight against Bali particularly since Bali had committed no crime? The dying Bali asked the Lord;

"What was my crime? Even if I committed a crime (with my brother), what is your right to kill me?"

The third question that Bali asked shows his disapproval of the way Lord Rama killed him. He says,

"I was fighting with some other person and was not careful enough when you shot me. Why didn't you fight against me with valour from the front and instead attacked on me like a hunter from a hiding position?"

The replies of Lord Rama were:

"The younger brother should be treated like a son. Even if he made a mistake you should forgive him, especially when he promised to respect you for your whole life."

Lord Rama forgets that the fight in which he himself participated was a result of the challenge by Sugreeva to the authority of Bali and not out of respect for an elder brother by a younger brother.

About his authority, he said he had permission from King Bharat to spread righteousness and punish evils. He does not feel the need to explain what was so evil with Bali and so righteous with Sugreeva. From where does this King Bharat come in picture in this scene?

In response to the third question, he quoted how great kings did hunting of deers in the past and justified that hunting kings did not care if the deer was careful or not. He justifies that since Bali was a monkey, he could be treated like a deer and hunted. So, why not Sugreeva, was he not a monkey?

Why did Lord Rama take the support of a traitor brother Vibheeshan to kill Ravan? What is so ideal and righteous about Lord Rama helping Vibheeshan takeover the kingdom and wealth of his deceased brother and marry his wife Mandodari?

Why did Lord Rama feel the need to ask his wife to pass through the burning fire to test her chastity and fidelity but did not feel the need to pass through a similar test himself? What is so ideal and righteous about it? Why did he, on the basis of gossips and flimsy provocation of an intemperate man of low intelligence and knowledge, banish his pregnant wife from his home despite having made her go through the fire test of fidelity? What is so righteous about it?

Why did he not fight his mighty sons Luv and Kush to defend his Ashwamedha Horse after these boys had already defeated his army led by his brothers and his lieutenant Hanuman? Why did he take the easy route, while he was almost at the verge of being defeated, to remind the boys that they were his sons and instead of fighting them, invited them to his kingdom?

Why did he feel the need to ask Seeta to once again prove her fidelity when she was brought back to Ayodhya from Balmiki's ashram? Was it not a repeated public humiliation and mistrust on a lady who had consistently displayed an exemplary character? What ideal did Rama want to display before others by doing this again and again? Why did he do this contrary to the advice of his teacher Rishi Vashishtha? Why did he feel the need to order his younger brother Laxman to commit suicide who had completely surrendered himself to his elder brother? Rama ordered death punishment on Laxman in response to his lifelong service to him. Laxman not only accompanied Lord Rama in his exile but did everything else, without ever applying his own brain. Because of his loyalty and dedication to Lord Rama, Laxman did not care even for his wife and was ready to fight with the other brother Bharat. What did he get in return? Lord Rama commanded him to commit suicide. What is so ethical and righteous in it? Why did he forget his sermon to Bali about treating a younger brother like a son while ordering death penalty on Laxman? Why did Lord Rama himself commit suicide by drowning himself in river Sarayu?

On the other hand, Ravan, who is supposed to have been depicted as the most evil person, to the extent that he is portrayed as a demon, comes across as a very pious and virtuous person. He wanted to avenge the humiliation to his innocent sister and therefore kidnapped Seeta. Instead of keeping Seeta in his palace, he accommodated her at a different place. He did not force himself on Seeta against her will even though she was in his total physical control. Despite knowing the intentions of Lord Rama to kill him, Ravan helped him perform the rituals to complete his worship of Lord Shiva's Rameshwara Lingam to please him before he built a bridge across to Lanka.

Ravan was a great source of wisdom as well. The story goes that after firing the fatal arrow on the battlefield of Lanka, Lord Rama told his brother, Laxman, "Go to Ravan quickly before he dies and request him to share whatever knowledge he can. A brute he may be, but he is also a great scholar." The obedient Laxman rushed across the battlefield to Ravan's side and whispered in his ears, "Demon-king, do not let your knowledge die with you. Share it with us and wash away your sins." Ravan responded by simply turning away. An angry Laxman went back to Ram, "He is as arrogant as he always was, too proud to share anything." Lord Rama asked him, "Where did you stand while asking Ravan for knowledge?" "Next to his head so that I could hear what he had to say clearly." Lord Rama smiled, placed his bow on the ground and walked to where Ravan lay. Laxman watched in astonishment as his divine brother knelt at Ravan's feet.

With palms joined, with extreme humility, Lord Rama said, "Lord of Lanka, you abducted my wife, a terrible crime for which I have been forced to punish you. Now, you are no more my enemy. I bow to you and request you to share your wisdom with me. Please do that for if you die without doing so, all your wisdom will be lost forever to the world." To Laxman's surprise, Ravan opened his eyes and raised his arms to salute Ram, "If only I had more time as your teacher than as your enemy. Standing at my feet as a student should, unlike your rude younger brother, you are a worthy recipient of my knowledge. I have very little time so I cannot share much but let me tell you one important lesson I have learnt in my life. Things that are bad for you seduce you easily; you run towards them impatiently. But things that are actually good for you, fail to attract you; you shun them creatively, finding powerful excuses to justify your procrastination. That is why I was impatient to abduct Seeta but avoided meeting you. This is the wisdom of my life, Ram. My last words. I give it to you." With these words, Ravan died.

Ravan comes across as the most ardent devotee of Lord Shiva and does not hesitate to offer even his own heads to him. He also comes across as a king who is really concerned for the welfare and pride of the subjects of his kingdom. He is one of the most self-respecting persons and does not hesitate to sacrifice everything that he has, including all his kins and his own life, despite repeated advice from his trusted well-wishers and advisors to the contrary. So what is the message in the story of Ramayan?

Any attempt to trace history in these stories would not lead us anywhere and we would simply get confused if we would try to apply reason and logic to these stories and their literal meaning. Without going into the details and without resorting to a religious discourse, it would suffice to hint that people on the path of truth would certainly be able to find the essence of truth in this story. Here, Lord Rama is the ultimate essence of cosmic consciousness, the Purush or the Brahma that is present in everything and everywhere. He is the divinity that is omniscient, omnipresent and omnipotent. He is the source of bliss in every conscious mind. He is the ultimate source of energy. Seeta is Prakriti, time (Kaal), or Maya through which the world appears the way it does. She is the creative potency of the Lord. It is through Maya or Kaal that the events and incidents appear to be taking place. Ravan represents ego. Hanuman is a representation of the mind. The samsara goes on due to maya and ego. The moment ego is annihilated, samsara comes to an end. The mind is the tool to control and annihilate ego. Any rational thinking logical mind would instantly realise that Hanuman, i.e. a monkey would never be able to do all those things which is ascribed to him in this story. The Hanuman has been depicted as monkey since the nature of mind is like that of a monkey. The mind would always be restless like a monkey. The mind would continuously keep on thinking and worrying about past and future and would not rest in present to attain a state of bliss. This is very similar to a monkey continuously jumping from one branch of a tree to the other without ever coming to a state of rest. The mind has unlimited and infinite power. Any task, howsoever difficult it may be, can be accomplished by focused attention of a positive and persistent human mind. There is absolutely nothing impossible for a motivated and focused human mind although human beings are generally not aware of this unlimited potential of their mind until they are awakened to this fact by someone else. Similarly, Hanuman is normally not aware of his own unlimited potential however when he is reminded of his unlimited powers, it becomes like a child's play for him to jump across the sea or to bring the mountain with the medicinal herbs to revive Laxman. The mind derives its power from the ultimate source of cosmic energy or God like Hanuman derives his power from his devotion to Lord Rama.

This story was fabricated, most probably, to induce people to start their journey on the devotional path with subtle hints about the TRUTH. However, unless people achieve a state of true devotion and gain the knowledge of TRUTH and thereby achieve a state of renunciation or detachment from all their actions by shedding their ego, this story does not serve any real purpose. In the present days, the fake religious leaders and story tellers exaggerate the events and incidents in this and many other religious stories with a sole motive to run their business of religion by exhorting the sense of faith and belief of people. In their attempt to keep people under their total control, they do not hesitate to portray God in a way which is diagonally opposite to the concept of a compassionate and kind divinity. In many stories, to inculcate a sense of fear with an intent to blackmail the masses, these people have fabricated stories wherein God is portrayed as an egotistical man sitting somewhere in the clouds who is continuously watching his own business and is ever eager to punish and cause pains and hardships to those who do not offer gifts, prayers and obeisance to him. At the same time, God showers gifts, material pleasures, boons and fulfills the wishes of those who are ready to pay homage to him in accordance to the rites and rituals prescribed by the priests and Brahmans. One such story, which is very very popular, is the one in the context of worshipping Lord Vishnu in his form as Satya Narayan (TRUTH – The Lord). The tradition of worshipping Satya Narayan started as worship to the nature, as an offering of gratitude to Lord Vishnu, during the times of achievements, however it became one of the tools of regular extortion and blackmail by the Brahmans in the name of God. I will quote one of the stories which is regularly recited during the ritual of Satya Narayan worship in which God is depicted as an egotistical person mainly interested in sycophancy.

> This story consists of a childless merchant and his adventures. There was a wise king named Ulkamuk. He had a pious and beautiful wife. He would go to the temple daily and would give charity to the Brahmans. One day near the banks of river Madhushala, where they were performing Lord Shri Satya Narayana's vratham, a wealthy merchant was passing by. He anchored his boat, went to the king and asked him, "Oh King, please let me know the details about the vratham you are performing with such devotion". The king replied that he was performing the Lord Satya Narayana Swami's vratham. He said that one who performs this vratham will gain worldly pleasures and attain salvation. The merchant asked him the details stating that, "Oh King, I would like to know the details as I am childless and would like to perform this vratham". The king gladly gave the entire details about the vratham and its rituals.
>
> After acquiring the entire details of the vratham, the merchant and his wife decided to perform the fast if they get a child. Sometime later, his wife Lilavati became pregnant and she delivered a girl who they named Kalavati. The merchant's wife Lilavati reminded him about his promise to keep the fast and perform the vratham. The merchant postponed it saying that he would do so when the daughter grows and is ready to be married. The merchant told his wife that during the time of Kalawati's wedding, it would be easy to do the fast because at the moment he was

busy in his business. So saying, he left for his business trip to various villages.

Kalawati grew up to be a beautiful girl. When the merchant saw his daughter was of marriageable age, he called the match-maker and requested him to search an ideal match for his daughter. Hearing the merchant's request, the match-maker reached Kanchan Nagar. From there, he brought the proposal of a young handsome boy. Agreeing to the proposal and after speaking to the boy's parents, Kalavati's marriage was performed with much fanfare and religious ceremonies & rituals. All this while and even at this time of his daughter's wedding, the merchant forgot about the promise to perform the Satya Narayana vratham. So, the Lord decided to remind the merchant about his promise by teaching him lessons.

The merchant, after a few days, left for his business trip with his son-in-law by boat. They anchored their boat in a beautiful village, named Ratanpur ruled by King Chandraketu. One day, the thieves robbed the wealth of the king. After robbing, they went and stayed at the same place where the merchant was staying. Seeing the guards following them, they left the entire loot near the merchant and then hid themselves. When the guards reached the merchant's place, they saw all the king's wealth beside the merchant and his son-in-law. Thinking them to be robbers, they arrested them and brought them before the king stating that they were responsible for the theft. The king, without giving any chance of explaining their case, ordered both to be behind bars. Even their wealth was confiscated by the king.

Meanwhile at the merchant's house, the thieves robbed their entire wealth. This left his wife and daughter to beg for their daily bread. One day while begging for food, Kalawati reached a Brahman's house. At that time, the Brahman and his family were performing Lord Satya Narayana's puja. After listening to the prayer and taking the prasadam, she left for home. By the time she reached home, it was already dark.

Leelawati was worried. She asked her daughter Kalawati, why it took her so much time to come home. Kalawati replied, "Oh Mother, today I was at a Brahman's house where they were performing Lord Satya Narayana's vratham." On hearing this, Leelawati recollected the long pending promise by her husband and narrated it to her daughter. She soon began the preparations for the Lord Satya Narayana vratham. She did the fast & prayer and asked the Lord for forgiveness. She prayed that her husband and her son-in-law return home safely.

Lord Satya Narayana was pleased with the prayer and the fast. One day, he told King Chandraketu in his dream, "Oh King, You must release the merchant and his son-in-law as they are not the robbers. Return their wealth and set them free. If you do not do so, your kingdom will be destroyed." In the morning, the king called the people in his court and told them about the dream.

The people agreed that the merchant and his son-in-law should be released by the king. The king asked the guards to bring the prisoners, returned all their belongings and set them free. The king told them that due to their wrongdoings, they had to undergo this suffering, but now there was nothing to fear & they could go back home. They bowed down to the king & left for home.

These and many similar stories would not be acceptable to any rational mind. In fact, stories of this kind have the potential to kill the real thirst for TRUTH that is present in each and every human being and divert them on to a path of irrational and illogical fanaticism. The Mahabharat of Ved Vyas, which contains Shreemadbhagvadgeeta which is one of the fountainheads of knowledge about TRUTH, too is not free from such kind of irrational and illogical stories. The concepts of having sexual relation with Sun god by Kunti, the concepts of so many people having brute physical force equivalent to the ten thousand elephants, the arms and ammunition as sophisticated and intelligent as they are described to be like the Brahmastra or Ekaghni would never be palatable to any rational mind. To top it all, Krishna – the God incarnate, justifies a need to get so many people killed in the Mahabharat war when he could have prevented the war. Why would a God incarnate need sixteen thousand wives and how in his human form he would simultaneously sleep with all of them? In another epic

Shreemadbhagvatam, every small creature like a crow or calf which had a tiff with Krishna in his childhood is exaggerated to be like a big monster with names like Kaakaasur or Vatsaasur. This so glorified God, as Krishna is portrayed in these epics to be, is shown to indulge in extremely mean diplomatic and unethical activities when he schemes to kill people like Bhishma, Drona, Karna or even Barbareek. These stories would not and should not be palatable to any rational mind. These stories would not have any value other than pure entertainment to children. However the essence of creating Krishna lies in Bhagvadgeeta which is a fine source of knowledge about TRUTH. These stories certainly have the potential to initiate people on to the path of devotion and ultimately lead to a state of enlightenment through Geeta and to a state of renunciation or detached action. Unfortunately, the current state of affair is such that these stories do not serve any purpose other than running the commercial business shop of the charlatans in the name of religion and God.

It is not that these irrational stories are limited to the so called Hinduism only. The Jains, the followers of Vardhmaan Mahaveer boast that as per their scriptures, Mahaveer donated thousands of elephants and chariots before renouncing the life of a householder. They go on to say that he donated ten million and eight hundred thousand gold coins. Since normal gold coins are ten grams in weight, this means he donated 108 tons of gold worth 324 billion rupees at current rates. Little do these people realise that the kingdom, that Mahaveer is portrayed to have been a ruler of, could never ever afford to have such number of elephants, horse or gold coins. Here the intention is only to show that he renounced every worldly possession that he had. However, they feel a need to exaggerate the value attached to the asset that is shown to have been renounced lest it would not impress the listeners or readers. Similarly, Buddhists claim that Siddhartha Gautam walked for eight steps on his own feet immediately after his birth. This is only to assign some miraculous and special powers to Buddha to make him comparable to Rama or Krishna about whom such unbelievable and irrational stories are associated with their birth and infancy. This is so even when Buddha and Mahaveer had prescribed strict adherence to truth as one of the basic conditions of their path. Nanak is said to have drowned in a river for 3 days and then resurfaced with the knowledge of TRUTH. Unfortunately, Nanak did not feel a need to transfer this knowledge of underwater survival even though he spent rest of his life sharing his understanding of TRUTH.

This is the state of affairs with religious traditions which have strong philosophical knowledge and understanding behind them. Then we have faith based religious traditions which insist on their followers to shut their brain and blindly follow and believe in whatever their religious leaders interpret in the name of God from the books like Bible or Quran. Like most other scriptures, most part of Bible and Quran is irrational and illogical.

Bible expects people to believe that a virgin can give birth to a child. To make it plausible to doubting minds, they invent the story of impregnation of the Virgin Mary by Holy Ghost. Just by believing in Jesus, one can be saved from going to the hell as Jesus would be there to save him on the Day of Judgment. The man who could not save himself from being crucified is expected to save people from going to the hell for eternity. Christians would make you believe that once someone goes to hell, he has to be there till eternity. Then how did they know about the affairs of the hell since nobody has ever returned from there? The Bible is not based on any sound logic, rational and enquiry and therefore it expects people to have faith without questioning its authority. Christians tried to stunt the growth of scientific investigation when they forced Galileo to concede and accept the biblical assertion that sun revolves around earth even after Galileo had concrete evidence to prove to the contrary. When Galileo supported the heliocentric view of Copernicus based on his astronomical observations and experiments, the Christian church administration ordered for its investigation by the Roman Inquisition in 1615. This investigation concluded that heliocentric view was false as it was contrary to the scripture. It ordered for placing the works advocating the Copernican system on the index of banned books and reprimanded Galileo for advocating heliocentrism. Galileo was tried by the Holy Office, then found "vehemently suspect of heresy", was forced to recant, and spent the rest of his life under house arrest. Osho Rajneesh, in one of his discourses had spoken on this incident in the following words;

> "Galileo had asked, and he had cornered the pope: "You either prove that I am wrong on scientific grounds...because it is not a religious matter at all. What

has religion to do with whether the sun goes around the earth or the earth goes around the sun? It has nothing to do with any spirituality, it is a scientific area. If anybody can prove anything scientifically against me, then of course I will withdraw. But why are you afraid?"

Cornered in this way, the pope had to accept that the real problem was: "We are not concerned whether the earth goes around, or the sun. Our concern is that even if one sentence in the Bible is found to be wrong, the whole credibility of the Bible goes. Then it is not a work of God. God is infallible; God cannot commit such a mistake. He made the earth; he made the sun then how come he does not know who goes around whom.

The point is that one sentence proved wrong will create doubt about the whole authenticity of the Bible, so we cannot allow you to create this doubt in people's minds."

Galileo was very old, almost on his deathbed. He had been dragged from his deathbed to the court of the pope. He said, "I don't want to get into any unnecessary trouble. I am already dying. So I will cancel the sentence." And he must have been a man of a great sense of humor. He canceled the sentence. But in a footnote, he wrote, "Although I am canceling this sentence, the fact is that the earth goes around the sun. They are not going to listen to me, and they don't follow any religion and they are not Christians."

Certainly the earth is not Christian, neither is the sun Christian. And certainly whoever wrote the Bible is not omniscient and is not infallible."

If Galileo would have had faith in Bible, he would not have built the foundation on which Newton built what is known as classical physics and which is still so relevant that it is the knowledge behind the motions of the satellites that are being used in the present day communication and the information technology. Galileo was the founder of law of inertia which subsequently was adopted by Newton as his first law of motion while postulating his three laws of motion. Newton's laws of motion gave birth to the concept of universal gravitation and laid the foundation for Einstein to postulate his special and general theory of relativity. Einstein's relativity eventually revealed the nature of time which is contrary to the common sense concept of time. Just think of the consequences if Galileo would have succumbed to the proponents of Bible for whom earth was the center of the universe and there were different sets of physical laws operating on the earth and the heavenly bodies! As per Bible, Jesus wants everybody to be like a sheep and wants a role of shepherd for himself. Sheep are not supposed to apply their own brain in their activities. Bible would also expect its followers to remain in the ancient state of pastoral economy of shepherds. Some of the moral stories in Bible are also very interesting. As per Bible, King David slept with his neighbour's wife and then got his neighbour killed in a war. As a punishment, God made all the wives of King David to sleep with his other neighbours in full public view. Bible fails to explain what was the wrong doing on the part of wives of King David and why were they punished for something for which David was responsible? What kind of a punishment is this in which God himself punishes the ladies to be sexually assaulted in full public view? I wonder why did God choose to have only one son and then destined him to go back to him in the most painful manner of crucifixion. I also wonder why not God felt the need to send him back to earth after the messages that his son carried was over ruled by another messenger Mohammad.

Christianity and Islam are mainly faith based belief systems. They do not leave much scope for independent enquiry declaring their source books as the end of knowledge. Prophet Mohammad declares himself to be the last and final prophet. He declares all the previous messengers like Noah, Ibrahim, Moses, Jesus etc. as incomplete and assumes the role of being the last and final messenger of God. Quran is believed to be of divine origin brought to earth by Gabriel on the orders of Allah using Mohammad as the messenger. Anything that can be claimed to be originating from or rooted in Quran is not supposed to be questioned. Muslim scholars are aware of the fact that application of reason and logic, to many of the facts and beliefs which are attributed to Quran, has the potential to completely demolish its foundation in the light of modern scientific knowledge. Therefore, they are generally not open to discuss the teachings of Quran with anybody who is not a Muslim. They are trained, as part of their theological traditions, not to allow anybody to express his doubt about the wisdom that can be attributed to Quran, irrespective of the quality of reason, argument, facts and figures that may be presented by any such person in support of his assertions. When Salman Rushdie attempts to talk about Satanic Verses, a fatwa or diktat is issued by some people claiming to be the guardians of Islam for his murder. What are referred to as the "Satanic Verses" are a small group of verses that were part of the original Quran which Prophet Mohammad initially claimed to have received from Allah through Gabriel like all other verses in Quran. In these verses, Prophet Mohammad established the existence and reality of goddesses Al-Lat, Al-Uzza and Manat of Pagan tradition. This acceptance of the existence of goddesses besides Allah was in direct conflict with his theory of monotheism. Once Prophet Mohammad realized about these conflicts and contradictions, he declared that these verses were not actually from Allah but from Satan. These verses were subsequently replaced by new verses demeaning the three goddesses. Since Prophet Mohammad himself admitted in context to these Satanic Verses that there was scope for errors in what he believed to be the direct messages from Allah, then logically it could be derived that other verses in Quran too could potentially be of satanic origin or from some other dubious source. Allah is considered to be the creator of the whole universe and therefore, He is also supposed to be aware of all the facts about the physical objects that exist in the universe created by Him. However, now we are aware of many objective facts which appear to be in conflict with the assertions made in Quran, e.g. the existence of the heliocentric solar system rather than the geocentric universe. Allah being omniscient, it is simply not possible for any objective fact to be wrong, if it is considered to be coming in the form of a direct message from Allah. Since, Quran is believed to be a direct message from Allah, all the assertions in Quran ought to be true irrespective of the time and space. As per some researchers, Quran seems to be suggesting that the earth is flat and the sun sets at a particular place going inside some muddy spring. The Quran is interpreted to suggest that meteorites are the missiles that are fired to shoot the devils. Quran is also interpreted to suggest that moon is farther from the earth than the stars and the universe has only seven planets. Some of the other facts that can be inferred from the assertions in Quran which do not conform to the current day scientific knowledge and logical analysis are

   a.   earth was created before the stars,

  b. Sun is a flat disk
  c. Humans were created instantaneously from mud or clay
  d. Human were created in paradise to their perfect anatomy and then brought down to earth
  e. Sperm originates between backbone and ribs
  f. Only Allah knows the gender of a foetus
  g. Space flight is impossible

These are some of the points which suggest that assertions made in the Quran need to be analyzed in the light of the modern scientific discoveries. Interested readers can go through a compilation of such apparent errors in Quran on internet at http://wikiislam.net/wiki/Scientific_Errors_in_the_Qur'an or at http://www.faithfreedom.org. It is believed to have been prescribed in the Quran (Qibla) that people ought to face Kaba while offering prayer to Allah. I wonder what would happen to someone who would try to face Kaba while offering his prayers if he happens to live at a place which is on the opposite side of the diagonal of the earth, which joins Kaba and the center of the earth (antipode of Kaba). Will he offer his prayer by facing towards center of the earth? I cannot imagine a sitting posture for this place which would meet this requirement. (This place happens to be in South Pacific Ocean with many small islands and some military installations nearby). Prophet Mohammad was a simple person. He was not a learned scholar. Out of compassion for his fellow human beings, he tried to share the wisdom which he gathered in the process of his enlightenment. He, therefore, prescribed many practices without going into their philosophical analysis. His language was simple so that it could be easily understood by the masses. Because of his simplistic approach, it is possible to find out contradictions and fallacies in what he said. This can be demonstrated through this example. As per Quran, if a man dies leaving behind a wife, more than two daughters and both parents, then the inheritance of the assets is to be distributed as below. The daughters get two third, the wife gets one eighth and both the parents get one sixth each. The basic arithmetical rules would show that this kind of distribution is not possible. When one would ask a Muslim scholar to explain about all these fallacies, he would mostly say that such references are also available in scriptures of Christians and Jews. That does not seem to be a valid and reasonable explanation. The concept of shunning the sensuality on earth so that one can enjoy the company of Hoors (the virgin damsels) in "Jannat" (paradise) does not appear to be logically sound. There does not seem to be a valid explanation for why one man could have four wives. The social treatment of woman in the name of Islam is really deplorable. The concept of "Jehad" or holy war (can a war ever be holy? Isn't it an oxymoron?) to spread Islam by the use of brute force and violence is condemnable. Intolerance towards non- Islamic view point is barbaric. The great tradition of fasting for a month during Ramadan and to focus one's mind on Allah during this period have been substantially diluted and modified to suit the convenience of many individuals. All these observations here about Quran or ISLAM are not meant to demean the tradition. It has been compiled here only to highlight that what the enlightened masters received and then tried to convey to the masses and what is presently being preached in their name is not the same thing. It is an established fact that Prophet Mohammad did not have extensive exposure in terms of how to present answers to the philosophical questions. His physical exposure of the world and knowledge about the society was limited to a small geographical area confined within the Arabian Desert. Yet, he received the ultimate TRUTH. After his own enlightenment and out of compassion for his fellow human beings as a result of the understanding of the universal brotherhood, he tried to share the essence of his understanding and presented the TRUTH in a manner suitable for his time and place so that people would accept it and get benefitted out of it. This could have been one of the probable reasons why he invented the story about the satanic verses as he realised that those verses were not leading the people towards where he intended them to go.

The intent to present these facts here is not to sneer at any religious tradition. All faith based religious traditions like Christianity or Islam started with a sense of compassion to help people overcome misery and grief in their personal and social life and to help them progress on to the path of devotion which could ultimately awaken them to the TRUTH and lead to enlightenment. The message of unconditional love that Jesus spread continues to be an undisputed tool to achieve the ultimate state of devotion and the world needs to be grateful to Jesus for spreading this message amongst so many people. In their attempt to make this message acceptable to the masses, many stories and references were created which were not expected to be important but unfortunately those stories and references are now being projected as the main plank of these religious traditions. The message of one God or Allah that Mohammad conveyed to his followers is still the essence of any philosophical or scientific enquiry. His message that Allah is Kind and compassionate (Raheem and Rehman) is such a profound and beautiful concept about divinity. This is a message to ask people to accept everything that happen in their life, irrespective of whether it appears to be good or bad, as divine grace. The concept of "Salat" or praying five times a day is such a great prescription to remember God almost continuously which can annihilate the sense of ego and thereby lead to the ultimate state of realization of TRUTH. The concept of "Sawm" or fasting continuously for a month during Ramadan to purify the mind and body and to focus the mind on the attributes of Allah is sure to reveal the TRUTH if someone strictly adheres to the fasting and indeed focuses his mind on Allah, the Compassionate and Kind. The concept of "Zakat" or donating at least 2.5% of one's income to the poor people in society comes out of concern for people who are all considered to be the children of the same God and originates from the concept of universal brotherhood. These are all so profound and beautiful spiritual concepts which are still as valid as they ever were. The sufi tradition of Islam is such a beautiful display of devotion and renunciation at the same time. Yet again, the stories and references and the way these messages have been delivered has become more important than the essence of the message. This has become so, mainly because of the vested interest of those who wanted to exploit the masses for their very own selfish and personal gains. The fake religious leaders wanted to enjoy power, prestige and material wealth and in their attempt to gain this, they have corrupted the whole religious traditions. This corruption of religion is not limited to any particular religious tradition and can be traced across almost all the so called religions which are in practice on this planet at the moment. We would look into this process of corruption in Hindu religious traditions.

Let us look at the origin of corruption. Before we can delve deep into this question, we need to understand the origin of the social structure, family and the concept of personal property. During the stage of human evolution when the only known profession of mankind to satisfy its physical need of hunger was hunting and gathering, people lived in groups and continuously kept moving from one place to the other in search of fresh stock of animal prey, roots and herbs. There was no concept of family, individual house or personal property and all males and females in the community were available to all for their sexual needs and support. Since it was not easy for the pregnant women to run chasing the animals, they stayed back at the places where the group camped. They collected the wood and other wild materials to make their place of stay safe and secure and thereby the concept of secured shelter got introduced into the life of mankind and women assumed the role of home maker. Their staying at a place for longer period provided them the opportunity to observe the natural process of growth of wild grain plants from the seeds. It helped them understand the process of agriculture and motivated them to adopt agriculture and domesticate animals. Agriculture and domestication of animals for milk, food and other needs ended the dependence of mankind on hunting and gathering and allowed them to stay at one place for longer period giving rise to the villages and society. The surplus produce from the agriculture, from what was instantly required by people for their immediate survival, gave rise to the system of commerce and barter. It also ushered in the concept of private assets and resources. With the concepts of private assets and resources coming into the affairs of mankind and availability of surplus assets and resources than what was required for immediate survival, people started worrying for the ownership and inheritance of these assets and resources after their death. This led to the development of the concept of family. It is claimed in scriptures that the concept and institution of marriage in India originated after Shwetketu, the central figure in Chhandogyopanishad could not bear the sight of his mother's hand being caught amorously by a Brahman while his father Rishi Uddalak remained a mute spectator to the whole incident. He propounded the various dos and don'ts for both the wedded men and women and enforced a dictum for the proper institution of marriage. After the agriculture, family and the institution of marriage had established itself and people were not constrained to think only for the immediate physical needs of their body, i.e. food, clothing and shelter, they got an opportunity to focus and concentrate their mind and observe various other phenomenon of nature. This led to the development of sciences like astronomy, meteorology, medicine, physics, chemistry, biology, metrology and many other streams of knowledge which could be gained through the observation of physical senses, analysis and rational thinking of conscious mind. However, they were not satisfied only with the external experiences and started to look for the reason behind the mind being constantly in a state of craving and desire. They started focusing their mind or meditating on the nature of TRUTH, the ultimate reality and the means to be in a state of eternal and perennial mental bliss. This led to what is known as varnashram vyavastha or social order associated with the goal of life and the stages of life.

As per the original concepts of varnashram dharm or goal of life, the ultimate goal of life is to achieve the state of Brahman or the state of eternal and perennial mental bliss. As per this concept, a Brahman is the one who has achieved the ultimate state of evolution and who has transcended the states of desires and cravings. A Brahman is the one who understands the true nature of the cosmos and remains unperturbed irrespective of the events and incidents in his immediate physical environment. A Brahman is the one who is not at all concerned about his physical possessions and assets and is not bothered even about the physical needs of his body. For a Brahman, the entire world is his own family and for him there is absolutely no place for ego or "Aham". A Brahman lives in a state of constant detachment from whatever is done through his body. A Brahman lives a life without fear and worries and lives in a state of equanimity. A Brahman is the one who has awakened to the ultimate truth and has become enlightened. As per the original concepts of Varna Vyavastha, anyone could achieve the state of being a Brahman irrespective of whether his family name had Jha, Mishra, Sharma, Chaturvedi, Trivedi, Dwivedi, Mukhopadhyaya, Chattopadhyay, Badyopadhyay, Thakur, Pathak or Namboodiri or not. There was absolutely no restriction on anyone achieving the state of Brahman without any consideration of them having a Paswan, Ram, Dom or Mushahar as their family name. To reach to the state of being a Brahman, people normally had to pass through four stages of life. These four stages were Brahmacharya or the stage when children lived and studied with those who have already achieved the state of being a Brahman, the stage of Grihastha or the stage when one was expected to pass through the experiences and responsibilities of a householder and contribute towards production and generation of resources, the stage of Vaanprastha or the stage when people transitioned their householder's responsibilities to the next generations and started withdrawing from being a family man and prepared towards becoming a Sannyasi, the fourth and last stage where they would indulge in austere spiritual practices to achieve the state of being a Brahman. In the original Varna Vyavastha, the social order started from being in the state of a Shudra wherein people were mainly constrained to look after the physical needs of their bodies. The Shudras mainly indulged in the faculties associated with the manual labour; however all Shudras had a natural desire and conscious awareness of their need to ultimately reach the state of being a Brahman. The natural desire to progress on the path of ultimate goal of life motivated people to voluntarily respect and serve those who were ahead of them on this path so that they could help them move forward and progress on the path. The second stage on the path was that of being in the state of a Vaishya, i.e. the stage when one has progressed from being constrained to work only manually and had progressed to a stage where people are still constrained to think of only the physical needs of the body; however they associated mainly with the services, trading and other commercial activities. Being aware of their natural desire to reach the ultimate state of being a Brahman, people obtained support from Shudras but voluntarily respected and served those who had gone up the ladder, i.e. Kshatriyas and Brahmans. The third stage was that of being a Kshatriya or a state when one has achieved all the physical needs of his body and has been able to create an environment around him which could help him move towards being a Brahman. They would focus their energy and efforts on maintaining the social order. They respected the Brahmans and commanded the respect from others in the society. There was absolutely no conflict in the society in this original varna vyavastha and there was no need for corruption as people voluntarily did whatever best they could to move forward towards the goal of their life. There was absolutely no class conflict in the society. People came to be associated with their preferred vocation as they learnt and adopted the vocation of their parents and that gave rise to the concept of castes. However, there was absolutely no restriction on a Shudra or anyone else to directly achieve the state of being a Brahman without passing through the intermediate stages. Anybody could become a Brahman if he could achieve the state of enlightenment and live like a Brahman. As per the norms of this original varna vyavastha, people like Kabir, Nanak, Dadoo, Sahajo, Ravidas, Mohammad, Lao Tsu, Buddha, Mahaveer, Jesus and many others are all Brahmans despite their journey of life starting from being a Shudra, Vaishya or Kshatriya. In the original varna vyavastha concept, all humans by birth were Shudras and depending on their effort, dedication and success, they achieved the various stages of being Vaishya, Kshatriya or Brahman or remained a Shudra. This was a social order based on the system of equality and equal opportunity for all without any kind of discrimination. However, as we are aware, the time changes everything and this excellent system too underwent a sea change when the corruption, probably for the first time, invaded and attacked this system and got so deep rooted in the society that we are still struggling to uproot it.

Some people, without actually having reached to a state of being Brahman, fraudulently declared themselves to be Brahman. Some others who had earlier reached to this exalted state fell down from it. These people, contrary to the normal practice of a Brahman to consider the whole world as his own family, started being concerned only for the very personal interests of their individual families. These people were the ones who declared that the varna vyastha shall be hereditary. They declared that the son of a Brahman would be a Brahman by birth and that of a Shudra would be a Shudra. They declared that the varna would be on the basis of birth and not on the basis of karma or action. Since all that the Brahman's said was accepted by the society without being questioned, these assertions too were accepted or rather forced on to the society. These fake Brahman's initiated the tradition of corruption in the society by declaring themselves to be the exclusive authorized agents of God. They told people that the only way to receive divine grace was through their agency service which was available to all for a service fee. They made promises not only to help people get the divine support for their material needs but also for their spiritual needs. They introduced so many rites and rituals at almost all stages of life and for all kinds of events and incidents that people had absolutely no choice but to remain their slave forever. The stories of an egotistical God who was omnipresent, omnipotent and omniscient and ever ready to punish those who did not submit to the orders of his agents and who was always eager to shower favours on those who submitted to him through his agents was widely circulated amongst the people. People were scared and threatened to pay the speed money and agency fee to these agents of God who would mushroom all around in the form of priests, gurus, pandas and mahants. Since the leaders of the society or the fake Brahmans initiated a process of perpetual corruption, it motivated others to adopt corruption as a way of life. Fake Kshatriyas started harassing and torturing those who did not submit to their muscle power and did not pay them part of their earnings. These people spared the Brahman's from their direct exploitation and extortion as they were still not a match to the wit, knowledge and leadership qualities of these fake Brahmans however they used all kinds of tricks and tacts to make the Vaishyas and Shudras surrender before them and submit to their undeserved demands and expectations. Whoever tried to resist them was dealt with brute force and violence as no one else could match them in terms of muscle power. Vaishyas had no one else to exploit but only the Shudras and they did this to the hilt. As a result, Shudras were exploited by one and all and they continued slipping down from their already marginalized position in the society. This system of corruption, exploitation and extortion got so deep rooted in the society that we are still struggling to expose its true character. With the passage of time, the fake Brahmans have adopted the profession of Baba, Guru, Media and Law, the fake Kshatriyas have become the bureaucrats and the politicians, the Vaishyas are business owners and industrialists and all the Shudras are found these days working as professionals, clerks and other employees, subordinates and suppliers of the other three class. Most of the people with their family names like Jha, Mishra, Sharma, or Chaturvedi today are Shudras whereas people like Ramkishan Yadav (Baba Ramdev) or Ram Jethmalani are acting like Brahmans, people like Ramvilas Paswan, Mayawati or even Devyani Khobragde for that matter are Kshatriyas and people like Mukesh Ambani or Narayan Murthy are Vaishyas.

The corruption of religious traditions have given rise to myriad social problems which in turn have generated a number of economic, political and administrative issues with which the society is afflicted with. As a result of this, most people in the society are living a life which is full of grief and misery. They live a life which is synonymous with unfulfilled desires, depression, hatred, guilt, shame, deceit, envy and such other emotions. The life, which ought to have been ecstatic, is full of sorrow. These undesirable states of life further motivate people to come out of these circumstances and they voluntarily fall prey to the vultures who live off the vulnerability of such people who are not able to accept the circumstances of their life. These vultures exploit the unsuspecting superstitious people in the name of religious rites and rituals, astrology, tantra and many other associated practices and traditions. This further obscures the true religious practices and continues to perpetuate in the society in a vicious cycle.

We would look into a few specific examples of this corruption. Anybody who has visited the temples of Tirupati Balajee or Mata Vaishnodevi is aware of the application of the speed money to expedite the meeting with or darshan of the deity. If you can pay more, you can jump the queue and an almost immediate appointment with God would be arranged for you by his managers. The agents of God have made him out to be like a corrupt official who is ready to meet your expectations provided you agreed to pay the fee of his agents for the required services and favour. The root cause of corruption is a belief that something which is not deserved and yet desired can still be obtained without actually deserving it. In other words, there can be shortcuts to obtain what one desires. This belief has been inculcated and enshrined in all of us as part of our religious and cultural training by our religious leaders. Our religious traditions encourage us to believe in such shortcuts. We can continue to commit sins all our life and get rid of all its effect by just donating a cow to a Brahman at the end. Now, is it not bribery or corruption? Our students can avoid studying the whole year and believe that they can still get a good result in the final exam by going to the temple and fixing a deal with the deity therein for good results in return for some offerings. Is it not corruption? Our cultural traditions prepare us to believe that we cannot only fix deals for this life but even for subsequent lives as well. We can fix deals even for our forefathers who would have died centuries ago by executing rituals in Gaya. We are used to commissioning Brahmans to complete a specific number of recitals of Maha Mrityunjay Mantra or Gayatri Mantra for some specific benefit to us or in other words we are trained to consume the fruit of someone else's efforts. Is it not corruption? People are openly cheated day in and day out in broad day light by the confident and super thugs in the name of spirituality, tantra, astrology and ayurveda using the bold and confident advertisements in the print and electronic mass media. Is it not corruption? Political and administrative authorities are not bothered about these cheats and remain a mute spectator to this broad day light criminal activites in the name of religious traditions and faith as they are afraid of its adverse effect on their vote bank and electoral prospects. Is it not corruption? I would not like to name any specific cheat here as doing so would mean being partial since it would not be possible to name all these charlatans in a work like this. It is sufficient to say that not a single person operating in the garb of a swami, baba, mahant, maharaj, panda, purohit, maulvi, mulla, maulana, sufi, father, jyotishi, tantric, spiritual guide, clairvoyant, tarot reader or other similar names who is formally running this business and that is his full time business and means of living is no different than the father-son duo who have been apprehended by Rajasthan and Gujarat police recently. Absolutely no one, who is in this business, is an exception. The degree and extent of fraud may vary from person to person in this business of religion, spirituality, astrology and tantra; however there should be absolutely no doubt about the fact that they all are fraudsters. There are some people who are actually offering some useful tools in return for the money and mental slavery like the ayurvedic medicines, some self-help tools or yoga and breathing techniques. They are the smart marketers and they cannot be excluded from the group of thugs and cheats as they run their commercial business marketing in the name of religious and cultural belief and on the basis of faith and devotion rather than running their business as pure commercial organisation. The general modus operandi of the thugs operating in the name of spirituality or religion is to claim some special powers, knowledge or attainment which could be applied to and utilized for bestowing peace and happiness on others. They offer these services to the masses for a service or agency fee which could be in cash, kind or in some other form like slavery. As a function of time, people are always afflicted with some kind of misery in their life related to health, wealth, relation, career, profession, social status or something else and they, therefore, out of their ignorance, feel constrained to develop a desire or aversion for specific events and incidents in their life. Once people realise that they do not have control over these specific external events and incidents which might affect their life for seemingly good or bad feelings, they turn towards these fake gurus, babas, astrologers, fakirs, tantriks, swamis, mahants and others to obtain their help to achieve the desired results in their life. Once they come into the influence circle of these thugs, they are completely brainwashed and hypnotized by these smart criminals. At this stage, despite having started from an undesirable situation in life which brought them in contact with these thugs, they lose all sense of discretion and rationality and voluntarily become slaves of these thugs. This results in serving these gurus with money, time, devotion and physical labour and in some cases even sexual services. The only interest of these fake gurus is to earn their livelihood through these gullible clients as these charlatans are not able to earn through any other legitimate means. They simply keep milking and cheating their devotees and disciples even when these innocent and ignorant people happen to be in a miserable situation. If some changes do occur in the life and situation of the devotees, it is because of the energy from their own belief and their own efforts to make things turn around for them. There is absolutely no role of the guru in any such development. This effect is summarized by Henry Ford when he said,

"Whether you think you can, or you think you can't--you're right".

However, any such success or even fabricated success stories and testimonials are widely used and advertised by the thugs to expand their business. This way, these thugs build big empires in the name of religion and spirituality. A bizarre example of the extent of corruption in religious belief has been witnessed recently when a fake Maharaj, alleged to have amassed properties worth rupees 1500 crore, is reported to have died in Punjab on 29th January 2014. Worried about the impact of his death on their business, his accomplices have declared that he has not died but has voluntarily gone into a deep state of meditation or Samadhi. They are alleged to have kept his body initially in a room on normal room temperature however when the signs of rotting started to appear on the corpse, they are reported to have shifted his dead body into a deep freezer in the name of providing a Himalayan environment to his body in mediation. The accomplices are not ready to accept the claim of the family members that their fraud guru had fled his home leaving behind his wife and infant son. The man claiming to be the son of this fraud Maharaj has appealed for a DNA test to establish the paternity of this fraud Guru. The accomplices of this fraud guru, who ran his business in the name of imparting Brahma Gyan, using a minor technique of hypnosis, claim that their guru had never married and never had a family. It is quite possible that this fraud guru would have colluded with his accomplices to spread the rumour about his death or Samadhi to expand his business and his accomplices may have influenced or bought the doctors to certify him clinically dead. It is quite possible that this fraud is still living a normal comfortable life and his accomplices are ensuring that nobody outside their fraud circle is allowed access to verify whether he is dead or alive. They probably never assumed that his family members might come forward to claim his body for the last rites. The emergence of the son of the fake Maharaj, contrary to the expectations of his accomplices, has made the things extremely difficult for his business to continue. Now, if he is actually dead, the accomplices would not be able to keep it under wraps for ever as the matter might be taken to the courts and then his body will have to be retrieved. On the other hand, if he is not dead and as a result of the court intervention, claims to have come out of Samadhi and presents himself before the masses, he may be forced to undergo a DNA test to establish his paternity which would expose his lies about having never married. This is one of the ongoing dramas at present related to the control over the ashrams and properties and the related business of a fake guru. More or less, all such ashrams of the present day babas are based on the business of similar frauds and cheating. To make their estates aka ashrams appear legitimate, some of these babas or gurus would start indulging in charitable and social activities like opening of school, college, university, hospital or starting of programs like provision for food and shelter for the poor. They may even align with the NGO kind of activities like preparation and distribution of mid-day meals for children or organisation of blood donation camps, flood relief camps and disaster management camps. However, even these social and charitable activities are misused to launder the ill-gotten wealth as a result of corruption and financial irregularities and to evade taxation. Such kind of cheats would always be interested in getting themselves photographed with celebrities related to the political, business, sports, media or entertainment areas and would use such photographs or even endorsements from these celebrities to further market their evil business. This also leads to a nexus between these so called godmen, antisocial elements associated with the management of the parallel economy and the unscrupulous people in politics and administration.

While presenting these specific examples, I do not intend to question the original source of wisdom associated with the traditions about which we have discussed above. Every tradition, when explored properly with focused attention in a meditative state of mind, reveals that it contains some very specific and profound meaning. However, at present, these traditions have degenerated in such a convoluted form that they have lost their original meaning and purpose and there is absolutely nothing to be gained out of them in the manner they are being practiced today. While anybody can directly find out the actual meaning and its association with the TRUTH for any religious tradition by meditating on it, we would restrict ourselves to explore only two specific items in this regard. We would explore the meaning of and the purpose behind worshipping Lord Shiva and reciting Gayatri mantra.

SHIVA

Lord Shiva is depicted as someone who has crematorium ash smeared all over his body. Crematorium is supposed to be the place of his playground in his form of Mahakaal. That is why the temple of Lord Shiva as Mahakaal in Ujjain is said to be in the midst of a great crematorium. The daily ritual in this temple includes "Bhasmarti" wherein the crematorium ash is supposed to be smeared on him to please him. He is also shown lying in the middle of the crematorium where his consort in the form of Mahakaali is shown to be dancing without any clothes on her body and only with a garland of human skull around her neck. She stops her destructive dance only when she comes across the blissful body of Lord Shiva who continues to remain unperturbed despite all the ferocious activities of Mahakaali going on all around him. He is also shown to have gulped the "Haalahal" poison which could have afflicted both gods and demons alike and does not let it go down below his food pipe. As a result of this poison, his throat area becomes blue in colour in contrast to the rest of his body which is depicted fair in colour like that of camphor. He is shown to have a crescent moon on his head and a very poisonous king cobra hanging from his neck and body. Continuous stream of Ganges water is shown to be flowing from his matted locks. He is shown to be riding an old bull. He has a damaroo (an hour glass shaped two sided drum musical instrument) in his hand. He is mainly worshipped in his phallus (lingam) form which is always represented alongside the vagina (yoni), a symbol of his consort goddess Shakti or the female creative energy. The lingam is worshipped mainly with the offerings of water, milk and some other items like bhang (leaves of cannabis plant), belpatra (leaves of wood apple tree) and dhatura (thorn apple).

In the present day practice, people worship Lord Shiva mainly with the offerings as mentioned above. Most of the time, people expect some favour from Shiva in return for the offerings and worship. There are numerous stories of Shiva fulfilling the wishes of those who complete his worship with elaborate rites and rituals as prescribed by the so called learned Brahmans. As per my understanding, which I have received by focusing my mind on Lord Shiva during one of my meditative state, the current practice of worshipping Lord Shiva is diagonally opposite to the tradition and purpose for which it would have started. The worship of Shiva is supposed to be a constant reminder for people to strive to achieve the state of being a Brahman. To achieve this state, people need to accept the crematorium as their home or in other words accept death of the perishable body with poise and grace. People need not be scared of the death of the body as signified by voluntarily accepting a poisonous king cobra hanging from their neck. Once death is accepted with grace, people are expected to transcend all kinds of fear including the mental, social or economic. The crematorium also signifies that all the physical possessions and material wealth has absolutely no meaning as none of these assets are of any further use to anybody when they are brought to the crematorium. The physical and material possessions and assets are not worth more than the ash in the crematorium and therefore desire for them or loss thereof need not disturb the perennially blissful state of mind. The old bull that Shiva has is of no use as it cannot be used either as a beast of burden or for agriculture. Shiva is a reminder for the people to be in a state of bliss irrespective of the material values of their possessions. Shiva's damaroo reminds people to be in an energetic state of joy, enthusiasm and excitement irrespective of the events and incidents in their life and induces them to indulge in dance and the music. They need to be in a state of equanimity despite being in a situation wherein Maya or Kaali (time) would carry on with its cosmic dance of destruction and killing. The Maha Kaali or time would change or destroy everything in this cosmos which is like a grand crematorium and would have a garland of human skulls around her neck which simply means that history would be testimony to the fact that everything that time would touch will have to undergo change, transformation and destruction. Everything that is there in this cosmos is under the control of Maha Kaali or time and is transient. The only thing that time cannot change is the conscious state of a

Brahman or Shiva where time will have to stop like Maha Kaali stops from her ferocious and destructive dance near the body of a blissful Shiva in the midst of the crematorium. In the state of being Shiva, people need to dedicate their life towards extinguishing the fire of Haalahal poison of anger, hatred, envy, greed, lust, deceit and violence that may be present in the society. Without letting these fire of poison affect their own consciousness (by stopping it from going all the way down to their digestive system), people need to douse and eliminate them from the society with the help of love, compassion, care, kindness and consideration which is depicted in the form of continuously flowing stream of cool, clean and holy water of Ganges. It is additionally depicted in the form of the soothing, soft and cool moon rays which is expected to bring calmness and peace to the mind of people. The tradition of offering of cold water or milk is to induce and remind people to achieve these attributes of Lord Shiva. His trident is a symbol to control or to be beyond the physical (daihik), divine (daivik) and material (bhautik) pains and afflictions that affect all the minds and body and also to balance the three gunas of Sat, Raj and Tam in the mind. The union of lingam and yoni represents the oneness of male and female or Purush and Prakriti (if we use the terminology from Sankhya philosophy) or the Brahma and Maya or in other words the passive space and active time from which all life originate. The more subtle meaning behind the tradition of lingam worship is to remind people to be in a state of mental bliss which people experience during sexual intercourse just before they achieve orgasm. In an ordinary sexual intercourse, people achieve a pre-orgasmic state of mental bliss wherein the mind becomes empty of all thoughts. People forget about everything around them including the consciousness of and identification with their physical body. However this mental state vanishes immediately after the orgasm. Yet people do experience this mental state every time they indulge in sexual intercourse. The lingam of Shiva which is perennially erect and surrounded by yoni is a reminder for people to strive to achieve a state of eternal and perennial mental bliss which they experience during sexual intercourse immediately prior to orgasm. This is a reminder not to be perturbed by the afflictions of the body or desires of the mind and be happy forever while being indulged in their routine chore. We have to remember that these are all symbolic only. No rational mind would ever accept someone to carry a moon on his head. If that would have been for real, just imagine the size of the cave in Himalayas which would be required to accommodate this man or god who can carry a moon on his head!

GAYATRI MANTRA

Now let us try to understand the tradition behind Gayatri mantra. This mantra is

ॐ भूर्भुवः स्वः तत्सवितुर्वरेण्यं भर्गो देवस्य धीमहि धियो यो नः प्रचोदयात् |

Om bhur bhuvah svah tat savitur varenyam
bhargo devasya dhimahi dhiyo yo nah prachodayaat.

This mantra is from Rigveda (3.62.10) and its origin is attributed to sage Vishwamitra. As per Swami Vevekanand, it can be transalated in English as "We meditate on the glory of that Being who has produced this universe; may He enlighten our minds.". Sir William Jones has translated this mantra as "Let us adore the supremacy of that divine sun, the god-head who illuminates all, who recreates all, from whom all proceed, to whom all must return, whom we invoke to direct our understandings aright in our progress toward his holy seat." This mantra is considered to be a highly sacred one and all new students when they commenced their study of TRUTH were initiated into this mantra by their teachers during a ritual which was known as Yagyopavit sanskar. This ritual is still in practice amongst the people of so called Brahman caste although its significance and the true understanding behind this ritual have been lost. During this ritual, students are made to go for begging for their own food and are also made to eat in the houses of the outcasts or Shudras. This is a reminder of the original tradition that everyone is born as a Shudra and he can proceed on to the path of becoming a Brahman by letting go of his ego symbolized by the begging ritual. The Gayatri mantra, which a new student is initiated into during this Yagyopavit or sacred thread ritual, is probably the most recited mantra amongst the Hindus. In the modern days of electronic music, it is the most commonly played mantra in the houses, shops and other establishments and during special religious occasions. There is an organisation by the name of Vishwa Gayatri Pariwar which has more than ten million people as its member and they regularly organize elaborate functions for group recitation and japas of this mantra. These people have even personified the Gayatri into a beautiful damsel with eight hands along with all other paraphernalia and attributes that is normally associated with a Hindu goddess. There is a lot of emphasis on reciting this mantra for as many repetitions as possible which is supposed to bring good fortune and favours from the gods. When I was a young child of around six years, my grandfather asked me to recite this mantra at least 21 times a day, if not more. He used to feel very proud to share with others that his grandson is a regular practitioner of Gayatri mantra and I also used to be happy to hear this. However, subsequently, after my enlightenment, I realised that that happiness was more of a child from being praised by his elders rather than anything else. It had nothing to do with Gayatri as I did not really know anything about it, not even its literal meaning. It was something purely alien to me at that stage. This is the kind of happiness in a child that programs his mind to strive to meet the expectations of his elders and subsequently of the society. This is also what ultimately converts him into being a puppet in the hands of the society and makes him feel constrained to live a life as per the expectations of the others rather than guided by his own wisdom and TRUTH. What I found about Gayatri was that Vishwamitra came to realise the truth during one of his meditative sessions. He understood the ultimate TRUTH. Out of his joy and excitement on achieving this, he was in an ecstatic mood. He wanted to share what he had understood. He said "OM". Now, those, who have already understood and experienced the TRUTH, they do not need any further verbal communication as "OM" was being used to denote the TRUTH. However for those, who had not understood it, he said, "BHU" or earth meaning that all that is there on earth is nothing but TRUTH. He realised that that was not complete and therefore said "Bhuvah" meaning that not only on earth but all that is there in sky is nothing but TRUTH. He still did not feel satisfied and then said "Swah" meaning that not only on earth and sky but everything that is there in this cosmos is nothing but OM or TRUTH. Yet, he realised that just by his verbal communication people may not be able to understand what exactly and which TRUTH he is talking about. So he further says "tat savitur varenyam" meaning that the radiance of TRUTH is something that we need to worship or praise. However, he still feels that unless people know and experience the radiance of TRUTH themselves, they would not be able to understand why it ought to be worshipped, praised or achieved. So he further adds "Bhargo Devasya Dhimahi" meaning that we need to understand and experience the radiance of

TRUTH directly into our consciousness through our intellect. Even at this point, he feels that people may not know how to achieve and experience this TRUTH that he is talking about and so he further adds "Dhiyo Yo nah Prachodayaat" which simply means that we need to focus our mind and meditate on what this TRUTH is all about and then TRUTH would reveal itself by inspiring our intelligence. Since Sanskrit was the commonly understood and spoken language amongst people during his time, so Vishwamitra conveyed this message in Sanskrit. It was presumed that the real message in this communication or mantra may not be understood by all by just listening it once as they may not be in a conducive and suitable state of mind when they hear it for the first time. Therefore, it was prescribed that people need to keep repeating it over and over again. In this process, while repeating it, people would be able to hear the message contained in this mantra under various external conditions and mental state and while doing so, the true meaning of this mantra would strike them sooner or later. Once they understand the meaning of the message in the mantra, people would proceed on to focusing their mind and meditating on what exactly the TRUTH is. This is all that is there in the Gayatri mantra. This is the reason it was given to the students when they started their studies and commenced on their journey of seeking TRUTH. Alas, what remains of it, in its current day practice, is nothing but its dead body which cannot do any good to anybody. Rather than doing any good, the practice of Gayatri without its true understanding is a waste of time, energy, efforts and money. Those who would understand the meaning of Gayatri would start meditating on the TRUTH and would not keep repeating its recitation like a parrot.

Experiencing and Understanding

Before we proceed further, we need to dwell on a very essential discrimination. While on the path of seeking TRUTH, we have to be clear whether we are interested in understanding or experiencing the TRUTH. The meditation can lead to its direct experience and knowledge about how it feels to be in experience of TRUTH. It can enlighten the seeker to an extent that he would be able to apply the TRUTH to his day to day life. As a result of this experience, he would align his activities as per the rules and laws of the nature relevant for his place and time and may create a code of ethics or dos and don'ts for himself. This set of rules or ethics may be called "Dharma". This would be recognized as a set of rules which would bring harmony, peace and progress in his life. He would then interact and interface with his immediate environment or nature as well as with other people, adhering to the set of the ethical rules or dharma, to fulfill the physical needs of his body and the desires of his mind. In this process, he would endeavour to gather wealth and assets (Arth) according to the rules of Dharma and fulfill the desires of his mind (Kaam). While going through this process of dharma, arth and kaam, he would maintain a sense of detachment or a sense of not actually being responsible for whatever is being done through his body or mind. This would give him a sense of being free from all kinds of bondage or moksha. His ultimate focus would be on moksha or liberation and all his actions would be guided by dharma. Between these two ends of dharma and moksha, he would endeavour to provide as much comfort to his body and as much fulfillment to his desires. This understanding should be sufficient for most of the people. It is like using the electricity and electrical appliances in our daily life. To use electricity and electrical appliances, we need not be aware of Ohm's law, Kirchoff's law or Coulombs laws. All that we need to know is how to switch on or switch off an appliance. These laws would do their work in the background as we use the electrical appliances. However, those who are interested in analyzing the TRUTH and going into why the TRUTH is what it is, they would need to develop intelligence and mathematical abilities to first understand the discoveries that the developments in physical sciences have made already available to all. It may have been difficult for those, who experienced the TRUTH before the developments of Elbert Einstein's Theories of Relativity and the Quantum Mechanics, to leap from the physical science to the analysis of the TRUTH they experienced as a result of their meditation. This probably led them to declare that TRUTH had nothing to do with the physical sciences. However, it is now available to all the physical scientists to leap frog from their understanding of what Einstein, Max Plank, Neils Bohr, Louis de Broglie, Heisenberg, Schrodinger, Paul Dirac and Satyendranath Bose and many of the other intelligent modern physicists have already made available in the public domain. I can declare with confidence that there is absolutely no difference between science and spirituality; however for this to be experienced and understood, someone needs to be equally adept in both the streams of meditation and the modern physics. The common sense concept of time and space that people normally live with would never let a man understand the underlying principle that governs all that is there in this cosmos. The understanding of the nature of time and the macro level mass energy interactions in the universe without a proper understanding of the theory of relativity is not possible. Similarly, the understanding of the interplay of the mass energy at a micro level is not possible without a proper concept of the quantum mechanics. Once someone masters the concepts of relativity and quantum mechanics and then continues his journey of seeking TRUTH with deep meditation, it should be not be difficult for him to understand the TRUTH.

Having discussed the outlines of religion and philosophy and their current state of affairs, we would now focus our attention on the society. As an individual, people have opportunity to explore how religion and spirituality are relevant for them and how it affects them as an individual. It is optional for them in terms of what they chose to be their individual path and how and what they want for themselves. Achieving one's own happiness or freedom could be the goal of all conduct of an individual as long as he is not concerned for the society. This is what the philosophers have termed as egoistic hedonism. However, when we look at it from the social perspective, wherein individual conduct of a particular person affects everyone else, and individuals cannot be left to their purely personal selfish choices as long as they are in a position to affect and influence the rest of the society. When we think of society, we have to think in terms of social hedonism which means that an act is right, if and only, if it results in greatest pleasure for greatest number of people. When we closely look at this assertion, we find that such assertion might lead to a life of misery and sorrow for some people particularly if they are not amongst those who have been counted amongst that greatest number and happen to be in minority. It is, therefore, imperative to analyse and study all the sociopolitical issues and problems that are prevalent in the society and which happen to be the apparent cause of pain to the people in the society. Once we study these issues and problems and analyse their root cause, we would need to look into what are the options for the people to come out of those situations.

MY INDIA

"We, THE PEOPLE OF INDIA, have solemnly resolved to constitute India into a SOVEREIGN SOCIALIST SECULAR DEMOCRATIC REPUBLIC and to secure to all its citizens: JUSTICE, social, economic and political; LIBERTY, of thought, expression, belief, faith and worship; EQUALITY of status and of opportunity; and to promote among them all FRATERNITY assuring the dignity of the individual and the unity and integrity of the Nation; IN OUR CONSTITUENT ASSEMBLY this twenty-sixth day of November, 1949, DO HEREBY ADOPT, ENACT AND GIVE TO OURSELVES THIS CONSTITUTION."

What has been reproduced above is the preamble of the constitution of India. Constitution of India is the source from which all the governments, judiciary and legislatures derive their power and authority. The president, the prime minister, the chief ministers, the governors, the judges of Supreme Court and High Courts, Ministers, MPs, MLAs and all the higher authorities who are responsible to run and administer the country derive their authority from this document. The preamble of the constitution is supposed to set out the purpose and guiding principle of this document. It derives its authority from "we, the people of India" meaning that it has been created by the representatives directly elected for this purpose by the people of India and has not been imposed by some external power or authority. The guardians of the constitution envisioned India to be a sovereign, socialist, secular and democratic republic. The word Sovereign means free from any external control. The word Socialist and the phrase "Justice – Social, Economic and Political" is supposed to promulgate absence of discrimination on the grounds of caste, colour, creed, gender, language and all such distinguishing factors and equal distribution of wealth, resources and all other means of living and earning opportunity amongst its people. It is also supposed to provide equal opportunity for all its people to participate in the political process. The word Socialist and Secular was added at the time of 42nd amendment to the constitution in the year 1976 to emphasize that state would not discriminate on the grounds of religion or creed. The constitution is supposed to promote fraternity or brotherhood amongst the people of India assuring the dignity of the individuals. Let us not doubt the integrity and capability of the people who were the founders of the constitution of India, as sitting here in 2014; we cannot fully appreciate the actual conditions and consideration that would have guided them to write what they wrote in the constitution. However, when we compare the goals that was supposed to have been achieved after the implementation of the constitution and what the actual condition of affairs are, after sixty four years have already gone by since it was "adopted, enacted and given to ourselves", we find that this document has completely failed in achieving what it was supposed to achieve. Sixty four years is not a short period of time. To grasp what has changed in the world in the last sixty four years, I would like to present an interesting story.

A boy in USA asked his grandmother, "Gramma, how old are you?"

The old lady replied, "I was born before we had television, penicillin, polio shots, frozen foods, Xerox, contact lenses and the pill. There were no credit cards, laser beams or ball-point pens. Man had not yet invented air conditioners, dishwashers or clothes dryers and the clothes were hung out to dry in the fresh air and man hadn't yet walked on the moon."

"Your Grandfather and I got married first, and then lived together. Every family had a father and a mother. Grandparents, uncles, aunts and cousins all lived together. We were before LGBT rights, computer-dating, daycare centers, and group therapy. We were taught to know the difference between right and wrong and to stand up and take responsibility for our actions. Time-sharing meant time the family spent together in the evenings and weekends and not purchasing condominiums. We never heard of FM radios, tape decks, CD's, electric typewriters or guys wearing earrings. We listened to Big Bands, Jack Benny, and the President's speeches on our radios. If you saw anything with 'Made in Japan' on it, it was junk. The term 'making out' referred to how you did on your school exam. Pizza Hut, McDonald's and instant coffee were unheard of.

We had 5 &10-cent stores where you could actually buy things for 5 and 10 cents. Ice-cream cones, phone calls, rides on a streetcar, and a Pepsi were all a nickel. If you didn't want to splurge, you could spend your nickel on enough stamps to mail 1 letter and 2 postcards. You could buy a new Ford Coupe for $600, but who could afford one? Too bad, because gas was 11 cents a gallon."

"During our days "grass" was mowed, "coke" was a cold drink, "pot" was something your mother cooked in and "rock music" was your grandmother's lullaby."Aids" were helpers in the Principal's office, "chip" meant a piece of wood, "hardware" was found in a hardware store and "software" wasn't even a word. We were the last generation to actually believe that a lady needed a husband to have a baby."

At this point, the grandfather intervenes and says, "Why can't you simply say that you were born in 1952."

The year our constitution was adopted, the world had not known about human organ transplants, artificial intelligence, electronic fund transfer or nuclear power plants. Space flights, personal computers, genetic engineering, digital media, mobile phones and internet were not even considered a possibility in the near future and were beyond imagination of the masses. While our constitution has been in practice, the walls between the East and West Germany have collapsed, the cold war and the non aligned movement is no longer a topic of discussion and a country by the name of USSR is no longer in existence on this planet. India has fought four wars with its neighbours since independence. During this period the population of India has grown from 35 crore to 120 crore. The life expectancy has gone up from 33 to 66 years. The democracy in the country has sustained all along this period. 14 different people (J L Nehru, Guljari Lal Nanda, Lal Bahadur Shastri, Indira Gandhi, Morarji Desai, Charan Singh, Rajiv Gandhi, Vishwanath Pratap Singh, Chandra Sekhar, Narsimha Rao, Atal Bihari Bajpeyee, H D Devegowda, Indra Kumar Gujral and Manmohan Singh) have been in the role of the prime minister of the country belonging to 7 different political parties during this period. The country has witnessed 12 five year plans during this period. Can we conclude that this period should have been much more than sufficient for the country to achieve the major goals and direction that the founding fathers of the constitution had in mind when they adopted and enacted this constitution on behalf of people of India? Let us explore where the constitution wanted to lead us and where actually do we stand today.

SOVEREIGN DEMOCRATIC REPUBLIC

Despite the accusations of dynastic rules and the corruption in the political system, there is absolutely no doubt in the mind of anyone about India being a sovereign democratic republic. Despite many shortcomings in its electoral and public representation management systems, India's people and politicians across the country have continually displayed a commitment to the democratic procedures as stipulated in the constitution. There may be substantial scope and opportunity for improvements in the political process in the country to establish a government **of the people, for the people and by the people** in its true sense, however, it is beyond any doubt that democracy has established itself to be the only system of governance in India. The most powerful post independence political dynasty in this country has experienced, more than once, what the wrath of people in this country can do to the political autocrats. We have also witnessed the emergence of non political entities like N T Ramarao or Arvind Kejriwal who, with the support of the ordinary citizens of this land, forced the established political formations to lick their wounds and mend their ways. It has consistently displayed its internal and external sovereignty ever since its independence. During the last 66 years, the country has aligned with the NAM, SAARC, USSR block and with the United States of America as per its needs and requirements without succumbing to any external pressure. It has carried out its nuclear and missile tests and had supported the Muktivahini in Bangladesh, again without bothering for how these activities were viewed at by the external forces. There is no debate about India being a sovereign democratic republic. That leaves the two other descriptors of the Indian state to be evaluated. These two are "secular" and "social". Let us look into our secularism and socialism.

SECULARISM

The constitution expects the country to be secular. The dictionary meaning of this word is "not connected with religious or spiritual matters." The term "secularism" was first used by the British writer George Jacob Holyoake in 1851. Although the term was new, the general notions of "freethought" on which it was based, had existed throughout history. Holyoake invented the term "secularism" to describe his views of promoting a social order separate from religion, without actively dismissing or criticizing religious belief. This is probably one of the most controversial and most debated terms in the Indian political context. While one set of politicians claim to be secularists, the others allege them to be pseudo secularists. Both groups have learned lawyers and good orators in their fold and they can go on debating this issue forever without coming to any conclusion. Such kinds of debates and arguments are more like jalpa and vitanda as opposed to vada or samvaada to come to a conclusion in this regard[1]. Before evaluating how secular our state or governments have been, we need to understand what is meant by freethought which is considered to be the origin of the term secularism. Freethought holds that individuals should not accept ideas proposed as truth without recourse to knowledge and reason. Thus, freethinkers would strive to build their opinions on the basis of facts, scientific inquiry and logical principles independent of any logical fallacies or the intellectually limiting effects of authority, confirmation or cognitive bias, conventional wisdom, popular culture, prejudice, sectarianism, tradition, urban legend, and all other dogmas. A line from "Clifford's Credo" by the 19th-century British mathematician and philosopher William Kingdon Clifford perhaps best describes the premise of freethought wherein he says, "It is

---

[1] Samvaada is the discussion between the teacher and the taught as in Krishna-Arujuna samvaada in Geeta. The student does not question the teacher's authority but questions his understanding for clarification. This type of discussion can occur only when the student surrenders himself completely to the teacher.

Vada is the discussion between equals to establish the truth / to resolve the conflict. Both parties are open minded even though they are convinced that they are right. They are ready to listen and to accept the opponents' version. Learning takes place at the end of vada since the truth is established to the satisfaction of both parties.

Jalpa or vivaad is the discussion between the two who are also convinced that each one is right and the opponent is wrong. Unlike in vada, the purpose is not to discover or establish the truth, but only to convert the other party. The outcome of this whole jalpa is a lot of noise. Even if it appears that one has lost an argument, he will not accept it, instead he goes back to get some more materials or concocts some other arguments only to establish that he is right and the other is wrong.

Vitanda is the discussion with the sole purpose of defeating the opponent. The arguments may lead to establish that the opponent is not qualified to discuss. There is no leaning for anyone at the end and it is also not worth listening.

wrong always, everywhere, and for anyone, to believe anything upon insufficient evidence." Having understood the rationale behind the origin of the term, let us further explore it in Indian context. The concept of secularism in India is borrowed from the French idea of laicite, which denotes the strict separation of Church and State or the absence of religious involvement in government affairs and government interference in the religious affairs of its citizens. It is based on the consideration that people lead two, mutually exclusive, lives: one public, over which the State may exercise its authority, and one private, encompassing the religious beliefs and other such customs, which the State will not legislate upon. This definition has been under sustained criticism in France once postcolonial immigration flows began changing the religious character of the French nation. As Sikhs and Muslims in France have found out, the definition of laicite means the boundaries that the Judaism and Christian traditions have erected between the private and the public life. A cross can be worn in French government schools, but not a turban or hijab. The Indian secularism has its roots in the French separation of Church and State; however, here it is defined to mean that the state has no official religion, and that it will not discriminate against any citizen on the basis of his religion. Every religion is supposed to be valued equally by the state. But in the political discourse of our times, secularism has come to mean something quite different. For most political formations claiming to be secular, it means opposition to the electoral appeals made on the basis of Hindutva or the "saffron" policies that are made to be the primary electoral plank of parties like the BJP or Shiv Sena. Having established the origins and the underlying concepts of secularism, the decision with regard to whether this meaning of secularism is right or wrong may be left to the readers. I believe that after the Left's winnowing to irrelevance, there is not a single major secular party in India. What we have in practice is the ethnic party system. In this system, parties ride to power on the basis of appeals to ethnicity related to religion, region, caste or some interplay of these factors. Every pronouncement by a political analysts or a psephologist on how various community or caste groups will vote en masse is a blow against secularism. In the last 66 years, the parties claiming to be the champions of secularism in India have made appeals and calculations all over the country on entire gamut of Indian ethnicity – a feat of electoral gymnastics that is quite unmatched. I would prefer not to go into any further analysis of the term "secularism". Doing so may give rise to another debate and discussion on this, particularly amongst the social scientists and political analysts whose main emphasis would be to prove something this way or that way. We would refrain from passing any judgment here and would simply present the facts and leave it to the people to decide whether we have been secular and if so then to what extent. The first fact is that this term was not there in the preamble of the original version of the constitution. A specific need was felt for its inclusion in the preamble during the 42nd amendment to the constitution which was probably the only time in the independent India's history when it's democratic and republic aspirations were under serious threat. We do not have parliamentary or assembly constituency delimited on the basis of religion and there is no provision for reservation in the name of religion for the posts of public representatives. While the constitution has been in practice, the practice of polygamy amongst the Hindus has been declared illegal. Divorce amongst the Hindus has been made legally acceptable. Some other significant changes that have been effected by the state and which has affected the Hindu social order are abolition of the child marriage, legal recognition of inter-caste marriage, prohibition of the practice of animal sacrifice inside the temples, abolition of the devdasi system in the temples, rights for Shudras to enter the temples and many such other reforms. The management and administration of the largest Hindu temples like Vaishnodevi in Katra, J&K and Tirupati Balajee in Andhra Pradesh have been taken over by the state. All the legislative and administrative changes that the state introduced with respect to the reforms mentioned above did not lead to any major protest and was accepted by the affected people without much fuss. In contrast, the country has also been a witness to the Shah Bano case. Shah Bano was a 62-year-old Muslim lady and a daughter of a police constable and mother of five from Indore, Madhya Pradesh. She was divorced by her husband in 1978 and denied any maintenance. Her husband refused to pay maintenance of rupees 500 per month that she demanded as she had no other means to support her. The case went up to the Supreme Court of India which ordered the husband to pay her the maintenance. This order of the Supreme Court was vehemently protested by the Muslim community in the name of interference with the Muslim personal law. Despite this order of the

Supreme Court, the lady was subsequently denied alimony because the Indian Parliament reversed the judgment under pressure of Islamic orthodoxy. The judgment in favour of the woman in this case evoked criticism among Muslims, some of whom cited Quran to show that the judgment was in conflict with Islamic law. It triggered controversy about the extent of having different civil codes for different religions, especially for Muslims in India. This case caused the congress government, with its absolute majority, to pass the Muslim Women (Protection of Rights on Divorce) Act, 1986 which diluted the judgment of the Supreme Court and, in reality denied even utterly destitute Muslim divorcees the right to alimony from their former husbands.

While we are on the topic of secularism, we need to keep in mind that secularism is expected to check the growth of fanaticism and manage the conflict between various groups identifying themselves in the name of religion. We have had numerous communal riots in the name of religion and hundreds of thousands of people have been killed as a result of the same. We have witnessed the demolition of the so called Babri Masjid structure in Ayodhya. We have also witnessed the burning of a train in Godhra wherein Hindus were burnt alive and which resulted in the Gujarat riots of 2002 in which thousands of people were killed. Only recently, we have seen the communal riots in Muzaffarnagar in UP. The country has also witnessed the pundits having been driven out of the Kashmir valley. All this has happened, despite the term "Secular" being a part of the preamble of the Indian constitution. While the constitution guaranteed the freedom to the minorities to protect their religious practices and faith, the successive governments have been going beyond the protection by conferring special rights and privileges on the religious minorities, probably with a sole motivation of using the communities as their vote bank. This has led to the polarization of the majority community as a protest and has created an environment of distrust and deceit. While nobody in the political arena or even the so called religious leaders have had any actual interest in the true religious practices, they have been indulging in this identity politics in the name of religion with a sole motive to use the age old "divide and rule" formula to perpetuate their exploitation and rule. From the above examples, it is evident that the secularism or whatever it is that is in practice in the name of secularism in India has definitely not served the purpose for which it would have been incorporated in the constitution and therefore, we certainly need some different model and mechanism to address the religious issues while dealing with its interface with the administration and governance.

Instead of the secular model that is in practice by the state, can we think of a different model of interface between the state and the various religious communities which could peacefully and effectively tackle the long standing issues like dispute in Ayodhya about Babri Masjid/ Ram Janmabhoomi temple, uniform civil code, religious intolerance, communal riots, minority appeasement and so many other issues which are supposed to be linked with the religion or religious beliefs and practices? We will explore.

SOCIALISM

Socialism is a social and economic system characterized by social ownership of the means of production and co-operative management of the economy. This was one of the ideals which had brought the farmers and the labour force of the country to help the freedom movement of Gandhi in India. After the independence from British rule in 1947, the Indian government took some of the major socialist initiatives like the establishment of heavy industries in the public sector, land reforms and the nationalisation of the major industries and the banking sector. Independently, Vinoba Bhave and Jayaprakash Narayan worked for peaceful land redistribution under the Sarvodaya movement, where landlords granted land to farm workers out of their own free will. In the 1960s, the Communist Party of India formed the first democratically-elected communist government in the world when it won elections in the states of Kerala and later West Bengal. However, when a global recession began in the late 1970s, economic stagnation, chronic shortages of resources and bureaucratic red-tapism led to the disillusionment with state socialism. Trade unions often paralysed national life with crippling private and public sector strikes. In response to this situation, the Indian state by late 1980s and early 1990s began to systematically open the Indian economy for private capitalistic exploitation. It was probably supposed to end the bureaucratic red-tape and authoritarianism in economic development which had become the characteristic of the state owned enterprises; however, it has given rise to a very ugly dimension of the capitalism. The private entrepreneurs, in their attempt to maximize their profit, have resorted to extremely unscrupulous means. They have corrupted the entire bureaucracy and the political leadership. Let us explore the socialism that we adopted and where it has taken us to.

The socialists like Jawaharlal Nehru, who led our Independence Movement, were the leaders who genuinely wanted to banish the poverty which they associated with British colonialism. However, these leaders were under serious inferiority complex as a result of having been under colonial subjugation for 200 years. They did not have confidence in India's ability to export its way to prosperity. As a result, Nehru sought economic independence by retreating from international trade into a cocoon of self-sufficiency. These socialists associated the poverty of India with British colonialism but conveniently and completely forgot that it was the international trade that had made India an economic world power prior to the commencement of British rule. When it was pointed out that other developing countries like Korea and Taiwan had opted for export-oriented growth rather than the self-sufficiency model which India had adopted and they are being rewarded with much higher GDP growth rate in comparison to India, our socialist leaders were not open to listen. They argued that these countries were neo-colonial puppets falling into an imperialist trap and they would have no future. These supposed puppet countries soon became richer in terms of per capita income than their colonial masters. India continued to remain a poor country after decades of independence.

The initial model of socialism that was adopted in India was supposed to protect Indians from the greed of the capitalist businessmen and promote prosperity as in the Soviet Union through planning and government domination of the economy. As a result, India was converted into a land of a million controls with extremely business unfriendly environment. Everything was forbidden unless specifically allowed. Government bureaucrats, with no business experience, were supposed to know better than any businessmen in terms of what should be produced, where and how. They were supposed to know better than consumers what was good for the consumers themselves. No citizen had free choice in buying anything: The government chose on his behalf the list of goods that could be produced or imported. It was all supposed to be in public interest. It was presumed that prosperity would be best achieved when nobody had the freedom to do anything other than what they were told. Citizens were told that the world was a dangerous place full of predators. The closed economy was justified in the name of protecting the interests of the Indians against the perceived threats from these capitalist predators. These extreme controls on the economy led to serious failures in achieving the targets. Literacy, infant mortality, life expectancy, poverty and every other social indicator in socialist India was far worse than in the Asian miracle economies. Vast sums spent on public health and education was wasted. Teachers and health staff had high rate of absenteeism, however they were protected from disciplinary action by strong trade unions. This model of socialism that India adopted failed to provide either economic growth or social justice for Indians. While this socialism was in practice, most of the political leaders and bureaucrats became incredibly wealthy by using controls imposed in the holy name of socialism to line their pockets and create patronage networks. As a reaction to this extremely tight control in the economy and in response to the lessons learnt that this model was not meeting the desired objectives, a need was felt for freedom of choice in the economic marketplace. The balance of payment crisis in 1991, which forced the government of India to airlift its gold reserves as a pledge with the International Monetary Fund (IMF) for a loan to service its imports, proved to be the proverbial last straw on the back of the camel. The new government that came to power in 1991 under the leadership of PV Narsimha Rao appointed a noted economist (Manmohan Singh) as its finance minister. Under his leadership, the markets were opened and liberalized. His economic reform efforts were termed as unshackling of the caged tiger by the media at that time. The result of this liberalization is that at present we have 65 billionaires[2] in India in US$ terms lead by people like Mukesh Ambani (US$21 Billion) or Azim Premji (US$ 13.8 Billion). We also have people like Shiv Nadar in this list with a total net worth of approximately US$ 8.6 billion. He was an ordinary engineering employee of DCM till 1976. There are 12 Indians in the Forbes list of 300 richest people in the world. The current GDP of India is approximately US$1.824 trillion which was US$ 275 billion in 1991-92. India enjoyed high growth rates for a period from 2003 to 2007

---

[2] Net worth calculated till October 2013 as per the India's richest list published by Forbes

with average growth rate being around 9% during this period. The per capita income has increased from ₹12,000 in 1991 to more than ₹85,000 at present. The foreign exchange reserve which was US$ 1.2 billion in 1991 is approximately US$ 293 billion at present. In 1991, we had 0.5 million telephones in the country, today we have around 900 million. The life expectancy and infant mortality rate today is 69 years and 30 per thousand which was 59 years and 79 per thousand in 1991.

However, we have to remember that the US$ exchange rate in 1991 was @₹18 a dollar which is approximately ₹62 a dollar now. We still have around 22% of our population below poverty line. The top 10% of wage earners now make 12 times more than the bottom 10%, up from a ratio of six in the 1990s. Every second malnourished child in the world is an Indian. The growth in economy has further widened the economic disparity which is apparent through the consistent rise in the Gini index. Still more than 50% of the population is dependent on agriculture which produces only 14% of the GDP whereas 30% of the population dependant on services sector account for 67% of the GDP. Spending and consumption by the richest 5% has gone up by over 60% between 2000 and 2012 in rural areas while the poorest 5% saw an increase of just 30%. In urban areas, the richest segments spending increased by 63% while the poorest saw an increase of only 33%. These data clearly indicate that the income gap between the rich and poor in the Indian society has continuously been widening. This is definitely not the socialism that the constitution prescribes. Despite having gone through a dozen of five year plans and so many political sloganeering about socialism and poverty alleviation, the economic disparity in this country has been increasing. No concrete or specific effort has ever been made during the last 66 years to address this injustice in the society. The just and equitable distribution of the natural resources or common wealth of the country has never been viewed from a religious angle. Any scheme for the benefit of the poor has been made to look like as if it is being given as a charity rather than as the legitimate right and share of the poor in the common wealth.

This widening economic disparity and unjust social order in the society has been one of the root causes of some of the complex socio-economic problems plaguing the country. The economic justice or socialism would have been the catalyst to bring in an era of social and political justice; however all that has been done so far in the name of socialism or social justice is nothing more than the political expediency motivated by purely selfish interests. The political class at present is only interested in carrying on with the divide and rule policy to perpetuate their rule. This politics of vested interest has perpetuated or given rise to a number of socio political problems. Some of the major socioeconomic problems that the Indian society is faced with are fundamentalism, regionalism, terrorism, Naxalism, corruption and poverty, etc. Everyone is worried about his job security. People are unsure of the future and therefore, always are eager to make the best out of any opportunity to make money without any concern for the social, moral or ethical values. Morality and ethics in public life is seen more like a constraint rather than being seen as a virtue of the individual. The gulf between the haves and have-nots, the social discontent and the degeneration of the collective consciousness coupled with the displacement of the ethical and moral values have substantially increased the incidents like theft, robbery, cheating, contract killing, abduction for ransom and rape. The Society has started running like a mad horse with blindfolds on its eyes without knowing where it is going. The man in this society has become a hopeless, hungry and impatient animal. We will examine some of these issues being faced by the society.

FUNDAMENTALISM

Fundamentalism is a demand for strict adherence to orthodox theological doctrines as a reaction against openness, rationalism and radical thinking process. The term usually has a religious connotation indicating unwavering attachment to a set of irreducible beliefs claimed to be originating from the scriptures and epics of authority. As a result of fundamentalism, anything which does not meet a preconceived notion or belief of a select group of people is vehemently opposed. This opposition may be purely in the name of religion, faith and belief without any concern for rationalism, justice and its impact on individual and society. The fundamentalists are ready to pay any price to protect their belief. Their intolerance motivates them to indulge in activities like violence; sabotage, incitement of mob frenzy, arson and communal riots. As a result of fundamentalism, all norms of a civilized society are abandoned in the name of faith.

The opposition to the Setu Samudram Project in the Indian Ocean by citing the references to the stone bridge built by the army of Lord Rama as mentioned in Ramayana is a typical example of Hindu fundamentalism. People associated with organisations like Bajrang Dal, Vishwa Hindu Parishad or Shiv Sena under the leadership of people like Pravin Tagdia can be often seen defending criminal activities in the name of faith and religion. Their response to any question which can be raised in the name of rationalism or on the basis of scientific thought process would be that this question is related to faith and rationalism may not be allowed to creep in here. Killing of scores of people in the name of religion and faith and inciting the mobs for arson and riots are all examples of fundamentalism.

The omissions and commissions on behalf of the state based on divide and rule policies of the state actors and political leaders is one of the main reasons for perpetuation of the fundamentalism. The constitution of the Sachar Committee to investigate the social status of Muslims by identifying and isolating them as a separate identity group and then implementation of its recommendations in the form of 15 point minority welfare programme is a typical example of how state activity can deliberately create a divide between the people in the society. Another typical example of pushing a permanent wedge between the so called upper and lower castes in the society was constitution of the Mandal Commission to investigate the status of other backward castes by identifying and isolating them as a separate identity group. The Mandal commission coined a new term in the name of OBC or other backward castes which was hitherto unknown to the society. Once the Mandal report was submitted, the term OBC became a political tool which was used by the VP Singh government in the name of social justice and which seems to have created a division in the society for ever. The refusal by the state to enact and implement a uniform civil code in the country is another example of how state activity or inactivity can aid the fundamentalism. Preventing the implementation of the Supreme Court order in the Shahbano case by passing special law in the parliament in this regard is another typical example of state aided fundamentalism.

Fundamentalism has led to some of the long-standing socio-political issues like Ram Janmabhoomi- Babri Mosque issue in Ayodhya, communal riots, caste related violence, honour killing orders of the Khap Panchayats etc. Nobody has any doubt about the historical facts and assertions of the Hindu groups that Muslim invaders to this country looted the wealth of the temples and also converted many temple complexes into mosques. The case of Gurudwara Sisganj in Chandani Chowk in Delhi has been a typical example of this phenomenon. This place had been in use as a Gurudwara or Mosque several times during its history depending on the physical might of the Sikh and Muslim community at that particular point of time. This dispute was settled through an order of the Supreme Court and this place has ever since been used as a Gurudwara. However the temple complexes in Ayodhya, Mathura and Kashi continue to be bone of contention between the Hindu and Muslim fundamentalist groups. While these complexes appear to have been temples converted into mosques, no fundamentalist group is ready to let go of their claims on these premises. The Babri Mosque structure was claimed to have been built in Ayodhya in 1528 allegedly after demolishing a temple. In 1949, some idols associated with the life of Hindu god Lord Rama mysteriously appeared inside this structure. This led to a civil suit and government declared the area disputed. In 1984 Hindu groups formed a committee to spearhead the movement for the construction of a grand Lord Rama temple at this site. In 1986, a district judge ordered the gates of the structure to be opened and allowed Hindus to worship inside it. A Babri Mosque Action Committee was formed as Muslims protested against this move. In 1990, L K Advani took out a cross-country rathyatra to mobilize the volunteers for the temple construction movement. In 1992, the volunteers or Kar Sevaks started pouring into Ayodhya and their mob demolished the structure known as the Babri Masjid. This resulted in communal riots across India and consequently hundreds of human lives were lost and substantial assets and properties were looted, damaged or destroyed. The matter was brought into The Allahabad High Court which pronounced its verdict on the four title suits relating to the Ayodhya dispute on September 30, 2010 considering the claims and counter claims of all the parties; however the issue is still far from over. Besides the specific incidents in Ayodhya, the issue has created a permanent environment of doubt and suspicion in the minds of the people identifying themselves with the one group or the other and this sentiment can be incited anytime by any unscrupulous political formation in the name of religion and faith.

The caste systems have consistently been exploited by the political groups for their vested interest. While the old social evils like the system of untouchability in the name of caste was in the process of being eradicated, a new issue of caste based identity politics and caste conflict in the name of social justice has been created using the Mandal Commission as a tool. The political parties like DMK, AIADMK, BSP, LJP etc have only caste based identity politics as their root. Caste consideration has become one of the major determinants of candidate selection for political parties. Politics in the name of caste, community and religion has become one of the major tools in the hands of the current day political formations to implement the divide and rule policy. Another example of fundamentalism in the society is visible in the form of Khap Panchayats which is prevalent in the north western part of India. These Khap Panchayatas often display scant regard for the rules and laws of the land in the name of tradition and custom. These groups have been allowed to get away without any punishment despite having indulged in heinous and serious crimes like brutal murders in the name of social and community honours as any antagonism with such groups may have serious impact on the vote bank politics of the unscrupulous political formations.

REGIONALISM

Regionalism is another plank of identity politics in India. This country is rich in its cultural and physical diversity. With the spread of the country in 3.1 million sq kms between 8°4' and 37°6' north latitudes and 68°7' and 97°25' east longitudes with 3214 km north south and 2933 kms east west expanse, it is almost like a continent in itself. It can be divided into five distinct physiographic regions like northern mountains, indo-gangetic plains, western deserts, peninsular plateau and the coastal plains. All these regions have their distinct environmental, climatic and physical properties which have given rise to a variety of distinct life style and cultural traditions. The lifestyle and cultural traditions of people in Goa would be in stark contrast to the lifestyle of the people in Arunachal Pradesh. The aspirations and expectations of the people in Leh region are entirely different from that of people in Kanyakumari. These varying regional aspirations and expectations have led to various socio-political issues. Regions like Uttrakhand, Chhatisgarh and Jharkhand accused their respective state governments of UP, MP and Bihar of draining out their resources and not investing back much for their development. Hence, these states were born in 2002. Similar demands have been emanating from regions like Telengana, Vidarbha, Bundelkhand, Darjeeling, etc. The historical unruly scenes including the chilly pepper spray which was recently witnessed in the lower house of Indian Parliament was part of the regional identity based politics in the name of Telangana. The Telangana issue spearheaded by TRS claimed that this region contributed 76% of the Andhra Pradesh state revenue but received less than a third of state budget allocation. They also claimed that this region contributed majority of water supply which was disproportionately used for benefits to coastal Andhra Region through canal irrigation and the region was also neglected in terms of educational funding and government jobs. These issues were raised to force the government to carve out a separate state. The Congress led UPA government in New Delhi obliged as they felt an opportunity for the vote bank politics in doing so. The same consideration motivated the opposition BJP to support this move. The regional aspirations of some of the vested interest groups engaged in the identity politics does not stop at asking for a separate state. At times, it goes to the level of asking for the creation of a separate country as has been witnessed in the case of Jammu & Kashmir and Punjab where some of the separatist groups had been demanding the creation of separate countries in the name of Kashmir or Khalistan. As a result of such demands, the whole society has been held to ransom at times. These movements for separate countries lead to violent insurgent activities plunging the whole state into an environment of terror. This has happened till very recent past in Punjab, J& K and some parts of the north eastern region. This has also resulted in large scale migration of people from their traditional ancestral homes. The Kashmiri pundits were forced to leave the valley. These issues have led to a huge wastage of valuable resources to maintain law and order in such situations. The cost of clearing Punjab of insurgency and the cost of an estimated half a million Indian security forces that are deployed in the Kashmir Valley for almost two decades now could have been utilized for some productive purpose but for this wasteful expenditure arising out of the regional identity politics. These same aspirations are visible when Raj Thackeray of MNS talks of driving the Biharis and UPites away from Mumbai or when people from North East feel a need to flee Bangalore to save their lives. Very recently, a number of Bihari migrants were killed in Assam as a result of the regional identity politics. The issues related to regional aspirations also give rise to secondary issues like human rights violations or the misuse of the provisions of the Armed Forces Special Powers Acts in these regions.

TERRORISM AND NAXALISM

Terrorism is the calculated and planned use of unlawful violence or threat of violence to inculcate fear. It is intended to coerce or to intimidate governments or societies in pursuit of goals and objectives that are generally political, religious, or ideological in nature. The two key elements of terrorism, i.e. direct physical violence and intimidation is adopted by the terrorists to produce terror in its victims. This is normally resorted to when the state actors refuse to listen to the demands of the groups of people or fail to satisfy them with their responses. The terrorists have normally very strong motivation to carry out the activities which their ideologues assign them. Most of the people are drawn into terrorism since they are made to believe that they are left with no alternative to protect and safeguard their interest other than resorting to active and violent methods to force the state to meet their demands. The underlying causes of terrorism could be socio-political, religious or strategic. One of the reasons that turn individuals into anti-state violent activist is when they have a sustained and persistent feeling of being humiliated or denied justice. Such issues normally arise out of state apathy, inefficiency, corruption, injustice or nepotism and favoritism.

Naxalism is another major issue related to violence with which India is faced with. The term Naxalites or Maoists are used to refer to the far-left radical Communist groups inspired by the principles and ideologies of Mao Tsetung which was further documented in Eight Monographs prepared by Charu Mazumdar in 1967-68. Naxalites have a vision to overthrow the government and upper oppressing classes by the use of arms and violence. The Naxal movement started in a small village named Naxalbari in West Bengal in 1967 under the leadership of Kanu Sanyal but has since spread to the rural areas in most of the central and eastern India. Naxalites have been attacking police establishments and infrastructures such as public transportation causing insecurity and instability in the area. It has been reported that between a period from 2006-2010 alone, there were nearly 9,000 Naxal related incidents in which around 3,000 civilians were killed. The Naxals are reported to be active in approximately 40 percent of India's geographical area and they control large portions of remote and densely forested areas. The land areas with high Naxal concentration have been named as the "Red Corridor". This is the area where the conflict between the tribal rights on land and their traditional way of living has been in direct conflict with proposed mega projects under private and public sector. The fast economic growth in the country during the last two decades has increased the pressure on the natural resources like land, minerals and forests for fresh projects; however, the accompanying economic disparity and concentration of wealth in only a few pockets has facilitated the Maoists to motivate and recruit more people for direct armed conflict with the state to stop the perpetuation of the uneven economic growth. The conflict between economic progress and aboriginal land rights continues to fuel the Naxalite activities. The strongest bases of the Naxals are in the poorest areas of India. They are concentrated on the tribal belt such as West Bengal, Jharkhand, Odisha, Chhattisgarh and Andhra Pradesh where locals experienced forced acquisition of their land for developmental projects. Naxalism is also viewed as a fight between the two extremes of the poorest and the richest people in this country. The Naxals take up the cause of the poors against the mighty lobby of the industrialists. Naxalism is viewed as a reaction of the poor people to present their dissatisfaction with what they expected from the governments and the industries and what they actually got from them. The attempts of the governments to forcibly neutralize the Naxalites have so far back fired. There been a great loss of life on both sides since the conflict began between the ultras and the security forces. Addressing the problem through violence has a potential to further polarise people on both sides. The continued Socio-Economic alienation and the dissatisfaction with the widening economic and political inequality has so far been sought to be solved by brute force alone. This has failed to effectively address the issue and would continue to fail if the root cause of the issue is left without being addressed. The irony of curbing Naxalism with force is that it results in poor fighting the poor as the people fighting from both the sides of Naxals and central paramilitary forces come from the same poor and deprived class of the society.

POVERTY AND ECONOMIC DISPARITY

There have been substantial efforts in the direction of poverty alleviation by the successive governments. The most important and effective amongst all the poverty alleviation programs has been the Mahatma Gandhi National Rural Employment Guarantee Act. All these programmes have definitely helped to some extent however the fact remains that even after all these efforts, around one fourth of the population of the country is still living in abject poverty. The benefits of the economic liberalization policies that were introduced in the 1991 have percolated down mainly to the people living in the urban areas. The rural poor have not experienced much of what has been talked about in terms of India shining or Bharat Nirmaan. A 2013 UN report stated that a third of the world's poorest people live in India. In 2010, the World Bank reported that 32.7% of all people in India fall below the international poverty line of US$ 1.25 per day (PPP) while 68.7% live on less than US$ 2 per day. Approximately 117 crore out of a total of 123 crore or more than 95% of the total population of India live with less than US$ 5 or ₹300 a day. According to a 2010 data from the United Nations Development Programme, an estimated 29.8% of Indians live below the country's national poverty line. As per a report recently published by UNICEF, one in every three malnourished children worldwide is found in India and 42% of the children under the age of five years in India are underweight. It also shows that a total of 58% of children surveyed under the age of five were stunted.

This is the same India where as many as 70 Rolls-Royce cars were sold in the year 2010, many of them being the ₹4.5 crore Phantom models. In the same year, around 15000 luxury cars costing more than ₹20 lacs a-piece were sold including the Mercedes, BMW, Audi and Porsche. According to Credit Suisse's Global Wealth Report 2010, India had some 170,000 people whose net worth was more than US$ one million. According to this report, India had 25 dollar billionaires and 35 near-billionaires (with wealth in the $500 million–$1 billion range). 1.3% of the Indian population or around 1.6 crore people comprising of around 30 lacs households had an annual income of more than ₹17 lacs. The total wealth of India's top 100 rich people rose to US$250 billion in the year 2013 as compared to US$221 billion in the previous year. This means that these 100 people accounted for US$29 billion as their annual income for the year 2013 out of a total GDP of US$ 1758 billion. It also means that these 100 people or 0.000008% people account for 1.5% of the national income. According to a report published in the year 2003, the top 10% of the people earned more than one third of the total income of the country. This disparity has further widened which is clearly apparent in the following table.

Income Distribution in India in the year 2010

Families	Population	% of total Population	Annual Income Range
(in Lacs)	(in Crore)		(in Lacs ₹)
30	1.6	1.3	> 17
310	16.0	13.1	3.4 - 17.0
710	35.9	29.5	1.5 - 3.4
1350	68.4	56.1	<1.5
Total 2400	122.0	100.0	

CORRUPTION

Corruption has become almost like an integral part of the governance and administration in India. As per the Corruption Perceptions Index published by Transparency International, India ranks at 94 in a list of 177 countries. The corruption in India is prevalent in the form of bribes, tax evasion, exchange controls, embezzlement and pilferage of funds meant for social welfare schemes etc. Some of the consequences of corruption are the loss to the state exchequer, an unhealthy climate for investment and an increase in the cost of government-subsidized services. A TI India (Transparency International) study estimates the monetary value of petty corruption in 11 basic services provided by the government, like education, healthcare, judiciary, police, etc. to be around ₹21,068 crores. India still ranks in the bottom quartile of developing nations in terms of the ease of doing business, and compared to China and other lower developed Asian nations, the average time taken to secure the clearances for a startup or to invoke bankruptcy is much greater.

Some of the major causes of corruption in India are high rates of taxation, excessive regulatory controls, discretionary powers and authority of the bureaucracy and lack of transparency in public functioning. The multiplicity of the authorities and numerous regulatory bodies with the power to stop any citizen or business from going about their daily affairs is another reason that compels people to indulge in corruption to expedite their work.

The discretionary powers of the government authorities to search and question individuals create opportunities for corrupt public officials to extract bribes. They force each individual or business to evaluate and decide in favour of paying bribe which appears to be an easier and cheaper option in comparison to the effort required in due process and the cost of delay associated with such process. In the cases of high taxes, paying off the corrupt official is cheaper than the tax. In real estate industry, the high capital gains tax in India encourages large-scale corruption and also encourages people to deal in black money. The desire to pay lower taxes than those demanded by the state explains the demand side of corruption. The net result is that the corrupt officials collect bribes, the government fails to collect taxes for its own budget, and corruption grows. In addition to tax rates and regulatory burden, the corruption results from opaque process and paperwork on the part of the government. Lack of transparency allows room for maneuvering for both the demanders and suppliers of corruption. Whenever objective standards and transparent processes are missing, and subjective opinion driven regulators and opaque/hidden processes are present, the conditions encourage corruption. The dimension of corruption in public places and the question of black money economy have become so huge that almost the whole country had come openly in support of Anna Hazare when he sat on an indefinite fast in the year 2011 to compel the government of India to bring in a strong anti-corruption legislation in the country. The public sentiments against corruption in public places was the one and only issue which helped the Aam Aadmi Party to win 28 seats in the Delhi legislative assembly in dec 2013 by displacing the congress party which had been ruling the state for the last 15 years. The magnitude and scale of corruption and scams in public place have been steadily increasing. The Indians have become accustomed to the culture of corruption and scams in public place. The long list of scams related to the coal block allocation, 2G spectrum allocation, Commonwealth Games preparation and management, Reliance Gas Price deal, NRHM, Fodder Scam, Adarsh Housing Society, Augusta Westland Helicopter deal, Bofors Gun deal, DIAL (Delhi International Airport Limited)-GMR Scam, Delhi Jal Board procurements, Vodafone Tax issue etc. have become almost like an integral part of our governance and administration. The tradition of scams in independent India was probably started in the year 1948 by the then Indian High Commissioner in Britain V K Krishna Menon in active collusion with the then Prime Minister of India Jawaharlal Nehru. This scam later came to be known as the Jeep Scandal. It was linked to the pilferage of public funds related to the procurement of jeeps worth rupees eight million only. Menon was subsequently rewarded by Nehru by being inducted in his cabinet. He became the defense minister of India. This tradition of corruption in high places has continued ever since then almost without any break. However, the magnitude and scale of the corruption has been continuously increasing and has reached to a level where the loss to the public exchequer runs in lacs of crores. The petty instances of bribery in places like the police station, block or district collectors office, municipal offices, revenue and tax collectors offices or officials concerned with the disbursement of funds to the public have been accepted as a norm by the public. This rot in the administration has given rise to the culture of touts and lobbyists who specialize in facilitating this nexus between the unscrupulous and greedy bureaucrats, politicians, businessmen and industrialists. I would refrain from naming the people associated with the trade of corruption in public places as it would not be justified to name only a select few leaving the others. At the same time, it would not be possible to name all the people related to the high profile corruption and scams as the list might run in several pages. It would be sufficient to remember that an independent MLA like Madhu Koda, the son of a poor tribal farmer, could rise to the level of being the chief minister of a state as a result of the political manipulation. He was the chief minister of a poor state like Jharkhand and that also for a brief time span of two years only and yet he is alleged to have amassed wealth in excess of Rupees 5000 crore through corrupt means. If this is what a person of very humble origin like Madhu Koda can do, just imagine the scale of corruption by those who have been in active politics continuously for several decades and generations and whose only motive to be in politics has been to amass wealth for themselves. Corruption in high political circles has also been used as a tool by the successive governments to sustain their respective governments. The cash for vote in parliament and the bribing of the Jharkhand MPs to vote in support of Narsimha Rao government to defeat the no confidence motion against it have directly demonstrated this aspect of the corruption. The anti-corruption agency like CBI has been directly used by the governments in power to threaten the political rivals. The CBI has been forced repeatedly to initiate fresh cases of corruption or to issue clean chits to politicians. Such actions of CBI for or against the politicians have been more in line with the political requirements of their masters rather than on the basis of actual investigation or evidence. This was amply clear when the Supreme Court of India had termed the CBI as a "caged parrot with many masters" and had asked the government to file an affidavit on how to free the agency of its control.

Another aspect of corruption has been in the form of black money. Black money refers to funds earned on the black market or parallel economy, on which income and other taxes have not been paid. The total amount of black money deposited in foreign banks by Indians is claimed to be in excess of US$1.4 trillion. Most of it is alleged to be stashed in the banks of Switzerland and some other countries which provide opportunity to park such ill gotten wealth. In February 2012, the then CBI Director A P Singh, speaking at the inauguration of first Interpol global programme on anti-corruption and asset recovery, had said, "It is estimated that around 500 billion dollars of illegal money belonging to Indians is deposited in tax havens abroad. Largest depositors in Swiss Banks are also reported to be Indians". In a hint at scams involving ministers, Singh had said: "I am prompted to recall a famous verse from ancient Indian scriptures, which says – यथा राजा तथा प्रजा or in other words, if the

King is immoral so would be his subjects". The CBI Director later clarified in India's parliament that the $500 billion of illegal money was an estimate based on a statement made to India's Supreme Court in July 2011. It is alleged that most of the FDI investments in India is actually the funds of the Indians which was earned through illegal means as part of the large scale corruption in the system. It has been like an open secret in the business and industry circles that most of the money coming to be invested in India in the form of FDI which is being routed through the tax havens like Mauritius or Cyprus belongs to Indian politicians and bureaucrats. Since the interest of the entire political class is linked to the corruption and black money industry, no serious attempt has ever been made by any government to trace the actual source of origin of all these FDI funds. A senior revenue official once claimed in a private circle that most of the FDI in India can be traced linked to the Indian corruption and black money industry if the source of the fund is traced back to the ten steps behind from where it is transferred to the Indian industry in its laundered form.

GENDER INEQUALITY

Gender inequality, insensitivity and discrimination against women are another major social problem that this country has been faced with. India ranks 132 out of 187 countries on the gender inequality index – lower than Pakistan (123), according to the United Nations Development Program's Human Development Report 2013. The traditional norms of a patriarchal society have relegated the women to live like a secondary citizen in their own home. The discrimination against the females in homes and also at the work places has drastically affected their health, financial status, education, and political involvement. Women are normally married off at a younger age and are constrained to face the responsibilities of a stringent domestic and financial burden. Women typically are the last member of a household to eat and the last to receive medical attention. As a result, they end up with medical conditions which could have been easily avoided in a gender sensitive society. The literacy rate amongst the woman is also low in comparison to the men, as the society is still not prepared to consider the woman equal to men even when it comes to the intellectual and mental capabilities.

A strong "son preference" exists in the country which is evident in the practices of female infanticide and female foeticide. In the informal and unorganized sector, it is estimated that an average woman's wage is 30 percent lower than a man's wage working in a similar position. The UNDP study shows that only 29% of Indian women above the age of 15 in 2011 were a part of the country's labor force, compared to 80.7% men. In Parliament, only 10.9% of lawmakers are women. Only 26.6% women above 25 years received a secondary education in 2010, compared to 50.4% of men. A government healthcare report, released in February 2007, showed that 90% of parents with two sons didn't want any more children. Of those with two daughters, 38% wanted to try for another baby.

Violence against woman is another gender specific social issue that plagues India. Most of the cases of violence against women in India is in the form of domestic violence, dowry related murders, acid attacks, honor killings, rape, abduction, and cruelty by husbands and relatives. Crime and violence against woman related to the evil custom of dowry has been one of the major problems in the Indian society despite the enactment of the Dowry Prohibition Act and the Protection of Women from Domestic Violence Act and also the provisions against cruelty under Sec 498A of the Indian Penal Code. In 2012, according to the National Crime Records Bureau (NCRB), dowry deaths – or murders of women by the groom or in-laws because of unmet high dowry expectations – constituted 3.4% of all crimes against women. In other words, on an average 22 women were killed per day because their families could not meet dowry demands. The NCRB statistics indicate that an Indian woman is most unsafe in her marital home with 43.6% of all crimes against women being "cruelty" inflicted by their husbands and relatives. Of the 24,923 rape incidences reported in India in 2012, 98% of the cases were related to the offenses by someone known to the victim. Between 2001 and 2011, the overall number of incidents of crime against women has risen steadily. There are only 84,479 women police personnel in India, constituting only 5.33% of the total police force which discourages the women to approach the police to report crimes against them. The criminals in the society have become so emboldened that news of rape has become like a constant feature on any electronic news channel. Because of such serious and grave situation, the Vasant Vihar bus gang rape case in New Delhi in Dec 2012 led to almost the whole country coming together against the administration to demand a safe living environment for the women. This public uprising forced the government to form the J S Verma Committee to look into these issues. The recommendations of justice J S Verma resulted in the enactment of the Sexual Harassment of Women at Workplace (Prohibition, Prevention and Redressal) Act 2013. This also led to recognizing acid attacks, sexual harassment, voyeurism, stalking and trafficking of persons as criminal acts under the amendments to the Indian Penal Code, 1860. However, the incorporation of the majority of Justice Verma committee recommendations into the criminal law amendments is not enough to change the fundamentals that drive anti-women discrimination. Stories of harassment, the rape of women – including of children as young as five or six years of age – and governmental incompetence or apathy continue to make their way into the front pages of Indian newspapers on a daily basis.

EDUCATION

Education in India is in the concurrent list of the constitution. Both, centre and state are responsible for the status of education in the country. The literacy rate in the country has risen to 66%. During the Financial Year 2011-12, the Central Government of India had allocated ₹ 38,957 crores for the Department of School Education and Literacy which was the main department dealing with primary education in India. Within this allocation, major share of ₹ 21,000 crores was for the flagship programme 'Sarva Siksha Abhiyan'. The literacy rate has gone up to 74.04% in 2011 from 65.38% in 2001. It was around 16% in 1951. However these statistics do not provide the insight into the actual status of education in the country. A 2013 study which surveyed school children across 500 districts, found that a fifth of 10-year-olds could not read sentences. Around 50% of seven-year-olds surveyed couldn't read letters and more than 50% of 14-year-olds were unable to divide numbers, the study found. A similar study on higher education last year estimated that fewer than 10% of graduates with master's degrees in business administration were employable. Those working in the education sector say that the education system in India emphasizes learning by rote like a parrot without any emphasis on development of life skills, practical learning or independent thought. People do attend the schools and colleges and obtain the certificates and degrees; however the basic question that remains to be answered is whether such enrolment is actually adding any value to their individual life or to the society as a whole. An education system which leads a person to live a more stressful life is definitely not leading the society towards its ultimate goal of happiness and freedom. The sense of unhealthy competition that the present system of education creates in the mind of the students leads them to put in their best efforts trying to defeat their fellow human beings at any cost. The educational institutions have become more like the factories producing the job seeking robots. These educational institutions have become more like business shops rather than an avenue to widen the imagination and creativity of the students. The development of temperament of enquiry in the minds of the students is limited to a very few educational institutions across the country. Most others are only interested in the statistics of the certificates and degrees they issue. The quantity has become the driving factor for the educational institutions with a very scant regard for the quality. The quality of education in the public sector at primary and secondary level has deteriorated to such an extent that anybody who can afford to do so would not like his children to enroll in the government schools. The schools and colleges in the private sector function more like a shop than an educational institution. These institutions in the private sector are mere instruments of profiteering rather than being an instrument to foster creativity, innovation, research and development. Education is no longer associated with developing a sense of enquiry, personal empowerment; character building, moral and ethical values, spiritual enlightenment, social service and sacrifice. While we are on the topic of education, it would be relevant to understand what an effective educational set up could be. A story that has been circulating on the internet with regard to how a primary teacher can make the difference in the life of a human being and how it can affect the society is worth sharing here. The story is set in the context of American society; however it is equally relevant and applicable to any other society. It goes like as below.

The first day of school, Mrs. Thompson faced her 5th graders and lied, "I'll treat you all the same." But that was impossible, because slumping in the front row, sat Teddy Stoddard. The year before, Mrs. Thompson had seen dirty, messy Teddy fight with others. How unpleasantly Teddy behaved in class! It got to where Mrs. Thompson found herself enjoying marking his papers with bold, red X's and F's.

Mrs. Thompson knew she was supposed to review each child's past records. After all the others' files, she finally read Teddy's, receiving a surprise. Teddy's first grade teacher wrote, "Teddy is a bright child with a ready laugh. He does his work neatly and has good manners...he is a joy to be around." His second grade teacher wrote, "Teddy is an excellent student, well liked by his classmates, but troubled because his mother has a terminal illness and life at home must be a struggle." His third grade teacher wrote, "His mother's death has been hard on him. He tries to do his best but his father doesn't show much interest and his home life will soon affect him if some steps aren't taken." Teddy's fourth grade teacher wrote, "Teddy is withdrawn and doesn't show much interest in school. He doesn't have many friends and sometimes sleeps in class."

Now, Mrs. Thompson understood more. She felt worse seeing Teddy's gift for her among other students beautifully wrapped holiday presents. His gift came in an old grocery bag with a tree drawn on it. Mrs. Thompson took pains to open it in the middle of the other presents. Some of the children laughed at the rhinestone bracelet with missing stones and the partly used bottle of perfume. But she stifled the children's laughter by exclaiming how pretty the bracelet was, putting it on, and dabbing some of the perfume on her wrist. Teddy Stoddard stayed after school that day just long enough to tell her, "Mrs. Thompson, today you smelled just like my Mom used to." After the children left she cried for at least an hour.

On that very day, Mrs. Thompson quit teaching reading, and writing, and arithmetic. Instead, she began to teach children.

Mrs. Thompson paid close attention to Teddy. As she worked with him, his mind seemed to come alive. The more she encouraged him, the faster he responded. By the end of the year, Teddy had become one of the smartest children in the class and, despite her lie that she would love all the children the same, Teddy became her favorite. A year later, she found a note from Teddy under her door, "You are the best teacher I've ever had in my whole life."

Six years went by before she got another note from Teddy telling her, "I finished high school near the top of my class. And, you are still the best teacher I've ever had in my whole life."

Four years later, she received another letter. "While things had been tough at times, I stayed in school, stuck with it, and will soon graduate from college with high honors. Mrs. Thompson, you are my best and most favorite teacher."

Another four years passed when another letter came. "After getting my bachelor's degree, I decided to go a little further in school. You have to know that you remain my best and the most favorite teacher." But now his name at the end of the letter was a little longer -- he signed the letter, Theodore F. Stoddard, M.D.

But the story doesn't end there. You see, there was yet another letter that spring. Teddy wrote he'd met a woman and they would soon be married. He explained that his father had died a couple of years ago and he wondered if Mrs. Thompson might agree to sit in the place at the wedding usually reserved for the mother of the groom.

Of course, Mrs. Thompson did. And guess what? She wore the bracelet with the missing rhinestones. And she made sure she was wearing the perfume that Teddy remembered his mother wearing on their last Christmas together.

They hugged each other, and Dr. Stoddard whispered in Mrs. Thompson's ear, "Thank you Mrs. Thompson for believing in me. Thank you so much for making me feel important and showing me that I could make a difference."

Mrs. Thompson, with tears in her eyes, whispered back. She said, "Teddy, you have it all wrong. You were the one who taught me that I could make a difference. I didn't know how to teach until I met you."

If only we could have more of Mrs. Thompsons as our teachers and our education planners and administrations could think of creating more of such teachers! This the same India about which Elbert Einstein once said, "We owe a lot to the Indians, who taught us how to count, without which no worthwhile scientific discovery could have been made". It is the same India which invented the decimal number system and where the time for the earth to go round the sun was calculated accurately hundreds of years before the European astronomers could do the same. It is the place where the first university in the world, Taxila, was established in around 700 BCE.

We have discussed in brief about what preamble of the Indian constitution envisaged about the Indian society and where has this society actually reached while the constitution has been in force. The above paragraphs give us some ideas about the socio economic issues that India is faced with at present despite having been under the aegis of the constitution for the last 64 years. During this period, the country has experienced the rule of various political parties and formations. The rules of various political parties and alliances have mainly focused on their party or alliance's political considerations and vested interests rather than being on the creation of a happy, healthy, peaceful, progressive prosperous, creative and constructive society. To understand what went wrong where, we need to discuss the state of affairs in the various political parties. We also need to explore whether we can expect these political parties to fulfill the aspirations of a happy and healthy society leading towards peace and prosperity on this planet. Let us look at those who claim to be the representatives of people's aspirations and expectations. We shall explore the politics in India and the prospects of the Indian society as well as the humanity as a whole in the next chapter.

POLITICS IN INDIA

After the results of assembly elections in Delhi were declared on 8th of Dec 2013, everybody who had got anything to do with the political landscape of India could not but only talk of and about Aam Aadami Party. Mohan Bhagwat of RSS had cautioned BJP not to ignore AAP. Congress did not only feel compelled to support the AAP government in Delhi but had been discussing at almost all levels to emulate the AAP style of politics. While Jairam Ramesh openly said not to make fun of AAP as that could prove wrong, Rahul Gandhi was open and willing to learn from the success of AAP while saying, "I think, we need to think in terms of empowering the people which I have been saying within the party. I am going to make this a central issue." Sharad Yadav of JD(U) linked the success of AAP in Delhi to its ability to effectively raise people's issues of corruption and inflation. Even people like Laloo or Mulayam, while making fun of AAP and ridiculing its leaders, were not able to ignore it.

The AAP government in Delhi is no longer in existence. However, the political party whose government lasted only for 49 days in Delhi has had its historical importance. They are considered to have reignited the political aspirations of the people in India. They are also credited with clearing an atmosphere of political cynicism. They have given rise to a hope that it is not impossible to change things despite the level of political and administrative degeneration that has deepened its root in the system. This is what has been probably the biggest blow to all the existing political parties. While AAP has forced the Congress and the BJP to re-evaluate their strategies, it has revitalized the think tanks of the left parties to consider this as an opportunity to regain their lost ground.

What was it that prevented the established political outfits to act in the same manner the way AAP did to get the results like AAP got in Delhi assembly elections? What was it that attracted more than ten million people to join AAP within a period of 60 days? After all, AAP did not have any special hidden strategy to win the elections. All that they did was what they have been talking about since Anna Hazare announced his decision to sit for an indefinite hunger strike pressing for his demand for a strong Lokpal to prevent corruption or to be more precise, prevention of bribery in public life. In the process, Arvind Kejriwal and his team of advisors chalked out their own route map, separate from what Anna Hazare had adopted, overruling the opinions of Anna regarding not to get into electoral politics. En-route, they made promises on issues like free water, reduced electricity tariff, a better Lokayukta for Delhi, an effective and efficient anti-corruption and vigilance team and over all a strong, efficient, effective and sensitive government FOR THE PEOPLE, OF THE PEOPLE AND BY THE PEOPLE with a vow to shun the VIP culture. So again, the question is what prevented the established political parties to do the same what AAP did to win the hearts of middle and lower class people in the capital of India? AAP was initially ignored, then scolded and subsequently ridiculed by the established politicians before being accepted as a formidable political rival and a force to be scared of.

Let us have a closer look at AAP. A number of well-known people from various walks of life have been flocking towards AAP to join it after its success in the Delhi assembly elections. Why? What has been the journey of AAP? One Arvind Kejriwal, a former IRS officer, repeated the fasting episode of Anna Hazare in Delhi. He, then, donned the outlook of an electrician and reconnected the power supply lines of those whose connection had been snapped by the electricity distribution companies. While doing so, he repeatedly conveyed to the people about his resignation from the plum job from where he could have made a lot of money if he indulged in the common and general practice of corruption that most others in that particular job are alleged to be practicing. He claimed to have given his life for the benefit of the people and came up with some innovative ideas like "Jhadu Chalao Abhiyaan". He led the demonstrations on some self-declared public issues in front of the PM house or other public buildings and in the process continued to be in the limelight and focus of the media. He is the national coordinator of the party. Despite so much of media coverage, not many people in the country, even today, are aware of the other names in AAP besides Arvind Kejriwal. Nobody knows who could be the face of AAP if something happened to Arvind Kejriwal. People like Yogendra Yadav, Manish Sisodia, Anand Kumar, Prashant Bhushan, Sanjay Singh, Ajeet Jha, Kumar Vishwas, Gopal Rai, Mayank Gandhi and others may think that they are one of the founder members of the party; however none of them could think of being an alternative to Kejriwal in AAP. AAP has drafted an organisation structure wherein national executive would elect one national coordinator from amongst them. In the absence of the present incumbent to this position i.e. Kejriwal, how would an individual be elected to this post could be an interesting and important event to watch. At present, there does not seem to be any single point, besides the point that was raised by the then "India against Corruption" movement, which can be considered to be the common minimum agenda and uniting factor for people in AAP. AAP is open for anybody to come forward, fill an online or offline form and become a member. They claim their membership drive is attracting a large number of people from across the country and people from almost all walks of life are thronging to join the party. And there is no exaggeration in their claim. They have regularly been showcasing some well known personalities as their latest members to continue to engage the media and to lure the potential new joiners. Who are these people who are so enthusiastic about joining this party and why?

The politics in India brings to the mind of people an image of power, authority, money, prestige and status and this is what the people of this country has been hungry and thirsty for. Most of the people who are thronging to the doors of AAP are the people who have had a dormant desire to enjoy this power, authority, money, prestige and status. In AAP, people are not being asked for any other qualification except for an assertion that they would fight against corruption and would not support the VIP culture associated with the hitherto political leadership class. It is so simple and so easy and therefore why would anybody let go of this opportunity? People are in a hurry to get into the positions of power, authority, prestige and status and therefore they are eager to join the party before anyone else. This has given rise to an spontaneous opening of AAP offices at district and block levels across the country where people have taken up the membership of the party and have proclaimed themselves to be the block or district coordinators and have formed the district or block councils, at times without any formal authorization from the party structure above those particular levels in the hierarchy. Even some of the state level councils have originated in this same way. Only time would tell what would be the response and reaction of such people once they would realise that their aspirations and expectations cannot be fulfilled. Today, anybody who has been in a comfortable position till date in his personal life thinks he has a legitimate claim to be a member of the parliament or national executive of AAP as his contribution in the party is not going to be less than some Yogendra Yadav, Manish Sisodia, Anand Kumar or Prashant Bhushan. Many of these new aspirants would come to the door of the party through and with references from these above named gentlemen but once they have donned the "Main Hoon Aam Aadmi" cap for 3 weeks, they would consider themselves at a level at par with these gentlemen and it might lead to a lot of personality clash, heart burns, churning and interpersonal issues which would definitely not be in the best interest of the party. So far they have had only one public episode of Vinod Kumar Binny being denied a cabinet birth and Loksabha ticket in Delhi, as a consequence of which, he compelled the party to expel him. Once they have a large number of people with different ideologies, principles, cultural backgrounds and personal agenda with clashing and conflicting interests, there are bound to be many more Binnys in the party. It would be an interesting scenario to watch how the party deals with such a development which is expected to be a major source of infighting in the party in the near future. The party, at present, seems to be deliberately avoiding announcing its policies on contentious issues. However, it would not be allowed to continue to do so for long by their rivals in the political arena. The real motivation, enthusiasm, consistency and cohesiveness of the people in AAP would be tested only after the party announces its plans and principles and agenda and ideals. Whether AAP would survive with distinction on the Indian political landscape or it would be like any other existing political party would be visible within six to twelve months after the Loksabha elections in 2014. Some signs of political opportunism are already visible in this party. Yogendra Yadav on behalf of the party had declared its support for the reservation for SC/ST/OBC/Minority in admissions and jobs. It did not feel a need to go for a public opinion or referendum on this issue like it did before deciding in favour of forming a government in Delhi with outside support from Congress. The party needs to clearly state its stand on the issues like temple in Ayodhya, article 370 of constitution or Section 377 of IPC, public sector, privatization and FDI, swadeshi, subsidy, women's rights, corruption, exploitation and other social evils in the name of religious and cultural traditions and beliefs, corruption of moral and social values and so on and so forth. Once the party makes its stand clear on these issues and declares its stand on foreign policy, economic policy, commerce and industry, education, public health and many other such issues, it would be an interesting scenario to watch how people inside and outside the party respond and react to the same. How is the party going to make its stand clear on all these issues? Nobody knows whether it would resort to the same way of obtaining the public opinion on all these issues like it did before deciding in favour of forming a government in Delhi with outside support from Congress or will it be a decision of Arvind Kejriwal alone like it was when AAP decided in favour of staging a sit out in front of the Rail Bhawan or before the submission of the resignation of the cabinet to the Lieutenant Governor of Delhi. Even if it goes for the public opinion route, the outcomes of such kind of subjective public opinion would always be under question. It would definitely not be beyond reasonable doubt and suspicion irrespective of what the outcome is unless the party adopts a technology driven transparent and objective way of obtaining such opinion from the public. Some early signs of where the party is headed are visible in the form of the party hobnobbing with the khap panchayats in Haryana, party recognizing a need for minority and SC/ST/OBC representation in its organisational structure, party openly expressing its support for the caste based reservations for SC/ST/OBC mainly to woo the Jats and Yadavs in Haryana during the forthcoming assembly elections in the state and the party deliberately keeping mum on the issues of religious and cultural linkage. Looking at these early signs, it seems party is more interested in building its organisation and winning the elections rather than focusing on and striking at the root causes of corruption and exploitation in the society. Unless the party is clear on these issues and has a clear manifesto, its fate would remain uncertain despite attracting people like Rajmohan Gandhi or Medha Patkar to join its fold. Good people would join it, would fast get disillusioned and then would not hesitate to leave it.

Let us look at some other political parties in terms of how, where and when they commenced their political journey and where they wanted to go and where they have actually reached. The Indian National Congress started its journey in response to a need felt by the then intellectuals and prominent social figures to present the demands of the people of India to the British rulers and to obtain concessions from the government for the Indians who did not have an opportunity to present their demands in a structured and formal way. It subsequently turned into a mass movement to gain independence from the British rule and to obtain "swaraj" and "suraj", if I can use the terminology used by the erstwhile Congress leaders. The origin and initial activities of Congress can be linked to the thought process expressed by Dadabhai Naoroji in "Poverty and Un-British Rule in India". In this book, the grand old man of India explained the process of the drain of wealth from India into England through colonial rule. Dadabhai believed that to solve the problem of the drain, it was important to develop industries in India and to examine the British and Indian trade in order to prevent the end of budding industries due to unfair trade practices. Over time, Dadabhai became more extreme in his comments as he began to lose patience with Britain. This was shown in his comments which became increasingly aggressive. He exposed the conflicts in British ideology by asking them if they would allow French youth to occupy all the lucrative posts in England. His work on the drain theory was the main reason behind the creation of the Royal Commission on Indian Expenditure in 1896 in which he was also a member. Dadabhai represented the aspirations of the Indians under British rule. Along with Dadabhai, Congress can boast of the heritage of thought leaders like Badaruddin Tyabji, Pherozshah Mehta, Surendranath Banerjee, Gopal Krishna Gokhale, Bal Gangadhar Tilak, Aurobindo Ghosh, J B Kriplani, C R Das, Jawaharlal Nehru, Kailashnath Katju and many others. It also had the commitment of the revolutionaries like Chandrasekhar Azad and Subhas Chandra Bose as a member of its team and cadre. It has had the contributions from able administrators like Patel, Shastri, Indira Gandhi or Biju Patnaik. The biggest mass movement leaders that the world has ever had like Mohandas Gandhi or Vinoba Bhave had their life devoted full time to the party. Even now, it has three internationally acclaimed economists (Manmohan Singh, P Chidambaram and Montek Singh Ahluwalia) at the helm of affairs in the party. It has the committed outside support and dedication of technology and management guru like Sam Pitroda. The young man who is being projected as its future leader has the courage to call an ordinance of his own government as "complete nonsense". However, despite having had access to such kind of resources and legacy, Congress is finding itself in a very tight corner today. It did achieve its initial objectives of representing the voice of people before the British Government and its subsequent main objective of achieving independence from the British Government. Whether it achieved its objectives of "Swaraj or Suraj" is no longer an important issue in the party. Why this party continues to be in the arena of politics even today despite the open assertion of its biggest leader ever, Mahatma Gandhi, to wind it up after independence is no longer a topic of debate in the party. The congress seems to have forgotten that Gandhi very clearly mentioned in his work "Hind Swaraj" that "swaraj" did not mean an English rule without the Englishman. In this work, he emphasized the importance of passive resistance as a pious tool of enforcing change in governance and administration. He also explained the need for the right means to attain the right ends however these things have absolutely no meaning for the present day Congressmen. The man who has been the Prime Minister of India for the last ten years on behalf of this party is considered to be one of the most spineless men that could ever become the Prime Minister of a country. He has been glad keeping his mouth shut while sticking to the PM's chair without any concern for his personal reputation and prestige. He has openly been called the puppet in the hands of the party president; however he had been happy with this adjective. His government has also been called the most corrupt government that India has ever had. When a young party leader belonging to the ruling family of the party openly called an ordinance of his government as a bunch of nonsense which ought to have been torn and thrown into the garbage bin, all that he could do was express his grief and whiningly complain to his mother despite being the prime minister of the country. This party is now synonymous with corruption, opportunism, dynastic rule and sycophancy. It is an open secret that the son in law of the ruling family of this party has been actively engaged in corruption, money laundering and other power brokerage activities. However, nobody in this party can muster enough courage to raise his voice against this man who has amassed wealth through these unscrupulous activities. The young man being projected as the future leader of this party can eat in the house of a tribal or scheduled caste lady or walk on his feet for many miles together to raise the issues of political importance; however when it comes to talking about the corrupt deals of his brother in law, he just ignores the issue. The largest real estate company of the country has been accused of being in collusion with this brother in law and the chief minister of the state where this company has its largest business has been alleged to act simply like a property dealer to help this man.

Looking at BJP, nobody would dispute the fact that its origin can be traced to the noble thoughts of "Integral Humanism" propounded by Pt. Deen Dayal Upadhyaya. This philosophy proposed to create a harmonious society which could provide the opportunity for people to satisfy the needs of their body (food, clothes and shelter), mind, intelligence and soul. Even today, anyone seeking membership to the party has to pledge that he or she does believe in "Integral Humanism" which is the basic philosophy of the party. Mahatma Gandhi stated a list of sins which can be considered as the fundamental thought behind the philosophy of "Integral Humanism". These sins are Politics without Principles, Wealth without Work, Commerce without Morality, Knowledge without Character, Pleasure without Conscience, Science without Humanity and Worship without Sacrifice. The stated objective of the party as per its constitution is

"The party is pledged to build up India as a strong and prosperous nation, which is modern, progressive and enlightened in outlook and which proudly draws inspiration from India's ancient culture and values and thus is able to emerge as a great world power, playing an effective role in the community of nations for the establishment of world peace and a just international order. The Party aims at establishing a democratic state which guarantees to all citizens irrespective of caste, creed or sex, political, social and economic justice, equality of opportunity and liberty of faith and expression. The Party shall bear true faith and allegiance to the Constitution of India as by law established and to the principles of socialism, secularism and democracy and would uphold the sovereignty, unity and integrity of India."

This party, at present, is considered to be the political front face of RSS whose vision and values can be traced linked to the faith in the oneness of the human race, the underlying unity of all religious traditions, the basic divinity of all human beings, complementarity and inter-relatedness of all forms of creation both animate and inanimate, and the primacy of spiritual experience. This party, too, can claim the legacy of thought leaders like Shyama Prasad Mukherjee, Deen Dayal Upadhyaya, K B Hedgewar, Golwalkar and Atal Bihari Vajpayee and has had the support of numerous RSS Pracharaks who vow to give everything that they have had in their life for the social cause. It has a battery of dedicated political thinkers, acclaimed lawyers, academicians and administrators in its present leadership team. The party does provide opportunity and space for people like Manohar Parrikar to join politics and become chief minister. Yet the party is not in a position to find a candidate with clean personal image without any controversy around him and is feeling constrained to project a person as its Prime Ministerial candidate who is considered by many to be an intolerant and ruthless opportunist and for whom there is absolutely no need for the means to be justified as long as he can justify his goal and who can stoop to any level and can resort to any means to achieve his goals. What his goals are, besides being in the chair of the Prime Minister of India, does not seem to be very clear either to him or to anybody else in his party. Whether the erroneous facts, information and statistics related to history, geography, culture, economics and politics of India that he presents before the masses, to lure them to vote for him and his party, are the results of his deliberate and conscious attempt to deceive and cheat the masses or they come out of his ignorance and poor intellectual capability has been a matter of speculation. This party too has been involved in corruption and politics of opportunism. One of its former national presidents was caught on camera accepting bribe to facilitate business deals through his political network. One of its chief ministers was constrained to resign as a consequence of the legal procedures related to cases of corruption and misuse of power. The party appears to be one of the most hypocritical organizations. It would stoop down to any level to better its electoral prospects while continuing to talk of high ideals and principles in governance and administration. There is a big disconnect between the talk and act of this party. To increase its shares of votes, this party would be open to divide the society on communal lines, induct the most corrupt people in its leadership team, allow the people to come back to the party fold who had to exit on very serious charges and would even change the historical facts and fabricate the new stories to mislead the people to vote in its favour. People join this party mainly to line their pockets and enjoy the power associated with the governance and administration. Anybody who can add to the vote percentage of the party is welcome here irrespective of his ideology, background and criminal record. This party is also alleged to be a tool in the hands of the big business houses and capitalists who are alleged to have used this party for their own vested selfish interests.

Lets us look at the communists. They have the ideology and philosophy of Karl Marx and Friedrich Engels which is comprehensively explained in the works like the "Communist Manifesto" and the "Das Capital". There is absolutely no doubt about the fact that the philosophy and ideology as explained in these works are still the best as far as the explanation of the class struggle and socio-economic dynamics of the society is concerned. This is why these ideals and philosophies appeal to anybody and everybody who can read and understand these works particularly if he is unmarried. It would be extremely difficult for any rational mind to refute the logic and explanation that has been used by Marx to present his philosophy. The concepts of social ownership of all land properties and application of lease rentals on land for public purposes, the concepts of progressively higher income tax slabs and abolition of all rights of inheritance instantly appeals to any rational and just mind unless it has been trained in a fashion to look for only personal and individual interest in everything. There could not have been a better world order than that which is envisioned in the communist literature if the individual needs of the people in the society would have been limited only to the needs of their body. Communism would have been the most favoured way of governance and public order if satisfaction of the physical needs of the body like food, clothes and shelter would have brought peace and bliss to the mind as well. The party in India has had committed and highly thought provoking leaders like M N Roy, S A Dange, EMS Namboodiripad, Ajay Ghosh, Indrajeet Gupta, HKS Surjeet and Jyoti Basu and even today has a lot of highly committed, learned and principled people as part of its cadre. It still has the commitment of people like Manik Sarkar, the man who assumed office as Tripura chief minister in 2013 for a record fourth successive term and whose personal net worth combined with that of his wife, who has retired from the central government service, is less than rupees twenty five lacs. He has never used the red beacon on his official car and washes his own clothes every morning. He donates all his salary and perks that he gets in his chief ministerial capacity to his party and his wife runs his household on a meager budget of five thousand rupees that he gets from his party in addition to a small amount of pension that she gets from the central government. The communists in India who started their journey in 1920s with high ideals have split so many times that it has become difficult to keep count of the splinter groups. The CPM, the CPI, The CPI (M-L), The Forward Block, RSP, SUCI and so many other groups are all centered around their particular leaders and have almost lost their relevance in the mainstream politics. The individuals in the party seem to have become more important than the ideology. Some of the ultra left political formations known as Maoists have adopted violence and guerilla warfare as their main tool of bringing in political change. This has resulted only in a constant conflict between the state security forces and the armed cadres of these outfits however no political solution seems to be attainable through the violent means, at least in the near future. All the communists are bewildered to see that the Indian society has distanced itself from their political activities. All the left parties are forced to think why they seem to have become almost irrelevant today in the Indian political landscape when the social environment seems to be most conducive for their growth.

Then there are parties which have come up on the basis of regional and local issues and identities. Parties like DMK, AIADMK, TRS, TDP, MNS etc. can be clubbed in this group. Parties like BSP or Shiv Sena are able to sustain by making a particular class or group of people relate to a particular and distinct identity and then keep on exploiting these classes on the basis of emotional appeals specifically applicable to these identities. Additionally, there are people like Mulayam, Laloo or Sharad Yadav who came into limelight as part of some mass movement and then continued to exploit every opportunity to keep themselves and their families in the positions of power and authority by exploiting every opportunity without having any specific ideology or philosophy. Devoid of any universal appeal and without having any well defined ideology or principle, these parties are continuously looking for opportunities to exploit public sentiment in their favour.

Having looked at all types of political formations in the country, now let us analyse the present sociopolitical environment in the country. We will start with the analysis of how and why a politically infant party like AAP without any resource to match the existing political parties could induce so many people in Delhi to vote for it. Surveys have revealed that the people who voted enmass in favour of AAP in Delhi were the urban middle and lower class people, the first time voters, the youth and the students. This is because the reasonably informed and politically conscious people in Delhi saw an opportunity to bring in a new era in Indian politics. The thick skinned bureaucrats and insensitive politicians had created an environment where people had almost resigned to the fact that there is no hope for the cleansing of politics and governance in India. Almost everybody had become cynical and had lost almost all hopes about good governance and politics. The frustration of people was aggravated by incidents like Nirbhaya gang rape and the lathi charge by Delhi police on the Baba Ramdev camp in Ramleela Maidan. The highest contributor towards motivating the people to press the broom button inside the polling booths was the hope generated by the "India against Corruption" movement led by Anna Hazare. The ridicule of the AAP leadership, by and on behalf of the established political parties, further infuriated the common man (Aam Aadami) who could identify themselves with the common man being fielded by AAP as their candidates. And despite having been accustomed and used to the bribery and corruption in public places, people still resent it. Our collective morality still does not allow even the most corrupt people to accept it openly in their social circle even if they do not have any issue with their personal conscience while indulging in corruption. In such an environment, the coalgate scam, the 2G spectrum scam, the Commonwealth games scam, the AgustaWestland helicopter scam, The Adarsh Housing Scam, Reddy Brothers, Bangaru Laxman, Yediyurappa and The Purti group Scam etc. acted as catalysts to draw the people to the polling booths in Delhi and press the broom button to teach a lesson to those who were considered as thieves, arrogant, insensitive and unreliable. Therefore, it can be safely concluded that the vote for AAP was a vote for hope out of frustration, vote for service against rulers, vote for common man against elites and above all vote for an alternative way of politics, governance and administration.

Let us look at why the established political parties have reached to a state where they have and why they seem to have lost the trust of the people. All the established political parties, irrespective of what ideology or objective they started with, have drifted away from their ideological positions and their main aim has shifted from achieving their long term vision to grabbing the political power and authority. Congress does not have a universal goal and ideology. BJP seems to have forgotten about the "Integral Humanism". Communists are finding it difficult to mobilize people to subscribe to their philosophy and are finding it difficult to survive without compromising from their ideological positions. All the parties are looking for each and every opportunity to grab the power and remain in the limelight and in the process induce others to match their strategy and winning formula. As a result, the only common thought process amongst all these pre-existing political parties is "divide and rule". The divide and rule formula is the most widely and commonly used formula by the political formations. Caste, creed, culture, religion, language, domicile, economic class, social class, nationalism, secularism or any other attribute which can be used to make people identify with a particular group identity is exploited to the hilt by the people practicing politics in this country in the existing political parties. Politics has become a full fledged business wherein financial investments are properly evaluated against the expected return. It has become a profession which can be transferred to the next generations. It has emerged as the most lucrative business and profession as even the highly successful businessmen and professionals keep looking for the right opportunities to make investment in this business. The people in this business or industry keep its doors closely guarded so that commoners are not able to gain easy entry into this exclusive territory and the places are kept reserved for their own kiths and kins. If these gates are not properly guarded, it would be extremely difficult for people like Akhilesh Yadav, Tejaswi Yadav, Chirag Paswan, Supriya Sule, Kanimozhi, Deepa Dasmunshi, Meera Kumar, Jayant Chaudhary, Sachin Pilot, Deepnder Hooda, Nitish Mishra, H D Coomarswami and even Rahul Gandhi for that matter to enter into this exclusive domain. The gate crashing into this exclusive domain by people like NT Ramarao of TDP, Prafulla Kumar Mahanta of AGP, Mayawati of BSP or Arvind Kejriwal of AAP causes serious turmoil amongst the existing occupants. At first, the existing players would do their best to prevent the entry of a newcomer in their club. Initially, they would ignore, ridicule or scare the candidate raising his head against them. If that does not prevent the newcomer entering into their domain, they would be prepared to pay any price for maintenance of their omerta code. The veterans would ensure that the newcomer is given whatever it is that would make him or her like them. They would give money, post, power, prestige or use personal relation, threat, coercion, murder, emotional blackmail, social pressure, religious and cultural pressure or any other tool which will force the newcomer to become like them. The existing players always end up transforming and converting the new entrant to play by their rules. Irrespective of the background and ideology of the newcomer and despite all the issues that one may have raised against the existing occupants, it has been observed that by the time the initial dust settles, the new entrant gets accustomed to the rules of the game being played by the existing players. He acclimatizes himself with the rules and then starts playing the same usual game and abides by the rule of keeping the doors of this exclusive domain out of bounds even for those who would have helped him get inside. A perennial and never ending long queue of power hungry, ambitious and enterprising people who want to join this exclusive club of practicing politicians keep waiting for their first opportunity to get inside this gate.

Last time, the people of Delhi voted in favour of Arvind Kejriwal. His ideology is what he has written in his book "Swaraj"; his compilation of thoughts and case studies on how local self governance could be the solution of all issues related to governance and probity in public life. Going by the contents in this book, it could have also been titled as "Suraaj". He has explained the various scenarios and solutions by giving examples like that of a tribal farmer Veer Singh Markam in a village in the Bastar district of Chhatisgarh, the functioning of Parliament in Switzeraland, the issue of opening of Wal-Mart in Middleton in USA and the management of Gram Sabha by Popat Rao Pawar of Hivare Bazar in Pune and so on and so forth. It is a good and honest attempt by Arvind to look at issues and solutions. I would give him 70 % for his efforts, 90% for dedication and 45% for success as far as evaluation and review of this book is concerned. While writing this book, he probably forgets that governance and administration is not that simple as he tries to portray it in his book. His promise has been fight against corruption.

By corruption, he seems to be meaning mainly bribery in the public place and pilferage of public funds. Whatever Arvind has personally done so far has confused people about his ideas and intentions. He comes across as a passionate, sincere and honest individual. At the same time, he also comes across as an impatient, adamant, arrogant, dictatorial, reactionary, shrewd and highly unpredictable person. Some of his decisions, utterances and activities seem to be originating from political opportunism. Despite all this, he comes across as a new and different breed of politician particularly since he does not seem to be motivated by purely selfish and personal interests. He also represents the aspirations of the middle class as he comes from this class. Additionally, he is also amongst the few individuals in the current day politics who can be termed intelligent and aware of the legal and constitutional provisions. He is capable of coming forward with innovative and creative original ideas related to the issue of governance and administration which hitherto seems to have been delegated to the bureaucracy by the political practitioners in the country. Arvind has been experimenting with the political process and is expected to learn from his experiments like sit-out outside the Rail Bhawan or the resignation of the Delhi cabinet. At present, he seems to be fully engaged with his focus on maximizing the electoral prospects of his party in the Loksabha elections. His main tool of winning the confidence of masses seems to be limited to raising an accusing finger on other political parties, business houses, media and other interest groups without going into the issue of how exactly he would solve the issues being faced by the society. His book Swaraj fails to address most of the major sociopolitical issues of the current day India and thinking about such issues does not seem to be on the priority list of Arvind and his party. Early signs indicate that AAP too would end up being a party of the political opportunists. Let us go a little deeper into this aspect of the issue.

Let us try to analyse what is there in it for the Indian society. The initial euphoria of the people to have voted for Arvind and his team by rejecting the thieves, arrogant, insensitive and unreliable is going to be over very soon. Many people have already started saying that AAP will simply fill the vacuum created by the Congress and then it will also run like Congress. If that happens, it would be a big blow to the hope that Arvind and AAP has given to the people. The most important issue is whether Arvind and AAP would be able to meet the expectations of the people or not. Will his book "Swaraj" match with works like that of Naoroji, Mohandas Gandhi, Deen Dayal Upadhyaya, Karl Marx and others in terms of providing the answers to the questions being faced by the society at the time of their creation? Will his key agenda items of Jan Lokpal, Right to Reject, Right to Recall and Decentralization of Power address all the issues being faced by the 1.2 billion people of India? Will he refrain from indulging in the divide and rule politics of his predecessors? Can he and AAP afford to ignore the issues like caste, class and creed which other parties would use as their tool? How will he challenge Mulayam and Laloo when they will claim their monopoly on MY (Muslim and Yadavs) or when BJP will ask for votes in the name of "Bhagwan Ram" and Hinduism? How would he respond to the claims of secularism of congress and nationalism of BJP? How would he respond to the people who would be asked to vote for BSP as Mayawati would claim sole responsibility to guard their interests? Will they speak of Biharis and UPites in Delhi as outsiders like MNS does in Maharshtra or will they speak for them in Mumbai? How would they counter the BJP when it would claim votes for their very clear stand on article 370 of the constitution? Will it continue to talk of referendum on Kashmir like Prashant Bhushan did and then quickly back out in the name of constitution when asked if the issue of Kashmir's cessation too ought to be decided by referendum? How will it meet the expectations of the students who are not able to get admissions and even after they have completed their education are unable to find jobs? Is it going to set some examples and precedents of personal sacrifice for public cause like Manik Sarkar or Indrajit Gupta or even Narendra Modi have done? Is Kumar Vishvas going to stop uttering nonsense in his Kavi Sammelans just to make people clap and thereby raise his rate for participating in such events? Is Yogendra Yadav going to appeal to people in Haryana not to vote for him on caste considerations? Is he going to refrain from deliberately bringing in a Jat to appeal to the Jat voters in Haryana to vote for him? Is AAP and its leadership ready to change its priority from winning the electoral politics to cleansing the politics and governance? Will AAP declare why it is in politics and how it would achieve it? Will AAP explain how it would not become like other political parties and would not adopt their culture in terms of running the party affairs and the governance? How will it ensure that politics does not continue to be a business like it is for the people in other parties? How the family expenses of those would be taken care of who would be joining AAP as a full time party worker? What would prevent the AAP people in power to favour their near and dear ones? Will it make it clear in terms of what would be the minimum eligibility criteria for someone to join the full time politics for and on behalf of AAP and what personal sacrifices would be mandatory for people before they assume the public positions of power and authority? Is it keeping its eyes and ears open for understanding the tacit and subtle expectations and aspirations of the people whom it plans to enroll as its active members and then is it geared up to manage those expectations and aspirations? Is it seriously thinking in terms of what it takes to be in the politics and governance besides a pledge to prevent bribery and pilferage of public funds and shunning the so called VIP culture? Airing the news of people like Milkha Singh's wife and daughter joining, IBN7's Aashutosh joining or Infosys's Bala joining the party would indeed pull more crowd towards the party but is the party prepared to assign productive and constructive roles to all the people who would be flocking to its doors? Is the party really serious about social change or is it simply going to create chaos and anarchy by just pointing fingers on others?

The main issue of Jan Lokpal Bill on which AAP was formed was hijacked by Congress and has already been passed in the parliament post the election results in Delhi and has even got the assent of the President. This bill, before being passed, has been debated and discussed thoroughly and openly amongst the members of the civil society as well as in the parliament. The erstwhile co-activists of AAP leadership, like Kiran Bedi or Justice N Santosh Hegde – the co-author of the original version of the Jan Lokpal bill, have expressed their satisfaction with the bill that has been passed by the parliament whereas Arvind and his team calls it Jokepal and believes that it would not have enough teeth to send even a mice to jail. In response, Anna, the original force behind the movement that gave birth to AAP, says not just a mice but even a tiger would be sent packing off to jail after this bill becomes a law. Now that the Lokpal bill or the central issue from which AAP originated no longer remaining an issue, at least until it is implemented and tested, all that remain on the front of corruption for AAP is the amendment in the laws related to the Lokayukta in Delhi, the issue which facilitated Arvind to sacrifice his government in Delhi. Was this the real consideration behind the resignation or was it simply an escape route for Arvind to come out of the tight corner that he had pushed himself into. Did AAP cabinet in Delhi resign simply to use this event to showcase it as its martyrdom to garner people's sympathy for Loksabha elections? Bribery and pilferage have become one of the motivating factors for the babus to expedite the works coming to their tables. However, in an environment where everyone appears to be ready with a sting operation tool and managing its anti-corruption public image becomes more important than anything else for the governments, it is quite possible that all the bureaucratic decision making process would come to almost a complete halt. The inactivity of the government functionary and their reluctance to take and own their discretionary decisions, until a specific and precise order is issued by the political leadership, might lead to a more serious problem to deal with than bribery and pilferage. If this happens, all these anti-corruption activism would immediately turn into a villain in the eyes of the common man. Is AAP sensitive to this scenario and does it have plans to act in an appropriate manner so that the snake is killed but the stick is not broken? AAP does not seem to have a solution to bring in an era of governance wherein decisions are taken and programmes are implemented without any scope of corruption.

Coming back to the sole issue of corruption which seems to be the focus of the alternative politics in the country at the moment, we would look at it from a different perspective. I believe that the roots of our society are corrupt without us being consciously aware of it. What AAP, Maoists or others are trying to prune is the leaves and small branches whereas what needs to be cleansed is the root.

Corruption is deeply rooted in our culture and no Lokpal, Lokayukta, CVC, CBI or vigilance infrastructure can uproot it. Unless and until there is a social movement wherein people are ready to sacrifice all their personal interest for this cause and are able to gather sufficient courage and strength to expose the root cause and true nature of corruption, this issue is not going to get addressed. It must be kept in mind that fear of punitive action for bribery and pilferage of public funds would not be able to help overcome this serious social problem. Such kind of actions would motivate people to innovate new methodologies for indulging in corrupt practices or to postpone taking decisions indefinitely which could bring all administrative functions to a grinding halt. What needs to be done is to prepare a society where people are internally motivated to cleanse the system and there could not have been an opportunity better than now to strike at the root cause of this issue. The developments in technology have provided an opportunity to strike at the very roots of all the social evils like this.

Today is the time of internet, Google, facebook, twitter, Skype and Whatsapp. Today is the time of iphone and android. It is the time of Samsung, Sony, Apple and LG. Today, no power on this planet can stop any idea from spreading across the globe. Today, people are genuinely fed up with the divide and rule model of politics. Today, it is the easiest to make people understand that any specific identity of a particular group which is created by man whether it is in terms of caste, creed, nationalism or belief has simply been created by exploiters to make people fight amongst them so that the exploiters or the so called leaders could continue to get the opportunity to lead or exploit. Today, it is the easiest to awaken people to stand for a spiritual model of governance and administration where there is no exploitation, there is no need for military and there is no undue restriction on free movement of men on this planet. Today, all the people of the world are almost ready to come together to create a world order where everyone is happy, healthy and smiling and where there is no hunger, no enmity, no jealousy and no need for weapons of mass destruction. Despite appearing to be too idealistic, too optimistic and too romantic, such a world order is possible. Some of the early indicators of this possibility are already visible to all. The technology has already broken almost all the barriers of communication between the minds of people on this planet. The world is increasingly becoming smaller and smaller as far as the spreading of ideas and beliefs are concerned. The model of globalization has already brought all the economies of the world to be in sync with each other. All that the people need now is to have a perfect sociopolitical model for governance and administration which could not only meet the physical and economic needs of the people but also their universal spiritual needs. The moment such an experiment takes place in a country, it would spread like a wild fire to the whole world. The whole planet would adopt that sociopolitical model for governance and administration. No government would be able to stop it. No opium of caste, creed, religion, nationalism or any other divide and rule formula would be able to stop this model from being adopted across the globe. Karl Marx's model failed because it was devoid of spirituality. Communists focussed on making the bread available to people; however, while doing so, they snatched away from the people their liberty to think and innovate. It failed because once the physical hunger of people was taken care of; their spiritual and intellectual needs were bound to raise their heads which was left unattended. Communists failed to look into the integral and spiritual aspects of the human beings. Capitalism has failed to create a happy world order because it is based on the assumptions of "survival of the fittest" which may be applicable to the jungle but not to a civilized human society. Osho Rajneesh's spiritual model has failed because he did not care to think for the physical and economic needs of the people falling in the realm of political and social changes. Today, when all the religious and political organizations are only interested in running their shops and maximizing their profits, AAP and Kejriwal have done a great job by creating an environment of hope and expectations in India. However, having looked at the agenda and priorities of Kejriwal and AAP, we can conclude that these people do not seem to be geared up to meet this expectation of the humanity. None of the existing politicians including Modi, Rahul or people like Laloo or Mulayam are ready to recognize these expectations and aspirations. Even the world leaders like Obama, Putin, Shinzo Abe or Lee Keqiang do not seem to be aware of these expectations of the humanity as a whole and therefore, they too, do not seem to be ready to utilize the opportunity that the technology has provided to establish a HAPPY, HEALTHY, PEACEFUL, PROGRESSIVE, PROSPEROUS, CREATIVE AND CONSTRUCTIVE society. If anybody could have done this in past then it could have been Mandela, Gandhi, Marx, Martin Luther King Junior, Ashoka, Akbar, Siddharth Gautam or Jesus Christ; however their time did not have internet, facebook, Twitter, google, Skype and Youtube. It is THE TIME, the opportunity has knocked once again for the mankind and this time it is in front of us. It is because, India is the democracy of 1.2 billion people and it is in the most enviable position to set the direction for the humanity as a whole. This is the opportunity for those who are ready to sacrifice themselves for the humanity and then jointly work together to create a world of dream. It is indeed a daunting task, it needs superhuman imagination and courage and it needs a true Brahman to lead it. Time would tell whether a true Brahman is available amongst us to rise to this opportunity to bring in a lasting peace and happiness for the humanity as a whole or not.

We would focus on what could be the route map and strategy to build a HAPPY, HEALTHY, PEACEFUL, PROGRESSIVE, PROSPEROUS, CREATIVE AND CONSTRUCTIVE WORLD. We would not engage ourselves in the academic debate of communism, socialism, capitalism, social equality, social justice, democracy, dictatorship, class, caste, creed social dynamics and society. We would simply focus on our end goal of creating a new world order which would be based on spiritual considerations. Some of our basic assumptions would be as below.

a. The whole humanity is a single family. The stronger and abler members of the family would not eat, sleep and enjoy until the needs of the weaker members of the family have been taken care of. There can be no lasting peace on this planet until humanity as a whole comes together and acts like a family. This assumption is summarized in two Sanskrit sholkas, i.e.

    i.   अयं निजः परोवेति गणना लघुचेतसाम् ।

         उदारचरितानां तु वसुधैव कुटुम्बकम् ॥

        This belongs to me and that belongs to somebody else is the thought process of narrow minded people. For enlightened people, all the people on this planet are family.

    ii.   मातृवत परदारेषु पर द्रव्येषु लोष्ठवत।

        आत्मवत सर्वभूतेषु यः पश्यति सः पंडितः॥

        The one who sees the image of his mother in the body of other's wife, the one who can see no value in the wealth belonging to others and the one who can see the same god in everyone else that is in him is the only enlightened person.

b. The nature has enough for everyone's need but not enough for a single person's greed.

c. A healthy society is the one where body is free of disease, mind is free of tension and the soul is free of ignorance. Once the body is physically strong, mind is calm and the soul is liberated, the society would automatically be in bliss.

d. We need to live rather than end our life preparing to live.
e. Most problems being faced by the humanity today are created by the humans.
f. The science and technology can provide the best and most optimum tool to overcome the problems being faced by the humanity.
g. There ought to be no place for superstition and unscientific belief in an innovative, creative, prosperous and progressive society.
h. There is absolutely nothing that can stand in the way of a persistent and positive human will.
i. Together, we can.

With the above assumptions in mind, we would endeavour to develop a universal and global manifesto to create a HAPPY, HEALTHY, PEACEFUL, PROGRESSIVE, PROSPEROUS, CREATIVE AND CONSTRUCTIVE world.

UNIVERSAL AND GLOBAL MANIFESTO

God grant me the serenity to accept the things I cannot change, the courage to change the things I can and the wisdom to know the difference between the two.   -   Reinhold Niebuhr

We have looked at the issues being faced by the society and the humanity as a whole and we have also looked at the current status of the political systems and the existing model of the governance and administration. If we have to play the same game that the existing political players have been playing, on their turf with the rules they have framed for the game, it may be difficult to defeat them and achieve the objective of creating a HAPPY, HEALTHY, PEACEFUL, PROGRESSIVE, PROSPEROUS, CREATIVE AND CONSTRUCTIVE social order. If we have to achieve our objective, we shall have to change the rule of the game and induce the existing players to accept these as our common goal. There is a saying as "unless you know where you are going, you would not be able to find a path to reach there". We, therefore, would try to paint a picture of where we want to go and then attempt to find the path. To create a new world of our vision, we can adopt the following as an initial draft manifesto which can act as the seed to stimulate the thought process of the concerned stake holders. After a detailed and thorough discussion on all the points mentioned in this manifesto, a final draft can be prepared to commence the journey. While the manifesto may keep changing in response to the changing time and environment, the basic aim to create a HAPPY, HEALTHY, PEACEFUL, PROGRESSIVE, PROSPEROUS, CREATIVE AND CONSTRUCTIVE social order shall remain unchanged. The Initial draft of the universal and global manifesto could be as below.

1. BASIC PRINCIPLE OF GOVERNANCE AND ADMINISTRATION TO BE "UNITE AND SERVE" IN CONTRAST TO THE CURRENT SYSTEM OF "DIVIDE AND RULE"

    Most of the models of governance across the world are based on the basic principle of divide and rule. People are first made to identify with a particular group in contrast to the other groups. The use of this technique or strategy is meant to empower the ruling class to control and exploit the masses. The ruled populations are made to believe that their interest is in conflict with other groups and therefore they need to resort to specific actions to protect and guard their interest by opposing and countering the activities and interest of the other groups. This often results in clashes between the different identity groups leading to the opportunity for exploitation and extortion by the vested interests. These vested interests would always keep on looking for opportunities to create groups with separate and distinct identity and would flare the emotions of the members of the group by giving rise to their sense of insecurity and fear about their group identity and interest being under serious threat. Unless there are different group identities with perceived interests which are in direct conflict and clash with each other, there would be no opportunity for anyone to exploit, rule and control the masses. Some of the most common examples which have been used to make people identify with different identity groups are in the name of nationality, religion, caste, language, state, physical features of the body and other similar attributes. This is basically based on the concept of "I am I and you are you and therefore, I and you are different and since we are different, I am better than you". The concept of jihad to spread a particular faith is a direct outcome of this thought process. This policy of "Divide and Rule" is one of the root cause of oppression and suffering of the mankind. In this model, instead of collaborating, human effort is directed towards pulling in different directions. As a result, humanity is not able to gain what it could gain otherwise, if it decided to unite, collaborate and serve rather than being fooled by some vested interests who would continue to apply the policy of divide and rule. The divide and rule policy not only results in exploitation and perpetuation of the rule of a smaller number of people on a vast majority, it also leads to a lot of wastage of the resources and efforts which otherwise could be utilized for the positive developments and betterment of the mankind as a whole. Discarding the policy of divide and rule would mean that state would not recognize any division between the human beings which could give rise to conflicting interest groups. It would mean that state would be completely neutral to the distinguishing attributes of the different identity groups and would endeavour to minimize the opportunities for people to indulge in identity politics leading to conflict amongst them. Wherever required, state would take control of any such situation by directly assuming the responsibility for management of any such affair which has a potential to develop into an identity politics in conflict with other identity groups.

2. ABOLITION OF THE CONCEPT OF PRIVATE OWNERSHIP AND SALE/PURCHASE OF ALL NATURAL RESOURCES INCLUDING THE LAND, WATER, AIR, SPACE, FORESTS, WILD LIFE AND ENVIRONMENT, MINERALS, ENERGY OR ANY OTHER NATURAL RESOURCES. PROCLAMATION OF COMMON AND COLLECTIVE OWNERSHIP OF ALL SUCH RESOURCES BY ENTIRE HUMANITY AND JUDICIOUS UTILIZATION OF ALL THESE RESOURCES FOR THE COMMON GOAL AND WELFARE OF THE HUMANITY AS A WHOLE.

Every human being, or for that matter, any living organism is dependent on the nature for its physical survival. Since every living organism needs the support of the nature and environment to sustain its body, it can be presumed that all living organisms, present and future, have equal right on all the natural resources available on this planet. It is, therefore, imperative that nobody is allowed to hoard these natural resources and these resources are preserved to the maximum extent possible so that the coming generations would not be deprived of these resources. Since all these natural resources are the common wealth of all the living organisms on this planet, it is crucial that nobody is allowed to control and hoard these resources beyond the immediate requirements to meet their needs as well as the needs of others for whom they may be working as an authorized agent. Some people may be better skilled and in a better position to utilize and manage these natural resources in comparison to the others and they may be given a reasonable and justified premium for their extra skills and extra efforts to make the natural resources available in the usable form for all others. However, this would not mean that people ought to be allowed to hoard and control these resources purely for their selfish interests depriving the rest of the people from enjoying the benefits of these resources. The state also needs to keep the needs of the coming generations in mind and therefore, instead of allowing the complete private ownership rights on the natural resources, people ought to be given only specific and controlled permission of its exploitation and use and that too with a specific condition that such exploitation should not be in conflict with the interest of those who are not directly involved in this deal between the private party and the state. It also needs to be ensured that the benefits accruing out of such utilizations are distributed amongst all in a reasonable and justified manner and the entrepreneur is not allowed to get more than what he would otherwise get as a common owner of this resource in addition to a reasonable premium for his investments, efforts and skills.

3. PROVISION OF MINIMUM AND BASIC NECESSITY TO LIVE FOR ALL
    a. FOOD
    b. SHELTER
    c. CLOTHES
    d. EDUCATION
    e. HEALTHCARE
    f. TRAVEL
    g. ENTERTAINMENT

Since all the wealth and assets that anybody would create on this planet would be as a result of their interaction and interface with the environment and natural resources which would be proclaimed under the common ownership of the entire humanity, it can be deduced that all the wealth and assets that is created by anybody has a substantial part of it under common ownership. Therefore, the entrepreneur can be given a premium for his skills and efforts however that premium can be decided only after the minimum resources required by all to help them live a dignified and respectful life is set aside from the total pool of assets and resources. While it would be important to keep in mind that people would need incentives and motivation to put in extra efforts and take extra pains to convert the raw natural resources into usable assets, the state need not forget that the basic ingredient for all such finished assets and resources are under common and collective ownership. It would, therefore, be an obligation on the state to provide the basic food, shelter, clothes, education, healthcare, travel and entertainment services to all as they happen to be the co-owner of the raw material for all the finished products and services. Once these basic needs of all are taken care of, the rest of the resources can be distributed amongst the entrepreneurs in proportion to their skills, efforts and investments. There need not be any fixed idea about what are the basic needs and requirements of the masses. It can be a dynamic consideration which could be a function of the advancement in science and technology, availability of the resources and the maximum premium that can be considered justified for an entrepreneur for his efforts and investments. A guiding principle could be that the ratio of recurring income between the most inefficient and unproductive person and the most efficient, skillful and enterprising person in the society need not be more than say 1:50. This ratio can be arrived at by a detailed debate and discussion between the economists and the technologists in terms of calculating the value component of the unfinished natural resources under the common ownership and the value component of the input contributed by the entrepreneur.

4. EQUAL OPPORTUNITY FOR ALL IN ALL AREAS OF LIFE WITHOUT ANY DISCRIMINATION WHATSOEVER IN THE NAME OF CASTE, CREED, RELIGION, SOCIAL STATUS, EDUCATION, ECONOMIC STATUS OR ANY OTHER ATTRIBUTE WHICH IS NOT NATURAL BUT MANMADE.

Once the divide and rule strategy is done away with, the state can afford not to recognize the individual distinguishing factors like caste, creed, religion and other such attributes which give rise to identity politics and social conflicts. State can be completely neutral in its approach in terms of providing equal opportunity to all its citizen in all areas of life without any discrimination whatsoever. The state's endeavour would be to be as objective and impartial as practically possible. In such a state, there would be no scope for a religion based personal law or caste based reservations. Universal and uniform rules and laws shall be applicable to all the citizens without allowing any scope for separate and personal laws for individual groups. While people may be allowed to do whatever they prefer to do in the individual private life, any collective and common affair and activity shall need to adhere to the uniform state rules and laws.

5. REWRITING OF THE CONSTITUTION AND ALL OTHER LAWS KEEPING THE CURRENT AND FUTURE TRENDS AND ADVANCEMENTS IN TECHNOLOGY IN MIND WITH EMPHASIS ON THE MODEL OF SELF GOVERNANCE AND ADMINISTRATION.

The constitution was written between 1947 and 1949. In the last 66 years while the constitution has been the authority behind the governance and administration, the world has undergone an unimaginable change. With due respect to the founding fathers of the constitution, it was simply beyond their comprehension, while they were drafting the constitution, that the constitution shall be required to serve a society wherein internet and information and communication technology would be an integral part of everyone's life. They could not have imagined of the technological advancements like human organ transplants, artificial intelligence, electronic fund transfer, nuclear power plants, space flights, personal computers, genetic engineering, digital media, mobile phones, internet and social media. They could not have imagined that technology would break all the barriers of communication and would substantially overcome most of the hardships that was being faced by the humanity during their days. It is, therefore, imperative that we rewrite the constitution retaining all its elements which have proven itself beneficial to the humanity as a whole and dropping all the rest which have become irrelevant and obsolete in the present day context. We need to reapply our brains to focus on what ought to be part of the constitution while keeping in mind the current and future trends in technology and its application in governance and administration. We need to realign ourselves as per the changing times and the need of the society. Most of the existing laws, governance & administrative process and legal provisions have lost their relevance and we need a fresh legal and constitutional framework and provision for the internet age.

6. ADOPTION OF THE CONCEPT OF DIRECTLY ELECTED PUBLIC REPRESENTATIVE AT ALL LEVELS OF GOVERNANCE. ELECTION OF PUBLIC REPRESENTATIVES THROUGH TECHNOLOGY DRIVEN SECURED ELECTRONIC IDENTITY OF VOTERS BEING REPRESENTED THROUGH ONLINE VOTING ELIMINATING THE NEED OF PHYSICAL BOOTH LEVEL ELECTIONS WITH PROVISIONS FOR CONTINUOUS AND UNINTERRUPTED CONTROL OF ELECTORATES ON ELECTED REPRESENTATIVES.

In the internet age, when the world has become a small village as far as flow of information is concerned, the process of election need not be what it has been till date. Anybody who is expected to serve a particular section of population ought to be elected directly by all those whom he or she is expected to represent and serve. In the present day election process, contestants are required to file nominations, which need to be manually verified and authenticated followed by door to door campaigning and voting at a central point on a specific day. Once someone is elected, he or she is considered to be the fate accompli for the electorates till his or her term (which is normally for five years) comes to an end. This system of election is afflicted with the use of money and muscle power, vote bank and appeasement politics and irregularities in the election management process. It also gives rise to serious challenges in terms of conducting an election in a fair and transparent manner. Because of the limitations of this system, there are discussions and debate on issues like right to reject and right to recall. There is serious cynicism amongst people about the effectiveness of such an election process. This system also leads to a lot of wastage in the form of mobilization of election management officials, cost of election offices and related consumables and stationery, campaigning, booth management and mobilization of the electorates. In this system, the voters have absolutely no control on their representatives once he or she has been elected. In the alternative system that is being proposed, there would be no need for any fixed date of election. Anybody could nominate himself or herself by filing an online web based nomination which would need to be automatically authenticated and verified based on electronic authentication of the individual through his biometric data linked electronic identity and on the basis of rules related to the fulfillment of the minimum eligibility and other criteria. This nomination process could be on and open for ever for all types of constituency without any restriction on anybody to file his nomination as long as they fulfill the specified minimum eligibility criteria. The eligible voters in a particular constituency can vote for any candidate who has filed his nomination and whose nomination is valid at the time when the voter wants to vote. A voter can vote from any voting enabled platform like an ATM machine or any other electronic public service platform or by using an internet based online terminal by getting himself authenticated through his electronic identity which could be linked to his biometric data and tagged to his constituency. A voter can vote and change his vote as many times as he wants in a day and can vote from any election facilitation electronic platform from any part of the country or world. Since his electronic identity would be tagged to his constituency, he need not be physically present in his constituency while voting. His valid vote would be the last vote that he has cast. There would be no requirement for him to go to a pre-determined public booth on a particular date and time to vote. In this election process, any candidate who polls the majority vote at a particular point of time would automatically get elected as the public representative and may continue to remain in the post as long as he or she is not displaced from this position. A public representative would automatically get displaced from his or her position if the number of votes polled by him or her falls below the number of votes polled by any other specific individual consecutively and without interruption for a specific period, say 90 days. Once a candidate has polled highest number of votes continuously for 90 days without any interruption, he/she would automatically replace the incumbent public representative and would continue to be in this position until displaced from this position or until his/her death or disqualification on some other ground.

7. STRINGENT MINIMUM ELIGIBILITY CRITERIA IN TERMS OF DEMONSTRATED AND COMMITTED PERSONAL SACRIFICE, COMMITMENT, DEDICATION AND PASSION FOR PUBLIC SERVICE FOR BEING ELECTED TO THE POSTS OF PUBLIC REPRESENTATIVES AND POSITIONS OF AUTHORITY AND POWER WHEREVER THERE WOULD BE ANY SCOPE FOR DISCRETIONARY DECISIONS. ELIMINATION OF ALL SCOPE AND POSSIBILITY OF NEPOTISM, FAVOURITISM, BIAS AND PREJUDICE IN THE DISCRETIONARY DECISIONS OF PUBLIC REPRESENTATIVES BY ADOPTION OF PREVENTIVE MECHANISM BEFORE ELECTION OF THE REPRESENTATIVES.

Most of the people who are or want to come in the public life today are motivated to reach to these positions mainly to exploit the system and misuse their discretionary powers and authority purely for their vested personal interests. They are mainly guided to earn as much as possible for themselves and their near and dear ones. This motivation not only leads to a dynastic tradition in public life but also vitiates the democratic system. Public positions become a platform for perpetuating the dynastic rule and for continuation of the exploitation of the masses. Such people would go to any length and would stoop down to any level to protect and guard the interest of themselves and their kith and kin even when it is directly in conflict with the interest of the masses. The system of nepotism and misuse of discretionary powers and authority for "I, me and mine" is one of the main reasons of general public looking at the so called political leaders with a sense of contempt.

Additionally, when incompetent people usurp the public positions of power and authority, they tend to indulge in unscrupulous activities which create a very dangerous trend for the governance and administration. It is, therefore, being proposed that the concepts of dedicated people for public cause as per the rules and regulations for the pracharaks of RSS, full time cadres of communist parties and the concepts of sannyas ashram of Hinduism be adopted and prescribed for the people aspiring to contest the elections for the public positions of power and authority, e.g. member of a state legislative assembly or member of parliament or sarpanch of a gram panchayat. The minimum eligibility criteria for public and political life could be stipulated as below

1. Political Party Sympathizer:

   Anybody, irrespective of their caste, creed, gender, nationality, religion, language or age can voluntarily commit to sympathize with the party ideals and can take upon themselves the responsibility to spread the vision and ideologies of the party and message of the party leaders. No formal registration or special commitment shall be required for being a party sympathizer.

2. Primary Member of the Political Party:

   The primary member of the party must commit to
   a. Refrain from indulging in any activity in any manner which is in conflict with the interest of the masses
   b. Contribute towards bringing transparency and openness in public domain
   c. Abide by the ideals, vision, policies and principles of the party
   d. Abide by the decisions of the party and maintain discipline in the organisation without compromising on personal ideals and values.

3. Party Executive Position:

To become eligible for holding an executive post in the party organisation, the minimum eligibility criteria could be

a. Must be registered as a primary member
b. Should commit to work full time for the party
c. Should be able to demonstrate that his or her family expenses would be taken care of, for a lifestyle and standard of living, at par with what it had been before the member assumes the Party Executive Position as a full time responsibility.
d. Should have achieved reasonable success in life prior to joining the full time party executive position. This success could be in any area or walk of life which the candidate would have chosen as the main source of earning livelihood for him and his family.
e. Should not have any legal or criminal case pending against him or any of his family members and should not have been convicted for any offence in the past. (Cases registered due to political and public activities without any direct personal interest of the candidate would not lead to disqualification).
f. Should be intellectually at par with someone who has formally studied at least till class 12.
g. Must be in perfect physical health without any chronic medical condition

4. Public Representative:

The eligibility criteria for being considered by the party for a public representative position (MLA or MP etc.) would be

a. The candidate must be eligible to be appointed to a party executive position.
b. Should legally transfer all his movable and immovable physical assets, resources, wealth and properties to someone else before filing his nomination as a public representative so that the total assets to be shown in the nomination paper is

nil and it continues to be nil as long as the member continues to hold the public post.

c. Commits not to live with his family and not to favour his family, relatives and friends as long as he continues to hold the public representative post. Treats his family members and relatives like any other citizen of the country and does not help them get any special treatment.

d. Commits to forego his affiliation to his caste, creed, religion, race etc. and swears in the name of universal power to stick to a life of service to humanity to bring peace and cheers on the faces of all human beings.

e. Commits to submit all his benefits and perks received in his capacity of a public representative for public cause and to live like an ordinary citizen with very basic resources and salary as considered appropriate by the political party.

f. Should be intellectually at par with someone who has formally studied to obtain a Bachelor's Degree in any stream of academics.

g. Would commit to the principles of Asteya (non stealing) and Aparigrah (not possessing anything beyond what is absolutely necessary)

5. <u>Minister / Public Executive Post Holder</u>:

The eligibility criteria for being considered by the party for a minister / public executive post position would be

a. Qualified to be a public representative

b. Should be intellectually at par with someone who has formally studied to obtain a masters degree in any stream of academics.

Candidates may be allowed to apply for tickets from more than one constituency; however they may be asked to specify their order of priority. Wherever more than one candidate seeks ticket from a particular constituency, the selection of the authorized candidates may be through an online voting by the actual voters of the constituency to eliminate the scope of any kind of favoritism in party ticket distribution at all levels of elections.

8. LEVELS OF GOVERNANCE AND ADMINISTRATION TO BE DECIDED ON THE BASIS OF TECHNOLOGY ENABLED, PROCESS DRIVEN, RULE BASED GEOGRAPHICAL, ECONOMIC AND DEMOGRAPHIC CONSIDERATIONS. CONSTITUTIONAL DIVISION OF POWER AND AUTHORITY AT VARIOUS LEVELS OF GOVERNANCE, E.G. NATIONAL LEVEL, STATE LEVEL, DISTRICT LEVEL, BLOCK LEVEL AND VILLAGE/COLONY/MOHALLA LEVEL TO BE BASED ON ELECTRONICALLY GEO-TAGGED POPULATION AND SERVICE CATCHMENT AREA.

At present the constitutional division of power is only between the state and the center. However, in this system, the specific local needs of the people, which are a function of their unique geographical, economic, cultural and demographic attributes, tend to get ignored. The centralized policy makers often tend to be unmindful of the specific requirements and availability of the resources at a local level. This leads to a lot of wasteful planning and inappropriate allocation of resources. There is a saying in Ayurveda as "यद्देशस्य यो जन्तुः तद्देशस्य तस्यौषधं" which means that for the treatment of the disease of an animal from a particular place the suitable remedial medicine also needs to be found in the same place. Therefore, it is being proposed that the constitutional division of power be reorganized by a careful study of what type of planning and execution can be implemented from what level. Instead of a fixed division of power between center and state as in the present form, the levels of governance could be decided on the basis of service catchment and population. For example, for every 10,000 people living in a contiguous geographical area, there could be a level of governance which could be named as panchayat government or colony government. The services like maintenance of local roads and lanes, street lights, maintenance of places of worship, parks and gardens, maintenance of resident security and safety systems, management and distribution of utility services like water and power, primary education, management of cultural and religious functions and other similar services of local nature could be the subject matter of governance at this lowest level. For every 10 panchayats or colony governments, there could be a local municipal or block level government. For every 10 municipal or block level governments, there could be a district level government and for every 10 district level governments, there could be a state level government. The areas of the governments at different levels and their service catchments may be automatically reorganized every ten years based on the changes in the factors like demography and economic activities. While the number proposed here and the methodology is only illustrative and indicative, the purpose is to devise an efficient system of governance and administration which would result in participation of the masses in deciding what matters most for them rather than the fates of the masses being in the hands of those who have absolutely no idea and understanding of the implications of their decisions. The funds for governance at each level could automatically be distributed from the central treasury based on the budgetary requirements of the governments at various levels. Governments at each level would prepare their own budget and an algorithm could be developed to allocate the funds to meet the budget expenses of various levels of the governments considering their respective budgetary requirements, the priority of the requirements for services of the governments at various levels, the collection of taxes from various catchment areas and the total availability of funds in the public treasury. The governments at each level would have their own permanent staff and paid employees to manage their affairs and would be free from the control of the governments at higher levels for their specific subjects of services and areas of governance. The governments at various levels would collaborate wherever some service area falls in their concurrent subject list of service or governance. No government at any level would be superior or inferior to government at any other level. All of them would function within their respective jurisdiction as per the division of service between them as defined in the new constitution.

9. GOVERNMENTS AT ALL LEVELS TO BE SENSITIVE TO THE LOCAL NATURAL, ENVIRONMENTAL AND CULTURAL NEEDS WHILE FORMULATING THE LAWS WITHOUT ANY SPECIFIC CONSIDERATION FOR RELIGION, CASTE, CREED OR ANY OTHER MANMADE ATTRIBUTE TO DISTINGUISH BETWEEN PEOPLE.

The government at all levels would be sensitive to the local cultural traditions and environmental requirements while formulating the rules and laws for their respective jurisdiction and service areas. There would be absolutely no recognition of the caste, creed, religion or any other similar manmade attribute which can lead to a system of identity politics or vote bank politics. However, this does not mean that governments would not be sensitive to the requirements of its service catchment in terms of their cultural and religious traditions or the requirements arising out of the local geography and environment. Protection of the nature, natural environment and resources would be at priority since these factors are normally linked to the local cultural traditions and customs. Emphasis would be on maintaining an ecological balance between man and nature. Development and growth would be considered only if it is not in conflict with the nature. For example, a local government can prevent tourism or construction of new houses or development of a particular industry in an area if they feel that such an activity can adversely affect the local environment which may be considered fragile and highly sensitive to such activities.

10. REPLACEMENT OF BUREAUCRATIC MODEL OF ADMINISTRATION WITH REAL TIME TRANSPARENT COLLECTIVE DECISION MAKING PROCESS WITH FIXED ACCOUNTABILITY. IMPLEMENTATION OF PERFORMANCE APPRAISAL OF PUBLIC SERVANTS BY PUBLIC THROUGH TECHNOLOGY ENABLED TRANSPARENT ONLINE PERFORMANCE MANAGEMENT SYSTEM.

Bureaucrats are the most important functionaries in the current day administrative system; however these bureaucrats are not accountable and responsible for their acts and deeds. They are supposed to act like the servants of the public but they tend to act like the masters of the public. Bureaucrats are mainly interested in completing their term, enjoying the power and status associated with their post and earn for their own family and relatives. They do not feel the pain which may be a result of an act of omission and commission on their part. They do not seem to be answerable to any one and may continue to keep raising issues which might lead to postponement of decision on any subject. Such actions are normally guided by the personal egos as well as the selfish considerations of these bureaucrats. Once the bureaucrats are made fully accountable for their actions and are made answerable to the public through transparent technology tools and are controlled by the public representatives at local level, the system of governance and administration would undergo a drastic positive change. If all the officials are made to act simply like the support functionaries for the public representatives in true sense and a continuous control is maintained over them by the public representatives without allowing for an opportunity for a nexus to be formed between them, they would be bound to act in the efficient, effective and productive manner. It is being proposed that officials at all levels work directly under the control of the local public representatives who should be authorized to control their service conditions. The service rules for an official at Panchayat level ought to be determined or legislated by the government at Panchayat level. The service rules for an official at district level ought to be framed by the government at district level rather than being imposed by the central government or the state government. The governments at all levels ought to be fully authorized to hire or fire any official for their respective service area. The panchayat, block, district, state or central governments may have their own employees and would frame the service rules for their respective employees. The administrative decisions at all levels of governments, from panchayat to central, shall be taken by the public representatives and the general body of the public. The officials would be merely the tools to implement such decisions and they themselves would remain under the administrative control of the public representatives. The performance of the officials at all levels shall be managed by an open and transparent web based online tool wherein all the public, who have had an opportunity to interact with the official or have directly or indirectly been affected by the acts and deeds of the official, shall rate the performance of the official. The salary hike, promotion, service benefits or even continuation in service for officials shall be decided on the basis of such performance management tool which would collate and compile the direct feedback from the public on the performance of the official. All the officials of all the departments including the senior most administrative officers shall be governed by this general principle. The official here would mean anybody who obtains a fixed monthly salary from the public fund in return for a specific service and would include all the service providers like teachers and other educational service providers, doctors and other health service providers, public transport employees, welfare officers, public utility and services employees, law and order maintenance service employees, judicial services employees, engineering services employees and all such people who have not been elected but selected to work for the people in return for a compensation.

11. SINGLE GLOBAL ELECTRONIC IDENTITY FOR ALL HUMAN BEINGS AND LINKING OF ALL SERVICES, RIGHTS, DUTIES, OBLIGATIONS AND OTHER PERSONAL RECORDS WITH THIS IDENTITY.

Today we have one Aadhaar card issued by UIDAI for all citizens. Aadhaar captures our biometrics and other details. These details are supposed to be linked to our bank accounts for direct transfer of government subsidy benefits in our bank accounts. A separate data collection is also under way in the name of national population register. Additionally, we have numerous other documents. We need one passport to go across the country border. We need a driving license as a proof of our authorization to drive vehicles across the country. We need a separate voter id card to vote in elections. We need ration cards, vehicles registration card, BPL cards, pension card, bank passbooks, credit cards, club membership card, party membership card, medical and health history card, medical insurance card, life insurance policy, educational certificates and marks sheets, railway reservation ticket, airlines boarding card and so many other cards. It is suggested that all these different and various schemes be scrapped and replaced by a single electronic identity device. This device could be operated with the biometric authentication of the individual and could be linked to all the services, rights, duties and obligation. This device could be a small solar powered device with a two way satellite as well as local peer to peer communication capability. The communication backbone for this device could be something like Outernet. (Outernet is a project of the Media Development Investment Fund of New York. They have plans to launch hundreds of low-cost miniature satellites known as "cubesats" into orbit around the Earth to create the Outernet, a wireless connection to the Web available for free to every person in the world. If everything goes according to plan, the Outernet could be here as soon as June 2015). This could be a low cost ubiquitous device similar to a SIM card in a mobile phone with additional features of biometric authentication for all transactional services. This device could store all the relevant information like personal details and bio-data, biometric identification details, linkages to all the public services like authorization to drive or to receive privileges, record of all relevant personal data like educational records and certificates, medical records, authorizations for public services like rail, bus or air travel, linkages to bank accounts and insurance policies, records of direct and indirect taxes paid and all such personal records which can be captured and stored on this device and linked to the public portals and servers. This could be a single, technology driven, one time solution which could eliminate a lot of wastage and duplication in the system. This would also act as a technology enabled crime prevention device as there would be absolutely no scope for any kind of impersonation, cheating or forgery and all relevant data would be readily available for verification and authentication by any one..

12. ABOLITION OF THE SYSTEM OF CASH TRANSACTIONS AND CURRENCY NOTES BY SECURED ELECTRONIC FINANCIAL TRANSACTIONS. RECORDS OF ALL PUBLIC AND PRIVATE FINANCIAL TRANSACTION TO BE AVAILABLE ONLINE IN PUBLIC DOMAIN FOR ANYBODY TO SEE.

Once we have enabled a single electronic identity for all and all personal records, rights, obligations, duties and services are linked to it, the next step could be abolition of the system of cash transactions. In the initial days of evolution of the trade services, people practiced the barter system wherein goods and services were directly exchanged. This system was replaced by valuation of each and every product and services in terms of some specific material like shells, metals or some other material which came to be used and widely accepted as the medium of exchange for goods and services. Later on, units of gold and silver became standard exchange facilitation medium. This was subsequently replaced by printed paper currency backed by the promises of the sovereign governments. The present medium of exchange is a mix of the electronic money and printed currency notes backed by the government promises. Technology has now made it possible to replace the currency notes by pure electronic transactions. The abolition of the currency note system would save a lot of trees from being felled which are required to make paper for their printing. It would also eliminate the serious problems of black money and fake and counterfeit currency notes. Additionally, forgery, cheating and all crimes related to financial transactions would instantly come to an end after this system is put in place. It is being proposed that all financial transactions be carried out using the biometrically authenticated personal electronic identification device. Such devices could communicate with each other by using some proximity sensor to initiate the mutual transaction which could be confirmed by the back end servers linked to both the devices through satellite communication. Being solar powered and satellite enabled, these devices could be used anywhere on this planet without being dependent on mobile telephony signals and grid electrical powers. On completion of the transaction, both the sending and receiving device would show their total balance and the amount credited and debited as the result of the transaction. This total balance in both the devices and the respective amount of credit and debit would instantly be updated in the back end server which could be linked to the bank accounts of the individuals. The copies of records of all such transactions of individuals may be kept in public domain for anybody to see which could eliminate the social and moral issues like expenditure on unlawful or immoral activities. The trail of money would always be available to see who received how much money from whom and then how that money was appropriated. This way, almost all funding for illegal activities would come to an end and all immoral and hypocritical activities would voluntarily be stopped by the people who normally indulge in such activities, because of the embarrassment that expenses on such activities can cause. Nobody would be able to take and give bribe without letting the whole world being aware of it, nobody would be able to ask for commission or cut from the public funds from the beneficiaries and nobody would be able to indulge in what is called underhand dealings. This would completely abolish the corruption in public place from its root and there would be absolutely no need of a Lokpal or Lokayukta, CVC, anti-corruption department, vigilance department or any other department to check the bribery, pilferage of public funds and any other forms of corruptions. All that people could obtain in return for discretionary favours would be in the form of presentation of gifts, jewellery, furniture, clothes and other consumables. While it may be difficult to curb the system of gifting of consumables and items of perishable and transient nature, the system of bribery in the form of costly items like jewellery or furniture can be curbed by insisting on showing the record of purchase whenever someone would try to redeem or encash it. All items in the possession of a person for which no financial transaction record would be available in the public domain may be declared as ill gotten and may be confiscated by the state as a public property. This would also eliminate the crimes like looting, theft, robbery, overcharging and all such activities since nobody would be able to get away after forcibly or fraudulently depriving someone of his legitimately earned money.

13. ABOLITION OF ALL TAX COLLECTION DEPARTMENTS AND THEIR REPLACEMENT BY AN AN IDLE MONEY TAX FROM ALL CONSUMERS AT THE TIME MONEY GOING INTO FIXED DEPOSITS

At present, we have income tax, excise tax, sales tax, service tax, road tax, value added tax, works contract tax, goods and services tax, minimum alternate tax, entertainment tax, life tax, death tax, this tax and that tax. All these tax departments have become a major source of corruption and the inspectors in all these departments encourage the tax evasion and corruption in collusion with unscrupulous elements. This leads to a lot of wastage of public funds in the form of collection efforts and the pilferage as a result of the collusion between the tax authorities and unscrupulous people. This also leads to a lot of harassment for the tax assessees and gives rise to unnecessary intermediaries like the chartered accountants and tax consultants. It is being proposed that all these tax departments be abolished and all these taxes be replaced by a single tax which may be called "Idle Money Tax". For this idle money tax to be generated and collected, every bank account may be programmed to automatically transfer any money in excess of a certain threshold, e.g. INR 10,000/- lying in a bank account beyond 30 days into a fixed deposit account. Whenever any money be transferred into a fixed deposit account from a normal savings or current account, an idle money tax at a predetermined rate may be imposed on it which may be collected automatically by the bank from the funds being transferred into the fixed deposit account the customer and the bank would credit it to the state treasury as the individual's tax contribution. This tax amount could be a predetermined amount based on the quantum of the amount going into the fixed deposit and the overall requirement of the tax for maintenance and provisions of the public services and the obligations of the state. The basic principle of this tax system would be (a) tax only on money not being used by the owner for productive economic activities (b) higher incremental rate of tax for higher levels of money being kept idle and (c) a single source of automatic tax collection at the point of money going into a fixed deposit account. This would ensure a boost to the overall economic activities as people would prefer not to keep their money idle. This would also reduce the price of almost all the goods and services by around fifty percent as all the taxes (except the customs/anti-dumping duty) would be abolished. Additionally, it would also create a more conducive business environment as there would be no tax terrorism and no unproductive activities like statutory book keeping and maintenance of other records not necessary to run a business.

14. ABOLITION OF REQUIREMENTS OF FORMAL EDUCATION AND DEGREES FROM EMPLOYMENT OPPORTUNITIES. JOB SPECIFIC, TECHNOLOGY DRIVEN, RULE BASED RELEVANT PROCEDURE TO BE DEVISED FOR ALL PUBLIC AND PRIVATE EMPLOYMENT OPPORTUNITIES MINIMIZING THE NEED FOR HUMAN INTERFACE AND ELIMINATING THE SCOPE OF DISCRETION IN SELECTION PROCESS.

The changes in the technology have made it possible to eliminate all scope of nepotism and favouritism in selection for jobs and services. The requirements of minimum educational criteria and all such other intellectual requirements for all the jobs and services in the country may be abolished. There could be an exhaustive pool of question bank for the relevant and job specific knowledge available in the central server of the job and recruitment management system. The system would also have places in all the districts where online computer based examinations could be conducted in controlled conditions round the year. Anybody could register himself online to take test for any job on any day and time as per his choice. The system could automatically generate an online test paper for him based on the pre-decided test pattern and the question bank available with the system. The results of such tests could be made available instantly and immediately after the test and the pass certificate for this test could be verifiable online from anywhere. All those who pass test for a particular class of job can opt and submit their choices, preferences and constraints for joining such jobs as and when an opportunity for such a job arises. Let us assume that someone passes the test for a bank manager's job and gives his choice for a particular district only and for a particular bank only. The test results may be kept valid for a pre-determined period, say three years. Now, within the next three years, whenever a new job opportunity comes in the district and the bank as specified by the candidate in his choice and constraint, he would be automatically considered by the system for this job. The job would automatically be offered to the candidate in order of their priority subject to their relevant test pass certificate being valid at the time of the job opportunity. The order of priority could be decided automatically by the system on the basis of age, economic conditions of the family, date of passing the test, score in the test, personal liability and the number of direct dependants etc. This system ought to be applicable for selection and recruitment for all jobs in the public and private sector and all job positions in the country ought to be filled by the central recruitment management system only. The hiring authorities at all levels of government and private employers shall have to subscribe to this system for their respective recruitment requirements to eliminate the scope of personal discretion in job opportunities and eradication of the scope of nepotism and favoritism in employment opportunities.

15. THOROUGH OVERHAUL OF THE EDUCATION SYSTEM TO MAKE IT MORE RESPONSIVE TO THE NEEDS OF THE SOCIETY WITH OPTIMUM UTILIZATION OF THE TECHNOLOGY TOOLS.

The system of class room based formal education shall be limited only till the level of secondary education or till the age of 16 years. Education till this level may be imparted in the local language. All the educational materials shall be standardized by preparing the standard audio-visual course materials which could be delivered through the streaming video channels so that the course material running in all the schools would be exactly the same. The teachers would be available in the classes to support and guide the students to help them grasp and understand the material that is being delivered through the standard video channels. There need not be any system of examination however attendance may be made compulsory in classes for every child till the age of 16. Beyond the level of secondary education, all higher education shall be delivered only through the online delivery channel. There would be no requirement of a formal classroom or campus beyond the level of secondary education. All course materials for all the streams of studies shall be standardized across the country in contrast to the current system wherein various universities have autonomy to devise their own course content. The best experts and authority in each subject shall be utilized for their contribution towards continuous improvement in the course materials. Course materials shall be required to undergo a constant change as per the new research and developments, discoveries and the changing needs of the society. Course improvement workshops shall be an ongoing process. Course preparation, delivery and examination management and administration shall be full time jobs for academicians and academic administrators. All practical courses, too, shall be delivered through online video channels only. Anybody desirous of obtaining special and higher knowledge in any subject or stream of education shall have the option to pursue the course of his choice as per the time available at his disposal. There would be no time limit to complete a particular course in any given duration. People would be able to study any course of their personal choice using the video course materials which would be made available free of cost through web based online delivery channels. This could be accessed through any internet enabled device from anywhere without any need for a student to ever visit a formal university or college campus. The examination centers shall be available in all the block headquarters wherein people could go after online registration for a particular course. People would be authorized to take up examination on the basis of electronic authentication of their identity based on their biometric attributes. All the examination centers shall be capable of conducting examination throughout the year for all subjects under controlled conditions. The computer systems in the examination centers would automatically generate a question paper for each examinee applying and registering to appear in the examination. The results of the examination shall be instantly available at the end of the examination. Certification for having passed all such higher education courses shall be only of academic importance and would not be linked to any other issue like minimum eligibility in the jobs. Additionally, there would be campuses for short and medium term residential courses from two to twelve week duration each wherein character building, personal empowerment and effectiveness, motivational and special skill courses shall be delivered in intense workshops to the inmates. Participation in some of the character building, empowerment or motivational courses or special skill courses may be made compulsory for all as a pre-requisite for enrolment in specific higher education course or as part of the eligibility conditions in public or private jobs. Options for vocational and practical training courses shall also be available in the form of intense short term residential course of two to four week duration each to impart the vocational skills to the students.

16. ALL PUBLIC RECORDS AND DOCUMENTS TO BE AVAILABLE TRANSPARENTLY IN THE PUBLIC DOMAIN FOR ANYBODY TO SEE

We already have a right to information act which authorizes the public to obtain any data from the public authorities. While this act has brought the opportunity for substantial change in the approach of the governance, there is still a long way to go as far as complete transparency and openness in the public affairs is concerned. It is being proposed that all the public services offices be directed to move towards a paperless organisation. All the governance and administration ought to be managed using the online and electronic tools based on the work flow management system. In this system, all the records and information which could be made available to the public as per the scope of the right to information act may automatically be made available in the public domain, to eliminate the need of filing an application under RTI to obtain the relevant information. To protect the data from corruption and to maintain its integrity, an online copy of all the public records may be made available to the public by keeping a read only copy of all such records in public domain while the original data may be hosted on the secure servers to which public access may not be necessary. In this way, all public records related to every item of governance and administration would be available in the public domain leading to a complete transparency and openness in the governance. Public would be able to see who did what and why on all issues related to the public. This would help implement the democracy in its true sense since once the public is aware of the stance of their representatives and their servants (officials and bureaucrats), they would be in a better position to decide their political course of action.

17. ALL THE PUBLIC SERVICES TO BE PROVIDED BY TECHNOLOGY DRIVEN, RULE BASED PROCESS MINIMIZING THE NEED FOR HUMAN INTERFACE AND ELIMINATING THE SCOPE OF OFFICIAL DISCRETION IN PUBLIC SERVICES.

The officials dealing with the public services need not be the policy makers for such services. The business of policy making and framing of rules should be left with the public through the public representatives or general bodies. The officials should be merely the support to facilitate the implementation of such rules rather than being the arbiter and controlling authority in such matters. One of the reasons for corruption in public life is because of the officials, in their role of being a public servant, normally tend to extort undue gratification from the public in cash or in kind. They do this by making the public feel that they are doing them a favour by actually doing what they are supposed to do as part of their normal duty and for which they are anyway being paid from the public fund. This can be totally eliminated by devising a system of delivering public service by online or technology driven tools which would automatically deliver the public services according to the rules implemented in the system. This system should eliminate all the scope of official discretion in such matters. As far as practically possible, all public services may be designed to be delivered through the technology driven tools, eliminating or minimizing the need for human interface in all such matters. Wherever there is any interface with the humans in the role of officials, an online efficiency and productivity report of such officials may be generated which should be available to the public to manage the performance report of such officials.

18. PEOPLE TO HAVE COMPLETE FREEDOM OF EXPRESSION AND OPINION. ALL PEOPLE TO HAVE COMPLETE FREEDOM TO FORM ASSOCIATION AND SPREAD NEW IDEAS AMONGST THEMSELVES AND INFLUENCE AND CHANGE THE MODEL OF GOVERNANCE AND ADMINISTRATION AT ALL LEVELS. THERE WOULD BE NO STATE INTERFERENCE IN THE EXPRESSIONS AND ASSOCIATION OF PEOPLE AS LONG AS THERE IS NO PHYSICAL VIOLENCE BETWEEN THE CONFLICTING INTEREST GROUPS. THE ROLE OF THE STATE OR GOVERNMENT AT ALL LEVELS WOULD BE TO MINIMIZE OR ELIMINATE THE CONFLICT AND DIFFERENCES AMONGST THE GROUP OF PEOPLE.

The state need not be scared of the new developments, transparency and openness. It should rather encourage the growth and development of ideas in public keeping pace with the development in science and technology and development of new ideas in the field of social sciences and management. To maintain a healthy growth of the society, the state would need to foster openness, transparency and flexibility to create an environment of innovation and creativity. The state ought to act as a platform to facilitate the exchange of ideas and openness. The role of the state would be to minimize and prevent the physical conflict and violence amongst the group of people; however, this would not be done at the cost of curbing the freedom of expression and opinion. The state may act as the moderator in situations where it may feel that there is scope for various opinions and ideas being expressed to lead to a situation of physical violence. The state would champion the cause of innovative ideas and opinions and would prevent the use of brute force coming in the ways of news ideas and openness.

19. ALL BUSINESS AND COMMERCIAL TRANSACTION RECORDS TO BE AVAILABLE IN THE PUBLIC DOMAIN FOR ANYBODY TO SEE AND VERIFY. A FIXED UPPER LIMIT PERCENTAGE CAP TO BE IMPOSED ON THE RETURN ON INVESTMENT ON ALL BUSINESS AND COMMERCIAL ACTIVITIES.

Similar to the requirements of placing all the data and information related to the public service in public domain, a system could be devised to make all the records and information related to all the private business and corporate affairs available for public scrutiny. Since private business cannot survive in isolation away from the society, it can be presumed that the private entrepreneurs take inputs from the society out of the common resources of the public and they add their special skills, knowledge and efforts to produce goods and services which again they have to sell to the public in the society. Since they grow on the back of the society and public, it is imperative that they do not exploit the society and do not obtain undue advantage out of their special skills and investments. It is proposed that all the records and information of private business be available in public domain for public scrutiny. The private business owners can be allowed to retain a fixed percentage of profit on their investment and a fixed premium or royalty for their innovation; however, they should not be allowed to decide on their own rule of the game. The affairs of private business should be completely under the control of the public. The private entrepreneurs ought to be treated as the agents of the public who have been authorized to engage in certain business activity on a pre-determined incentive for their extra efforts to add value to the resources under common ownership of the society. The simplest example is that the market is under the common ownership of the society and no private business entity can sell its product or services in the market unless the society as a whole agrees for the same. Any private business owner found violating such rules may be deprived of his ownership of such business and such business affairs could be brought directly under the control of the public. Similar to the system of allowing a profit of around 15% in item rate works contracts and supplies, private businesses can be allowed a certain percentage of profit and the rest may be assumed to be under the common ownership of the public. To implement this system efficiently, all the records and information related to the private business houses ought to be made available in the public domain for anybody to see and inspect rather than simply relying on an annual system of audit by individual vested private interests operating as the chartered accountants and company secretaries and other intermediaries.

20. MINIMUM INTERVENTION AND DISTURBANCE TO THE NATURE AND ENVIRONMENT

Since all the natural resources are owned by the humanity as a whole including the people in the future generations, it is imperative that the present generation does not utilize or exploit the natural resources beyond its bare minimum requirements. We need to preserve the natural ecosystem and environment for the future generations so that the coming generations of humanity does not have to struggle for the basic necessity of life like air, water, mineral and other basic necessities of life. We have a direct proof of having killed most of our major natural river and drainage systems and having polluted the air envelope around us to the extent that it is not fit for a healthy living. We need to take lessons from these and review our current model of growth and development. We have to ensure that human comfort is not achieved at the cost of items which had taken thousands of years to develop. If our ancestors left these resources for us, we need to leave these resources, as far as practically possible, for our descendants. The mega projects, dams, power plants, mining, roads and other industrial activities need not be carried out at the cost of environmental degradation. The cost of environmental factors ought to be given the highest considerations and priorities by parties specialised in such matters rather than leaving it to the discretion of the project proponents while preparing the financial models of such projects. Even in such circumstances, certain basic factors e.g. maintenance of uninterrupted flow in perennial rivers or the upper limit of pollutants in the air must not be compromised at any cost.

21. ABOLITION OF
   a. ALL PRIVATE FINANCIAL TRANSACTIONS IN THE NAME OF RELIGION, RELIGIOUS RITES AND RITUALS AND ASSOCIATED ACTIVITIES.
   b. ALL ADVERTISEMENT AND FINANCIAL TRANSACTIONS FOR ANY SPECIAL KNOWLEDGE AND INFORMATION BASED SERVICE WHICH CANNOT BE VERIFIED AND SUBSTANTIATED UNDER CONTROLLED CONDITIONS
   c. ALL VOLUNTARY, CONTRIBUTORY AND NON-VOLUNTARY FUND OR ANY OTHER RESOURCE COLLECTION OR RECEIPT, IN CASH OR IN KIND, IN THE NAME OF ANY RELIGIOUS, CULTURAL, METAPHYSICAL, SUPERNATURAL OR ASSOCIATED ACTIVITY OR BELIEF

The religion and religious rites and rituals have become a big perennial business and source of exploitation for the masses. People often face hardships and difficulties in their life and try out everything that they can within their means and control to come out of such situations. However, despite all their best efforts, people are constrained to live in the conditions that are not as per their expectations or desires. Therefore, people try to look towards self styled godmen and fake religious leaders who fraudulently claim to have powers or special knowledge to help people get rid of their problems and afflictions. Such people prey on the vulnerability of the masses particularly during their bad times. To exploit such people, these charlatans advertise through the print and electronic mass media as well as through managed mass gatherings to fool the people to fall in their trap. These charlatans would advertise claiming to own some special power or knowledge and would offer to make these powers available to the masses for a direct or indirect service fee. Most of such advertisements in the name of religion, astrology, tantra, mantra, spirituality and other special powers have absolutely no basis. These people have absolutely no way to substantiate their claim. However, people lose their rational sense when they come across these very well prepared and professionally managed commercial advertisements which are based on the principles of hypnosis and mind control and fall prey to these fake claimants of special power or knowledge. These people would then continue to exploit their gullible clients in the name of conducting special rites, rituals and religious practices, astrological or tantric remedies and other such activities. The unsuspecting and innocent clients are not only exploited financially but are often subjected to mental slavery and even sexual exploitation. Had there been any iota of truth in any such services, such kind of people would have claimed the one million dollar that the James Randi Educational Foundation (JREF) has announced to give to anyone who can prove the existence of any such special or metaphysical power under controlled conditions. JREF has sponsored a One Million Dollar Paranormal Challenge offering a prize of US$1,000,000 to an eligible applicant who can demonstrate evidence of any paranormal, supernatural or occult power or event under test conditions agreed to by both parties. Despite this challenge having been in place for the last more than two decades, nobody has been able to claim this prize money. This proves that all such claims of special power which is available for a fee, ranging from a lower limit of rupees ten to no upper limit, is nothing but a simple tool of deceit and cheating by the thugs. Yet, there is no way such practices can be stopped in the society since it is being carried out in the name of religion and faith. No government has taken any step to prevent these ill practices in the society as it is expected to have a serious impact on the vote bank politics of anyone who tries to clean the society of such evil practices of exploitation. To overcome such kind of social evils, it is proposed to impose a ban on all such advertisements in the name of special, supernatural, paranormal, astrological, tantric, spiritual or religious powers which cannot be substantiated under controlled test conditions. It is also proposed to ban any financial transaction, voluntary or involuntary, direct or indirect, in cash or in kind, in the name of religion, religious rites, special powers, spirituality and all such special powers which generate undue hope amongst people to help them come out of bad situations in life unless such claims can be substantiated under controlled conditions. This is aimed at preventing the thugs from spoiling the true religious and spiritual practices and to re-establish the path of truth which has been obscured by such unscrupulous elements who have turned religion and spirituality into a business.

22. STATE FUNDING AND MANAGEMENT OF ALL COMMON RELIGIOUS AND CULTURAL ACTIVITIES AT ALL LEVELS OF GOVERNANCE

To prevent control of the religious and cultural activities from going into the hands of the unscrupulous elements who misuse such events and occasions to perpetuate their exploitation of the masses in the name of religion using the manipulation tactics to fleece them and also to prevent the masses from being emotionally exploited in the name of religion and culture, it is imperative that the management and administration of all the religious and cultural activities within their respective service catchment is taken over by the relevant governments at various levels. The government could fund and manage the places of worship through its paid employees and run the affairs of the religious and cultural activities as per the requirements of the local community at public expenses. The government could use such opportunities to create an environment of trust and brotherhood between the people belonging to different communities and keep the traditions and culture from deteriorating and vitiating into undue and unwanted practices which is normally introduced by vested interests. State funding of such activities and affairs would not only help keep the tradition in pure form but would also lead to a better opportunity for communal harmony as state would try to coordinate and emphasize upon the common elements between the religion and traditions rather than catalyzing the conflicts by highlighting the contradictions. The state management of such affairs would also provide an opportunity for people from different community to come together and actively participate, cooperate and collaborate with each other. While the panchayat governments could manage the affairs of the places of worship within their jurisdiction, the block governments could manage the affairs of the places which are frequented by the people from all the panchayats in the block. Similarly, the places of worship of national importance could be managed by the central government and places of state wide importance could be managed by the state authorities. Since the governments at all levels can be expected to understand the expectations and aspirations of the people at their respective levels, it would be most efficient and productive for them to manage the affairs at their respective level. The religious and cultural functions at national level could be organized by the central government while the events important only for a small local community could be an affair solely within the jurisdiction of the local government. By preventing the private vested interest from taking the management of such affairs in their hands, the religion and culture can be safeguarded from being adulterated and misused.

All places of worship outside the houses of the individuals shall be open for all the members of the public. Everybody would be allowed to visit and worship in these places as per the rules and traditions of the particular place of worship. The affairs of these places shall be looked after by the full time paid employees of the state acting in the roles of priest, purohit, mulla, granthi or pastor. There would be no requirement for a Hindu priest to have been born a Brahman or for a maulvi to have been born in a Muslim family. All that they would require to be eligible for such jobs shall be their understanding of the traditions and customs which could meet the expectations and aspirations of the people who would be visiting such places of worship. All such places of worship would be funded, managed and administered by the state. All these places shall be of composite nature and shall have required places of worship for people belonging to different faiths in the local community. This would mean that a Shiva or Hanuman temple would also have a place for offering Namaj as per the Islamic traditions. A church in a community, which has majority of its members as Christian but also has Hindus, Sikhs and Muslims in the community, would also have a Hindu temple and mosque structure and proper place for Guru Granth Sahib inside the church complex. It would not be mandatory for a pastor in this church to be a Christian. As long as the person is well aware of the Christian traditions and can meet the expectations of the Christians visiting the church, he would be eligible for this job irrespective of the fact that he was born as a Hindu, Muslim or in any other faith. Since the majority population of this community is Christian, therefore the head priest of this temple complex would be looking after the affairs of the church whereas his assistants would look after the affairs of the mosque, Hindu temple, synagogue or Guru Granth Sahib and Sad-Sangat.

23. PROMOTION OF RATIONAL THINKING AND ERADICATION OF SUPERSTITION AND UNSCIENTIFIC BELIEF.

To prevent the unscrupulous elements from cheating and preying on to the masses and to safeguard the interest of the innocent and gullible people from getting trapped into the dangerous nets of the charlatans, it is important to promote a culture of rational thinking and to eradicate the superstition and unscientific belief from the society. Because of the ignorance of the people, vested interests are successful in manipulating and cheating most of the people in the name of tradition, belief, spirituality and many such other issues which can be collectively classified as superstition and nothing else. Most of these manipulations are done using the common emotions like social or divine fear and greed, the adverse situations in life like weak physical or economic state or disturbed mental conditions. It is important to create a society which is open and alert and does not fall prey into the hands of the thugs who are hell bent on cheating them. The governments at all levels ought to actively work towards eradication of the unscientific belief and superstition by organizing the actual demonstration and seminars for the masses wherein issues related to superstition could be explained by experts to explore and expose the truth behind any such uncommon phenomenon which could be utilized by the thugs for cheating the masses.

24. STRONG MONITORING AND PREVENTION OF MISLEADING, CONFUSING AND IRRELEVANT ADVERTISEMENTS AIMED SOLELY AT COMMERCIAL PROMOTION WITHOUT ANY VALUE ADDITION TO THE PUBLIC LIFE.

The age of commercialism and advertisement has started a practice wherein any junk product or service without any actual value is sold to the masses by simply creating an artificial need for such junk in the mind of the people. Using the hypnotic and mind control techniques and by creating an unnecessary craving in the minds of the people for product and services, unnecessary products are pushed into the market. To market such products, all kinds of tricks in the books of advertisement are used by the unscrupulous advertisers. Their motive is simply to push their product in the market and gain profit out of it without any consideration for the adverse and negative social impact of such advertisements. Normally, good looking female body is used as an object to create craving in the minds of people even when females have absolutely nothing to do with a particular product. The advertisements also directly and indirectly make people believe about such attributes of the products which have absolutely no relation with the actual properties of the product. Some of the advertisers also make false claims about the properties and benefits of their product. Some advertisers would claim about some irrelevant property in such a way that people may consider such irrelevant properties as something very important. Some advertisers would try to manipulate the masses by simply acting on their sense of greed, envy, fear, shame or sense of being inadequate. While pushing such advertisements, there is normally no consideration for any specific value addition to the public life. The only impact of such advertisements is profit for the advertisers and a sense of being deprived for the masses. Such advertisements have potential to increase crime and anti-social activities since people are being instigated to feel deprived and inadequate and consequently being forced to desire products, services or life style which is normally beyond their legitimate means of income. To maintain their social prestige and false image amongst their peer groups, many people get motivated to indulge in crime to obtain what is being marketed through the mass media advertisements. Because of the mass media advertisements, anybody can get attracted and develop a craving for a product or service which ought to have been targeted for only a limited and select class of audience. The advertisers do not care to apply discretion in considering what needs to be advertised for what class of target audience and what could be the possible and potential effects of such advertisements on the society. It is, therefore, being proposed to have a system of strong monitoring and prevention of misleading, confusing and irrelevant advertisements aimed solely at commercial promotion without any value addition to the public life.

25. PROMOTION OF SCIENCE AND TECHNOLOGY

The promotion of science and technology is the back bone of development of any society. It is the development in science and technology that can convert a constraint into an opportunity and provide new, innovative and disruptive technologies to overcome the problems of humanity which hitherto might have appeared like a fait accompli for the humanity. Development of science and technology would unravel the mystery of nature to help the humanity live a comfortable life in complete synch with the nature. It is the development in technology which has broken the barriers between the minds of people across the globe and has converted this whole planet into a small village specifically in terms of exchange of ideas and communication. The collaboration and exchange of ideas amongst the people across the planet has given rise to an opportunity for further rapid development in science and technology. It has also facilitated the growth of creative ideas and their exploration and testing. The development in science and technology can not only meet all the physical and material demands of the body of the people but can also bring peace to its mind and has the potential to unravel the basic philosophical questions that the humanity has been facing since the development of human society. There is absolutely no difference between the pure scientific enquiry and pure spiritual pursuit. Without substantial development in science and technology, it would be difficult to bring the essence of the true spirituality into the grasp of the masses. Unless the masses have an opportunity to understand the scientific philosophy, religion cannot be understood in totality and the thugs may continue to cheat the masses in the name of religion and spirituality. The development of science and technology and research and development activities in this area ought to be accorded the highest priority by any sensible society and the best brains of the society need to be encouraged and motivated to work in this field.

26. REORGANIZATION OF THE CURRENT SYSTEM OF MEDICAL AND HEALTH EDUCATION BY COMBINING THE ALLOPATHIC MEDICAL EDUCATION SYSTEM WITH THE TRADITIONAL AND AGE OLD KNOWLEDGE SYSTEMS.

The present system of allopathic medical education has proved to be a great boon to the society. It has facilitated the scientific research and development in the health and medical services and has worked towards eliminating the superstition and unscientific practices in the health care sector. However, along with all its virtues, it is also afflicted with some undesirable attributes which probably has cropped up due to rigidity and some vested interests associated with this sector. The system of allopathic medicine has been in practice for not more than 500 years; however, the traditional systems of medicine have been in practice ever since the development of the human society. It is claimed that the allopathic system of medicine merely attempts to treat and get rid of the immediate symptoms of the disease and fails to address the underlying cause of the disease or the disharmony produced by the underlying disease. It is also claimed about the modern system of medicine that it is limited to the application of some agents which can kill the bacteria, virus and fungus. Additionally, it is alleged that it tries to block the sense perceptions of disease symptoms by using stimulants and resorts to surgical procedures to clean and cut the parts which it is unable to heal or make good. While these allegations do not do justice to the modern medical science, wherein developments like stem cell therapy, human organ transplants and regenerative medical practices have created miracles and wonders compared to what had been available to the human society in the name of medical and health care services earlier, it is also true that the modern medical science has definitely not been open to adopt and adapt to the age old knowledge and wisdom available in the field of medical science and health care. There is no avenue for people to go to a medical services practitioner who would not only be trained in the modern system of medicine but would also be fully trained in the traditional knowledge system related to this field. Unless we have professionals who are trained in all these systems, we cannot expect to get the best in the medical and healthcare services. It is therefore, being proposed to merge the modern system of allopathic medical education with the traditional systems of Ayurved, Unani, TCM, Accupressure, Hypnosis and all such other alternative medical practices so that people are able to get the best care from the best medical professionals. It would also eradicate the rivalry amongst the different systems of medical practitioners and would lead to a rapid growth in the medical science as a result of collaboration of various knowledge traditions with the modern scientific approach of enquiry and research and development. Instead of having separate boards and authority for different systems of medical education and practice, it is proposed to develop a single authority which could regulate the medical education system and could bring the best of both worlds to the service of the humanity.

> Longer term vision after two or more adjacent countries come under the ~~rule~~ service of this manifesto.

27. FREE AND UNRESTRICTED MOVEMENT OF ALL HUMAN BEINGS ACROSS THE BORDER AND RIGHT TO SETTLE AND ENGAGE IN THE COMMERCIAL AND BUSINESS ACTIVITIES ANYWHERE ON THIS PLANET WITHOUT ANY DISCRIMINATION OR RESTRICTIONS WHATSOEVER EXCEPT TO PRESERVE THE NATURAL ENVIRONMENT AND CULTURE OF THE LOCAL GEOGRAPHY.

The vested interests have created the artificial boundaries between the people on this planet in the name of nation state by drawing lines on the face of the earth. This has happened as an integral part of the divide and rule strategy. As a result of this, people across the boundaries are trained since their childhood to live with a sense of false pride in the name of patriotism. They are also trained to hate the people from across the border. There is also a subtle assumption in this system for people to consider themselves superior to the rest of the world. This division of earth in the name of independent and sovereign countries is a result of a scarcity thought. In this thought process, it is presumed that nature does not have sufficient resources to sustain the humanity as a whole and therefore, more and more geographical areas and natural resources need to be kept under direct physical control of a particular group, in exclusion to the rest, to meet only their physical needs and requirements without any consideration for the rest of the humanity. This concept is in direct contrast to the assumption that unity and collaboration amongst people and their joint efforts would enable them to overcome any constraint in life and the nature in such a scenario would tend to be an ally rather than an adversary. While the development in science and technology particularly in the field of information and communication technology and space science has already broken almost all the barriers between the people on this planet as far as the exchange of ideas and communication is concerned, it is high time that even the physical restrictions and control which prevent the people from meeting each other and collaborate is completely removed. It is proposed that once two adjacent nation-state adopt this universal manifesto as their model of governance and administration, they would remove the artificial boundary between them and facilitate the free flow and intermingling of people within their service jurisdiction. The moment governance is transferred from the hands of those who are there only for their vested personal interest into the hands of those who come into public life out of their conviction for social service and sacrifice and with a commitment to serve the humanity as a whole without any consideration for divide and rule, the boundaries between the states would automatically get eradicated. As long as there are separate national identities and artificial restrictions on people to move across the globe, there cannot be a lasting peace on earth and the mass conflicts would continue to haunt the humanity.

28. ERADICATION OF MILITARY, WEAPONS OF MASS DESTRUCTION AND ALL OTHER DEADLY WEAPONS FROM THE PLANET. REDEPLOYMENT OF ARMED FORCES IN THE AREAS OF NATURAL CALAMITY AND DISASTER MANAGEMENT, EXPLORATION OF NEW AVENUES AND SOURCES OF NATURAL RESOURCE, EXPEDITIONS AND DISCOVERIES OF UNEXPLORED AREAS.

The world spends 2.5% of its GDP on military expenditure. This translates to approximately US$ 1.8 trillion per annum as the global annual military expenditure. This also means that all the 7.1 billion people on this planet are contributing approximately INR 1300 per month towards the military expenditure. India ranks eighth in terms of highest military expenditure in the world and spends nearly US$ 46.1 billion or 2.5% of its GDP on military which is approximately INR 275000 crore. Pakistan and Bangladesh spend nearly seven and 1.6 billion US$ respectively on their defence establishments. Such kind of expenditure on military and defence, just in response to an apprehension to guard against the external aggression, is a sheer waste of the valuable resources which could otherwise be utilized for the public welfare and other creative and productive activities.

Instead of spending on the negative and destructive activities like military, weapons, arms and ammunition, the resources ought to be utilized for raising the level of human satisfaction, comfort and peace. It is, therefore being proposed that the expenditure on military be minimized with a vision to completely abolish it. The military establishments between the two adjacent and geographically contiguous countries could be completely demobilized once both the countries adopt and come under the service of this manifesto. Once all the countries across the world adopt this manifesto, the concept of maintaining a state military power to guard against the external aggression could be completely done away with. At the time of demobilizing the armed forces, the people employed in the defence services could be redeployed in the areas of natural calamity and disaster management. They could additionally be utilized for the activities which require special training, courage, strength and discipline such as exploration of new geographical areas and avenues for the unexplored sources of natural resource. They can also be deployed for expeditions and discoveries of unexplored areas. After the existing work forces in the defence establishments retire from the service, the new intakes could be taken only for these creative, constructive and special requirements rather than for the destructive purpose. Once, the concept of maintaining armed forces against external aggression is done away with, manufacturing of all kinds of lethal arms and ammunition could be controlled and limited only to meet the requirements of maintenance of law and order by the local governments and to control the wild animals. All kinds of weapons of mass destruction ought to be annihilated from the planet. All kinds of fire arms in private possession ought to be brought under the control and in possession of the local governments and no fresh arms and ammunition could be made available to the private individuals unless they have specific needs to guard themselves against wild animals.

THE ROAD MAP

To achieve the vision and objectives as enumerated in the Universal manifesto, we would need to build a social change organisation or political party to directly intervene in the affairs of the governance and administration. The kinds of changes that have been envisaged in our manifesto are so radical in nature that we would need a team and organisation to bring about a revolution in the society. The organisation would need support of a leadership team capable of converting this vision into reality. To achieve this dream, the dream leadership team will have to be assembled out of the existing human beings on this planet. We have no opportunity to recall people like, Buddha, Socrates, Jesus, Mohammad, Mahaveer, Nanak, Kabir, Marx, Gandhi, Mandela, Martin Luther King Jr. or many others who could have been the leaders of such a dream vision or revolution if they had the support of the technological revolution that is available to the present generation. However, we can definitely assemble a team of the people who have comparable character attributes to these giant human beings named above. The character attributes that would be required to be present in the leadership team to achieve this vision would be

1) Intelligence
2) Courage
3) Will
4) Commitment and Dedication
5) Sacrifice
6) Openness

Out of the above mentioned six desired character attributes in a dream leadership team, we would need at least four character attributes to be individually present in each leader of the team. It would be more fruitful to have a non executive vision leadership team of people above the age of 50 years. The second line of leadership team may comprise of people in the age bracket of 35 to 65 years who may be required to work under the guidance of the vision leadership team. These people would be required to be part of the full time party functionaries. They may also be required to assume the roles and positions of public representatives and public authorities to implement the required changes in the society according to the strategy devised by executive team under the guidance of the vision leadership team. The younger people below the age of 45 years may be required to actively support and engage in the change activities at various levels. The age limits as mentioned above shall only act as a general guideline for assignment of various roles to the individuals however there would not be any hard and fast rule about this in the organisation. Individual suitability for a particular role in the organisation may be decided on a case to case basis rather than having a very tight and stringent rule in this regard related to the age of the people. The party may be functionally organized as per the plan being presented below to cover the entire spectrum of its functions. Proper consideration and focus has to be given to the various organisational elements to manage all its activities in a professional and efficient manner. The vision, mission and goals of the organisation shall be guided by the universal and global manifesto which may be further detailed under the guidance of the vision leadership team. The day to day operational and organisational management responsibilities shall have to be considered in their minutest detail before formally announcing the launch of the political formation. A detailed route map shall have to be chalked out to achieve the ultimate vision of "One World" wherein the entire humanity on this planet shall live a HAPPY, HEALTHY, PEACEFUL, PROGRESSIVE, PROSPEROUS, CREATIVE AND CONSTRUCTIVE life with a sense of global and universal brotherhood in complete synchronization with the rules and laws of nature. The functions of the party may be organized as per the graphics on the next page.

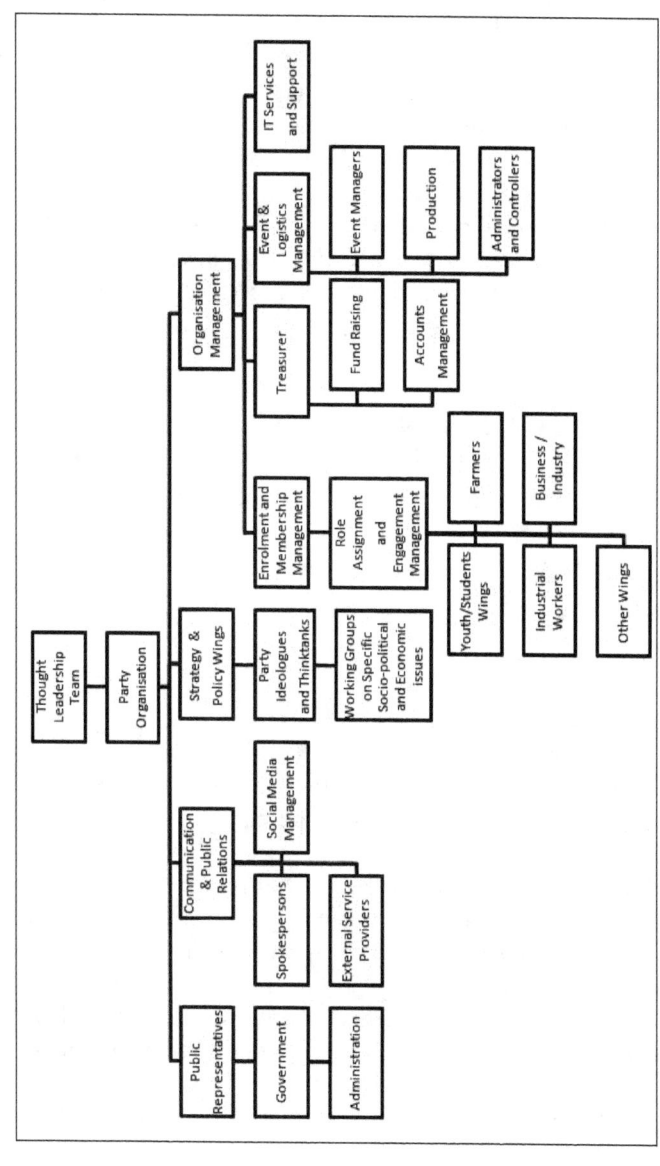

The dream Thought and Vision Leadership Team may comprise of the individuals who have not only had the six character attributes as mentioned above but also have had an impeccable image for them amongst the public in general. The mere presence of these individuals in the organisation and their blessings and support for the vision should inspire the people in the society to join hands with the efforts of the organisation to help it achieve its vision.

Based on the above considerations, a dream ten member Thought and Vision Leadership Team, from amongst the living legends in India, may comprise of the following individuals listed in the descending order of their age.

1. Dr. APJ Abdul Kalam
2. Prof. G D Agrawal (Swami Gyan Swaroop Sanand)
3. Sri Dalai Lama 14th
4. Dr. Sam Pitroda
5. Azim Premji
6. Bunker Roy
7. Manik Sarkar
8. Dr. Binayak Sen
9. Sugata Mitra
10. Sri Rajendra Singh

Before we move forward to discuss the roadmap for this vision, we would like to clarify that the individuals named above are only a part of the dream team. At the time of preparation of this work, these people may not be aware of this vision. They have not been approached so far to discuss their views on these ideas and no direct or implicit consent has been obtained from these people about their support and blessings for this vision. At this stage, it is being presumed that it would not be impossible to persuade these people to lend their name, face, mind and time for this revolution. It is being presumed that these people would happily agree to help build a happy, healthy, peaceful, progressive, prosperous, creative and constructive world. A brief introduction of all these people is being presented below.

Dr. APJ Abdul Kalam

The former president of India who used to be known as the missile man of India was born on 15th Oct 1931 in the house of a poor fisherman in Rameshwaram in Tamilnadu. The man who started his career as a child newspaper vendor went on to become the chief scientific advisor to the prime Minister of India and the secretary of the Defence Research & Development Organisation. As Chairman of (TIFAC) and as an eminent scientist, he led the country to arrive at Technology Vision 2020 giving a road map for transforming India from the status of a developing country to a developed nation. A recipient of Bharat Ratna, he has advocated an action plan to develop India into a knowledge superpower and a developed nation by the year 2020 in his book India 2020. The four books authored by him, viz, the "Wings of Fire", "India 2020 - A Vision for the New Millennium", "My Journey" and "Ignited Minds - Unleashing the Power Within India" have become household names in India and among the Indian nationals abroad. These books have been translated in many Indian languages. He is considered to be one of the most inspirational and highly respected thought leaders in India at present.

Dr. G. D. Agrawal (Swami Gyan Swaroop Sanand)

Prof. Agrawal, born on 20 July 1932 is a civil engineering graduate from IIT Roorkee and a Ph.D. in environmental engineering from the University of California at Berkeley. The first member secretary of the Central Pollution Control Board and the former head of the Civil and Environmental Engineering Department at IIT Kanpur, is one of the most respected environmental scientist in the country. The former scientist and present day sannyasi has made it  his life's mission to recall India to its traditional reverence for nature and to share that wisdom with the developed world. He has fasted several times for long periods demanding immediate halt to the construction of dams and other projects on the river Ganga and its tributaries which were causing environmental damage to the river system and disturbing the ecological equilibrium of the Himalayan region. He had sat on a fast-unto-death to demand that river Bhagirathi be allowed to flow in its natural form. He called off his first fast on the 18th day on 30 June 2008 and the second fast on the 38th day on 20 February 2009 when the Central Government gave a written commitment to suspend all work on the hydel projects with immediate effect. His last fast for "Aviral Nirmal Ganga" in 2013 lasted for more than 120 days.

Tenzin Gyatso - Dalai Lama 14th

Born on 6th July 1935 in Tibet, the current Dalai Lama, the spiritual head of the Tibetan Buddhism sect and a recipient of the Nobel Peace Prize in 1989 is a great advocate of compassion as the source of happy life. The Dalai Lamas are believed to be manifestations of Avalokiteshvara or Chenrezig, the Bodhisattva of Compassion.

Bodhisattvas are believed to be enlightened beings who have postponed their own nirvana and chosen to take rebirth in order to serve humanity. He has been living in India since 1959 and has been travelling across the world teaching the Tibetan Buddhism philosophy. He is considered to be a great humanitarian and an advocate of religious harmony, socialist economic theory, democracy and women's rights. He is also known for his concerns for the environment. He probably enjoys the highest global acceptability amongst the religious leaders. He has received over 150 awards, honorary doctorates, prizes, etc., in recognition of his message of peace, non-violence, inter-religious understanding, universal responsibility and compassion. He has also authored or co-authored more than 110 books. He has held dialogues with heads of different religions and participated in many events promoting inter-religious harmony and understanding.

Dr. Sam Pitroda

Satyanarayan Gangaram Pitroda was born on 4th May 1942 in Odisha in a Gujarati family. He has a Masters degree in Electrical Engineering from Illinois Institute of Technology in Chicago. He is regarded as one of the earliest pioneers of hand-held computing because of his invention of the Electronic Diary in 1975. It was reported that the man who founded and was first chairman of India's Telecom Commission had never made  a telephone call himself until he came to the US in 1964. This information and communication technology and business management guru is currently the advisor to the Prime Minister of India on public information infrastructure and innovations. He is also the chairman of National Innovation Council. As technology Advisor to the Prime Minister of India in mid 1980s, Pitroda is credited with heralding the telecom revolution in India. He is also considered to be the man who advised the then Prime Minister of India and made a strong case for using technology for the benefit of society. In 1987 during his tenure as advisor to the Prime Minister, Pitroda headed six technology missions related to telecommunications, water, literacy, immunization, dairy and oil seeds. He has also served as an advisor to the United Nations.

Azim Premji

Azim Hashim Premji, born on 24 July 1945 is the chairman of Wipro Limited and a recipient of the Padma Vibhushan. He has a Bachelor's degree in Electrical Engineering from Stanford University, USA. He is a business tycoon and philanthropist. He is one of the wealthiest Indians with his personal wealth estimated to be approx US$15.3 billion in 2014. In 2000, he was voted among the 20 most powerful men in the world by Asiaweek. He has twice been listed among the 100 most influential people in the world by TIME Magazine. His grandfather was a noted businessman and was known as Rice King of Burma. After partition, when Jinnah invited his grandfather to come to Pakistan, he turned down the request and chose to remain in India. An investment of ₹10,000 with Premji in his Wipro shares in 1980 was worth more than ₹500 crore in 2012. Azim Premji is the first Indian and the third non-American to sign up for the Giving Pledge. His declaration reads, "I strongly believe that those of us, who are privileged to have wealth, should contribute significantly to try and create a better world for the millions who are far less privileged. I will continue to act on this belief." By April 2013 he had already given more than 25 per cent of his personal wealth to charity.

Bunker Roy

Sanjit (Bunker) Roy, born on 2 Aug 1945 is an alumni of Doon School and St. Stephens College, Delhi. He established the Social Work and Research Centre (now known as Barefoot College) in 1972 emulating the work style and lifestyle of Mahatma Gandhi. The Barefoot College focuses on demystification of technology and placing control and ownership in the hands of very poor rural communities. It is the only college in rural India that is fully solar electrified. Its constituency includes people who have been rejected by society or have little or no formal educational qualifications. Within its programs—Solar, Water, Education, Health Care, Crafts, People's Action, and Communication—more than 37,000 men and women have trained and worked as Barefoot teachers, doctors, midwives, dentists, health workers, solar engineers, solar cooker engineers, water drillers and engineers, hand pump mechanics, architects, artisans, designers, masons, communicators, water chemists, phone operators, blacksmiths, wasteland developers, carpenters, computer instructors, accountants and recycling professionals. Bunker Roy is a recepient of Robert Hill Award from the global Solar Community, St. Andrews Prize for the Environment and the Jamnalal Bajaj Award.

Manik Sarkar

Manik Sarkar, born on 22 January 1949, is the icon of honesty and probity in public life. He took oath as the chief minister of Tripura for the fourth consecutive term in March 2013. He also happens to be a Politburo Member of Communist Party of India (Marxist). He donates his entire salary and perks as a public representative to his party. He and his wife live off a meagre allowance of ₹ 5000 that his party gives him as subsistence allowances in addition to the pension of his wife. He is the only Chief Minister in India who has no house or a car on his name. He and his wife do not use the official vehicles for their personal work and instead take a rickshaw for their local travel needs with no personal security guards. He had only ₹ 1080 as cash in hand and his bank balance stood at ₹ 9720 before the assembly elections in 2013. His wife, a retired officer of the central government, had a fixed deposit of ₹ 23,58,380 (major part being the money that came as her retirement benefit), jewellery of 20 gm of gold and cash in hand of ₹ 22,015. He inherited a home of 432 sq. ft with a tin-shed from his mother which he later donated to a relative.

Dr. Binayak Sen

Born on 4th January 1950, Dr. Sen is an MD in Paediatrics and an alumni of the Christian Medical College, Vellore. He is the national Vice-President of the People's Union for Civil Liberties (PUCL). He is the recipient of Jonathan Mann Award, the Gwangju Prize for Human Rights and the Gandhi International Peace Award. As a sympathizer to the Maoist Movement, he has been convicted for sedition and

sentenced to life imprisonment by Sessions Court in Raipur. He is out on bail granted by the Supreme Court of India. He is also a recipient of the Paul Harrison award for a lifetime of service to the rural poor which is given annually by CMC, to its alumni. He has also been awarded the R.R. Keithan Gold Medal by The Indian Academy of Social Sciences (ISSA) for his outstanding contribution to the advancement of science of Nature-Man-Society and his honest and sincere application for the improvement of quality of life of the poor, the downtrodden and the oppressed people of Chhattisgarh. His personal sacrifices, sufferings and selfless health care services for the rural poor and his dedication and passion for human rights for the downtrodden have won him all round appreciation.

Prof. Sugata Mitra

Sugata Mitra, born on 12 February 1952, is a Professor of Educational Technology at the School of Education, Communication and Language Sciences at Newcastle University, England. He is best known for his "Hole in the Wall" experiment and widely cited in works on literacy and education. Prof. Mitra has been described as a polymath by the University of London, as his 30 years of research spans a wide range of disciplines. He obtained his Master's degree and Ph.D. in Physics from IIT Delhi and is credited with more than 25 inventions in the area of cognitive science and education technology. His interest in computer networking led him towards the emerging systems in printing in the 1980s. He set up India's first local area network based newspaper publishing system in 1984 and went on to predict the desktop publishing industry. Prof. Mitra is a leading proponent of Minimally Invasive Education. He is a recipient of the Dewang Mehta Award for Innovation in Information Technology and Leonardo European Corporate Learning Award in the "Crossing Border" category. His interest in the human mind led him into the areas of learning and memory and he was amongst the first in the world to show that simulated neural networks can help decipher the mechanisms of Alzheimer's disease.

Sri Rajendra Singh

Born on August 6, 1959, Rajendra Singh is an environmentalist popularly known as 'Jal Purush' or Waterman of Rajasthan. He is a recipient of the Jamnalal Bajaj Award and Ramon Magsaysay Award for community leadership. The Guardian named him amongst its list of "50 people who could save the planet" in 2008. He is well-known for his efforts in water harvesting by building check dams across  Rajasthan. The efforts of his team have brought water back to more than 1,000 villages – spread over 6500 sq. km, and revived 5 rivers in Rajasthan – Arvari, Ruparel, Sarsa, Bhagani and Jahajwali. River Ruparel, that went dead, has started flowing again after a span of three decades. River Arvari which became perennial by 1995 was awarded the `International River Prize'. He has been the leader and organiser of the popular environmental programmes and movements like Ped Bachao-Ped Lagao padyatra, Jungle-Jeevan Bachao Yatra, Aravali Bachao Yatra and Rashtriya Jal Yatra. He has also been organizing Pani Panchayat or Water Parliament in distant villages in Rajasthan to make people aware of the traditional water conservation wisdom, the urgency of groundwater recharge for maintaining underground aquifers and advocating community control over natural resources.

Having chosen a dream team of ten people to act as our non executive thought and vision leadership team, we would need to develop a complete plan for achieving this daunting task. The plan that is being presented below may be treated as a draft plan which might need corrections and modifications based on the feedbacks that is obtained in response to the actions taken according to this plan. While the vision of creating a HAPPY, HEALTHY, PEACEFUL, PROGRESSIVE, PROSPEROUS, CREATIVE AND CONSTRUCTIVE WORLD shall not be changed, everything else that is being proposed below may be modified or replaced by some more appropriate step or strategy that may be required to achieve the goal being envisioned through this work. We shall endeavour to take one small step at a time; however, our focus would always be on the end goal of realising the ultimate vision to create a new world order. At this stage, it is being proposed to pass through the followings steps to achieve the vision of creating a HAPPY, HEALTHY, PEACEFUL, PROGRESSIVE, PROSPEROUS, CREATIVE AND CONSTRUCTIVE world.

Step – 1

A web site and a social media page shall be created for this vision and all the materials related to the vision shall be uploaded on the web site and the social media page. A Google hosted email group shall be created to disseminate the information related to the vision amongst the members of the group. A core team consisting of the pioneers of this thought shall share the responsibilities amongst them to create the web site, prepare the documents and enrol a select group of passionate and committed individuals to share and actively support this vision. The cost of all these initial activities shall be shared by the pioneers.

Step – 2

An audio visual dance drama programme shall be produced and digitally recorded on the theme of the poem "Himalay Ka Sandesh" by late poet Ramdhari Singh Dinkar. This programme may be screened before all subsequent events of the vision. The cost for production of this dance drama may be funded through sponsorship. A copy of this poem in Hindi and its English translation is being presented as an appendix to this work.

Step – 3

The next step would be to discuss and debate the vision and manifesto amongst a select group of socio-politically conscious and passionate individuals belonging to various schools of thoughts and ideologies. The minimum eligibility for anyone to be a part of this select group would be an open and firm commitment to help create a HAPPY, HEALTHY, PEACEFUL, PROGRESSIVE, PROSPEROUS, CREATIVE AND CONSTRUCTIVE world. This group may consist of academicians, activists, social thinkers, public servants, students, business people and professionals belonging to a wide spectrum spanning from the extreme right wing thinkers to the ultra left activists. It may have orthodox, conservative and dogmatic people as well as extremely radical, progressive freethinkers. The number of people in this initial select group may be limited to 50+10%. The current version of the manifesto and the other contents in this work shall act as the seed thought and initial point of discussion. It would also act as the starting point for preparation of the agenda for the various rounds of discussions and debates. The revised version of the vision and manifesto shall be prepared as a result of discussions and debate between these people. The debates and discussions shall be in the nature of Samvaad and Vaad and would not be allowed to go into the realm of Vivaad/Jalpa or Vitanda. The basic rule of all such debates and discussions shall be as below

a. Nobody would ever shout or raise his voice while presenting his point.

b. Nobody would lose his temper or composure during the debate and would speak in a calm manner without feeling a need to change the volume, pitch or tone of his normal voice.

c. Nobody would be interrupted while he is presenting his view.

d. No session of the debate would be allowed to come to an end until all the participants have come to a consensus or conclusion. Participants would be required to come prepared to continue the debate without any concern for time constraints. The film "Ek Ruka Hua Faisla" directed by Basu Chatterjee may be screened for all the participants to view before they sit for the first round of discussions and debates.

Whenever it would become necessary to end a session of the debate without having reached to a consensus or conclusion, the next session to resume the discussion shall have to be organised the very next day. It would be necessary for all the participants from the previous session to come for the continued session. The exception to this rule would be allowed only for extreme personal emergencies.

e. The participants shall be required to stick to the point of debate.

f. Arguments and counter arguments shall not be based on any fact or data which can not be verified and substantiated instantly and immediately. Live internet connection shall be available at the venue of the discussion to obtain any information available in the public domain. No secret, confidential or imaginary fact or data shall be used to support any point of argument.

g. No argument, logic, question or fact shall be presented in the course of the discussion which could individually and personally embarrass any other participant. Individual motive or ability of the participants shall not be questioned by any other participant.

h. Facility for audio visual presentations may be made available to the participants, if required.

i. The entire session of the discussion shall be video recorded and shall be uploaded on the youtube with a link on the website of this vision.

j. The cost of all the activities at step three shall be shared by the members of the select group

Step – 4

a. Teams consisting of up to five members in each team from the select group who have been part of the discussion at step three shall be assigned the responsibility to approach and interact with the people projected as the members of the dream vision and thought leadership team.

b. There will be ten such teams and each team will be assigned the responsibility to interact with only one specific individual out of the ten people projected as the members of the dream vision and thought leadership team.

c. The responsibility of each of these teams shall be to meet the specific dream vision and thought leadership team member and share the vision in detail with him. The team would develop rapport with the projected senior member and would invite him to share his views and ideas on this vision with the rest of the group members.

d. A series of ten lectures and talks by these ten members of the dream thought leadership team shall be organised on the theme of creating a HAPPY, HEALTHY, PEACEFUL, PROGRESSIVE, PROSPEROUS, CREATIVE AND CONSTRUCTIVE world. The theme lectures/talks shall also be focussed on the relevance of technological revolution to build such a new world. The background banners at each of these lectures shall read as "TECHNOLOGICAL REVOLUTION: OPPORTUNITY TO CREATE A HAPPY, HEALTHY, PEACEFUL, PROGRESSIVE, PROSPEROUS, CREATIVE AND CONSTRUCTIVE WORLD"

e. These talks may be limited to a maximum audience of 200 people.

f. All such lectures / talks shall be video recorded and uploaded on the youtube with a link on the website of the vision.

Step – 5

a. A two day seminar shall be organised on this theme in all the central and state universities across the country in association with the political science and sociology departments of the universities.

b. The leaders of the peoples movements, civil society members and social activists within the geographical influence areas of the respective universities shall be invited to participate in these seminars

c. At least two members from the select group who have been part of the vision at step 3 shall actively participate in these seminars and would manage these seminars in association with the local academicians of the university where these seminars would be organised.

d. Common PowerPoint presentations and audio visual materials related to the vision shall be used for all these seminars.

e. Further action items, research projects, academic dissertations and critical evaluation of the vision shall be developed in association with the academicians of the respective universities and members of local civil society.

f. Volunteers shall be enrolled from amongst the youth, social activists and civil society members to disseminate this vision to a larger population. At least 1000 volunteers shall be enrolled at this stage.

g. The cost for all the activities at this step shall be shared by the respective universities and through sponsorship.

Step – 6

a. All the volunteers from across the country shall be invited for training at a central place.

b. A one week intensive training shall be imparted to all these volunteers in communication and management of people's movements.

c. A detailed and formal course material and schedule shall be prepared for this training programme to fully equip the volunteers to do what they would be training for.

d. The thought and vision leadership team may be invited to speak and interact with the volunteers and share their life experiences in managing the people's movements and social projects.

e. Volunteers shall be equipped with printed and digital support materials to share the vision with the masses at large

f. Teams shall be formed of two to three volunteers to cover their respective geographical areas within a given time frame.

g. Specific targets shall be assigned to these teams in terms of number of villages/colonies visited and the number of people directly addressed.

h. Code of conduct and code of ethics shall be developed and implemented for the whole organisation.

i. It would be planned for the volunteers to connect directly with at least 10% population of India within a span of one year. Each team would be required to extensively travel and organise public meetings in their respective areas covering at least 200 households daily. This way 1000 volunteers divided in 400 teams would be able to cover at least 10 crore people within a span of one year.

j. A close coordination with the team of volunteers shall be maintained by a central executive and management team who would support the volunteers for their input and resource requirements and would receive the feedback from the volunteers in the field to adjust the plan and strategy.

k. A formal management structure with clearly defined and documented spans of control, roles & responsibilities and management protocol in the organisation shall be developed and implemented. The long term vision of the organisation shall remain creation of a HAPPY, HEALTHY, PEACEFUL, PROGRESSIVE, PROSPEROUS, CREATIVE AND CONSTRUCTIVE WORLD.

l. A social media management team of volunteers shall be raised across the country to help manage the feedback and inputs received through the social media and manage the people's perception.

m. The media shall be invited to interact with the team during the volunteer training program. Post the volunteer training program, regular and continuous media briefing shall be issued with the updates and experiences of the volunteers in the field.

n. All the updates shall be regularly and promptly uploaded on to the vision web site.

o. Volunteers shall be fully equipped to upload their reports and field experiences directly to the web site and social media pages.

p. Gateways for online voluntary contribution of funds to the organisation shall be activated on the website of the organisation.

q. All the expenses at this stage shall be taken care of by the voluntary contributions and sponsorships from the public

Step – 7

a. Offices across the country at village, block, district and state levels shall be opened in association with the local volunteers and well-wishers.

b. The organisational shall be managed professionally similar to a professionally managed large diversified corporate group.

c. Innovations and customisation in the management may be allowed to accommodate the specific local needs and requirements.

Step – 8

a. Mass movements shall be organised across the country to press for the implementation of the universal manifesto and for rewriting of the constitution.

b. The organisation will field its candidates in to the electoral arena as per its constitution and charter.

c. The highest priority for the organisation will be to realise its long term vision rather than winning a few seats in elections at the earliest.

Step – 9

a. Once the organisation has managed to have its presence in the parliament, it will continue to force the government to go for a complete overhaul of the constitution as envisaged in its manifesto.

b. The organisation will continue with mass movements to press for its demands to create a happy, healthy, peaceful, progressive, prosperous, creative and constructive world.

c. The organisation will spread its ideology in other countries and would engage with local population to induce them to adopt this manifesto

Step – 10

a. Once the organisation is able to form its government in India, it would implement its manifesto in toto.

b. The government would support the organisation to spread its ideas and engage with people in other countries.

c. Once a government is formed by the organisation in another country and its manifesto is implemented in that country, all restrictions on free movement of people between these countries shall be removed.

d. Once the government is formed between two adjacent countries, the military on the borders between the countries shall be demobilised.

e. The organisation shall continue to engage people across the globe to demolish all boundaries between the people on this planet and to eradicate all weapons of mass destruction from this planet.

The Tools

We need to discuss the mass movement tools that the organisation may adopt to achieve its vision. The following tools are being proposed for the organisation

a. Highest use of information and communication technology as well as other new age technology including the digital media, online social media, public meetings through online streaming videos and community radio

b. The non-violent civil disobedience and active resistance shall be the main tool of the organisation to realise its vision.

c. The organisation would prepare its volunteers to endure for personal sacrifice and suffering for its vision without ever indulging in physical violence. If the need be volunteers may be prepared to die rather than kill.

d. There would be no place in the organisation for self torturing manipulation tools like fast unto death or indefinite fasts for a specific demand. These tools may be adopted only symbolically for enrolling new members and for the purpose of self cleansing rather than expecting the other party to be influenced by such tools. If the other party is sensitive, reasonable and sensible, dialogues should be good enough to engage them. If they are insensitive and mentally strong, they would not be bothered to see the seeker suffering from the self inflicted torture.

e. Volunteers would be trained in spiritual understanding of truth. There would be no place for speaking lies and there would be no concept of embarrassment for the volunteers in the organisation. If someone commits some mistake, he would gracefully accept it rather than hide it to look good in the eyes of the others. Leaving the physical body for ever or living inside a jail would be gracefully accepted by the volunteers.

f. The movement need not succeed if such success requires compromising with the basic moral and spiritual values of truth and non-violence.

g. Volunteers would be trained not to focus on personal humiliation and embarrassment of those who may be seen as the villains. The attempts would be on converting and enrolling such people rather than causing personal pain and sufferings for them. Forgiveness and compassion would be the guiding principles of the organisation in such circumstances.

h. Individual as well as collective Honesty and Integrity shall be the basic requirements for anyone to continue in the organisation. The organisation and its vision may be sacrificed but not the ideals.

i. There would be no need for the organisation or its members to stick to the teachings or dictates of any scripture or religious authority or tradition. Rationality and consistency in its actions shall be the deciding factors on any question on such issues. The organisation shall gracefully accept the consequences of sticking to the rational viewpoint without succumbing to any kind of social, religious, executive or judicial pressure or action.

j. The organisation may not feel obliged to offer excuses or explanation for its decisions and actions to any external agency. It may refuse to respond to any question from the external source; however it would encourage an environment of open discussion and debate inside the organisation keeping them within the realm of Samvaad and Vaad.

k. The organisation would never endeavour to exploit the mob psychology and the principles of mob dynamics. It would endeavour to have a committed team of informed and disciplined volunteers rather than having a large uninformed, unprincipled, unruly and disruptive mob. The priority would be to enrol and train the volunteers with a sense of commitment, passion and sacrifice who would be ready to suffer personal pains and hardship rather than having a large mob of opportunists and sheep who may not be able to find their own path when the senior leaders may not be immediately available to guide.

With the above, I present this draft vision document before humanity. I would wait for the inspirations and instructions for the further course of action from the source which used my body to present this work before Him in his form of billions of people on this planet.

APPENDIX

The Message of Himalay

Poem by

Ramdharee Singh Dinkar

हिमालय का सन्देश

रामधारी सिंह दिनकर

हिमालय का सन्देश

HIMALAY'S MESSAGE

[चिंताव्यंजक संगीत]

[Anxious Contemplative Music]

कवि

तर्कों से तर्कों का रण छिड़ा,
विचारों से लड़ रहे विचार,
ज्ञान के कोलाहल के बीच,
डूबता जाता है संसार |
और सबका उलटा परिणाम,
बुद्धि का जितना बढ़ता ज़ोर,
आदमी के भीतर की शिरा,
हुई जाती कुछ और कठोर |

ज्ञान के मरू में चलता हुआ
आदमी खोता जाता है,
हृदय के सर का शीतल वारि
और कम होता जाता है|

बुद्धि तृष्णा की दासी हुई,
मृत्यु का सेवक है विज्ञान,
चेतता तब भी नहीं मनुष्य,
विश्व का क्या होगा भगवान?

[बांसुरी का आशाव्यंजक संगीत]
पहला स्वर

तेज करो मत धार चंचु की,
विष की बात न बोलो,
बाज़, पंख से बंधी
कँटीली तलवारों को खोलो |

Poet

In the tumult of knowledge,
the world is sinking
Oblivious of the arguments and
counter arguments and who, how
and what the men are thinking
Greater the intellectual debates
and discussion,
Higher the chaos and confusion.
Sensitivity is giving way to
illusion and seclusion

In the desert of knowledge,
humanity is getting lost
The soft and cool feelings in the
human heart is the one being
affected the most.

Intellect has become the servant
of desire and the science and
technology is serving destruction
O God, what would happen to
the world?
Humanity is still not conscious of
its direction

[Flute Music of Hope]
First Voice

Talk not of the hatred, Sharpen
not your pecker
O Falcon, open up your wings
and throw away the spear

बरसाओ मत आग नयन से,
शीतलता छाने दो,
ऊपर उड़ते हुए हंस को
भू पर अब आने दो |

बीत चली गर्मी, पावस के आने की बारी है,
शांतिदूत के स्वागत की घर घर में तैयारी है
|

[दूरागत समवेत गान]

दाह भू का हरो, पंथ शीतल करो,
विश्व का सर भरो वारि की धार से;

ओस का जाल दो, चांदनी डाल दो,
आदमी का हृदय सींच दो प्यार से |

शांति के हंस को, धर्म - अवतंस को,
अंक में लो, इसे प्रेम दो, मान दो ;

हो जहाँ भी ज़हर, क्षीर की दो लहर,
बाण की नोंक पर फूल को तान दो |

दूसरा स्वर
[विद्रूप हँसी के साथ]
शांति ?
कहीं दूध के बिना तरसती मानव की संतान,
कहीं क्षीर के मटके खाली करते जाते श्वान |
कहीं वसन रेशम के सस्ते,
महंगी कहीं लंगोटी,
कोई घी से नहा रहा,
मिलती न किसी को रोटी|

Do not spread hatred, let there be warmth of love
Let compassion of paradise be brought on earth by dove

Summer has already gone by, its time for the rain
Peace and love is welcome in every heart and brain

[Chorus: Coming from a distance]

Douse the fire on earth, let the path be cool, Fill the water of love in the worldly human pool

Cover the earth with cool moonlight and dew
Fill the human heart with love

Embrace, love and respect the dove of peace
Make space for true religion and perennial bliss
Replace the poison with waves of milk
Replace the bullet with flower and silk

Second Voice

[With squid laughter]
Peace?
Here human infants are craving for a single drop of milk
There the dog is busy emptying the big pot of milk
While some can't afford even a loin cloth, Some others don't even mind wasting a lot of silk

इस समाज की एक दवा है
आग और उत्क्रांति |
शांति !

तीसरा स्वर

हिंसा नहीं, हिंसा नहीं |
नर में छिपी जो आग है,
उसको न उतेजित करो,
जितना बने, संसार में माधुर्य, शीतलता भरो
|

है क्या उचित नर को चलाना
लाठियों के ज़ोर से?
सकता कभी हो व्यक्ति का
मन तृप्त नीति कठोर से?

बदला जगत का ध्येय,
साधन भी बदलना चाहिए,
तजकर घृणा, नर को
प्रणय पथ पर निकलना चाहिए|

बदलो मनुज को यों
कि वह अपनी कमी पहचान ले,
तुम चाहते जो कुछ,
मनुज उसको हृदय से मान ले |

जंजीर कसते हो जहाँ
वह आदमी की देह है,
बसता जहाँ मन, वह
बहुत भीतर हृदय का गेह है |
मन तक पहुँचने को नहीं
यह लौहमय रथ चाहिए,
इसके लिए तो गंध-स्यंदन,

While some are throwing away refined butter, some others can't afford even a simple meal,
The only medicine for this society is revolution and bullet.
Peace !

Third voice

No Violence, No Violence
Do not flare up the hidden fire in the human animal
As much as possible, fill the world with peace, love and compassion

Is it appropriate to drive the humanity with brute force?
Is the human mind ever going to be satisfied without liberty and freedom?
The end has changed and so should the means
There ought to be no place for hatred and humanity ought to proceed on to the path of love and compassion
Change the humanity in such a way so that people understand their weakness and voluntarily come forward to accept and do what may be expected from them

Brute force can only constrain the physical body however the mind and heart cannot be won by force

To win the mind, the power of gun and bullet is useless. The road to heart is made of the flowers of love on which only the

फूल का पथ चाहिए |

vehicle full of smell of compassion can run.

करके दलन नर में जगाओ
बंधु, प्रतिहिंसा नहीं |
हिंसा नहीं, हिंसा नहीं |

Stifling the human mind would only lead to violent reactions.
No violence, No Violence

चौथा स्वर

वृथा है यह पावन उपदेश |

हिंसा नर की मलिन वृति है,
किसको यह अविदित है?
नर के विमल शील की महिमा
किस पर नहीं विदित है?
किन्तु, शिला को भेद नहीं
पाती जब प्रेम - पुकार,
खुलता नहीं द्वार अंतर का,
विनय मानती हार |
तब मनुष्य की भुजा
पराजय वाणी की हरती है;
तोड़ लौह अर्गला
द्वार का उन्मोचन करती है |

हिंसा है तबतक
जबतक नर में पशुत्व है शेष |
व्यर्थ है यह पावन उपदेश |

Fourth Voice

This holy discourse is useless
Who doesn't know that violence is a negative vice of the humanity?
Who doesn't know the virtue of pure modesty and serenity?
However, when love calls fail to impress the brutes and become ineffective, the modesty gives up.

The use of force becomes inevitable when persuasion fails to achieve its goal. The bullet is used to break the locks of hindrances and to open the door to the destination.
As long as the untamed wild animal remains inside humans, violence cannot be completely ruled out.
This holy discourse is useless

कई स्वर
[समवेत गान]
भूख लगी है रोटी दो |
मन में नहीं प्रदीप हमारे, तन में दाहक आग,
हम न जानते हिंसा-प्रतिहिंसा का यह खटराग

Many Voices
[Chorus]
We are hungry, give us bread.
Our body is on fire and minds are dark. We don't care about violence and non-violence

Those whose stomachs are full can think whatever they feel like,

जिनका उदर पूर्ण हो
वे सोचें चाहे जो बात,
हम भूखों को सिर्फ चाहिए
एक वसन, दो भात |
भूख लगी है रोटी दो |

पाँचवाँ स्वर
[सोचने की मुद्रा में]
"भूख लगी है रोटी दो |"

कितनी कड़ी, मगर कितनी
सच्ची है यह आवाज
रोक सकेगा इसे कहाँ तक
कोई शाही ताज !
"भूख लगी है रोटी दो |"

सच है अगर लोग भूखे हैं,
भूख मिटानी ही होगी,
चाहे मिले जहाँ लेकिन,
रोटी तो लानी ही होगी

"भूख लगी है रोटी दो |"
सच तो है, रोटियां नहीं तो
क्या ये कविता खायेंगे?
थाली में धरकर विराट
कवियों के गीत चबायेंगे ?

छठा स्वर
इन घेरों को दूर करो |
मन के चारों ओर लकीरें,
नहीं सोचने भी दोगे ?
रोटी देकर क्या चिंतन का
भी अधिकार छीन लोगे ?
अजब मुसीबत! पहले तो
जन रोटी को बिललाता है,
और रोटियां मिली अगर
तो मन कैदी हो जाता है |
मन के ऊपर पड़े शिलामय

we the deprived ones need only
a piece of cloth and some grains
to sustain our body.
We are hungry, give us bread

Fifth Voice
[In contemplative mood]
"We are hungry, give us bread."

Hard fact but how true is this
voice! No government or
imperial force can stifle this
voice.
"We are hungry, give us bread."
Eradication of hunger shall have
to be the priority.
Whatever it would take to
eradicate hunger shall have to be
done.

"We are hungry, give us bread."
They can't eat poetry in place of
food. Poems of great poets and
great thinkers would not be able
to sustain their body.

Sixth Voice
Remove these boundaries.
Boundary all around my mind
and thoughts, won't you let me
even think? By giving me bread,
would you take away my right to
contemplate?
What the hell, people first cry
for food, however in the process
of taking care of the body, the
mind becomes enslaved.
Remove the ramparts of big
boulders around the mind.

प्राचीरों को चूर करो |
इन घेरों को दूर करो |

सातवां स्वर

चिन्तक, यह तेरा भ्रम है |

नहीं खींचते हम रेखाएं,
केवल राह बताते हैं,
बहके हुए विचारों को हम
ठीक बिन्दु पर लाते हैं |

चिंता सच्ची वही जो
कि जनजीवन में बल भरती है,
नर की बिखरी हुई शक्ति को
भू पर केन्द्रित करती है|

मिलती कौन वस्तु जन मन को
इधर-उधर भटकाने से?
पेट भरेगा कभी मनुज का
गीत स्वप्न का गाने से?

इस असंख्य भूखी जनता से
तेरी कला बड़ी है क्या?
जिस विलास का तू प्रेमी है ,
उसकी आज घड़ी है क्या?

पाप-पुण्य की कड़ी,
कल्पना नरक स्वर्ग की टूट चुकी,
देख,मनुज के नए भाग्य की
किरण गगन पर फूट चुकी|

इस मनुष्य का धर्म स्वेद है,
ईश्वर अविश्रान्त श्रम है,
समझ नहीं पता इसको तो

Remove these boundaries.

Seventh Voice

Thinker, it is your illusion.

We don't draw boundaries, we only show the path
We help set direction to the wandering thoughts and wild imaginations

The true concern is the one which empowers the society. It ought to help collect, concentrate and focus the unlimited power of human mind for peace and prosperity on earth.
Nothing can be achieved by thoughts strayed.
Physical hunger can't be satiated by singing dream songs of paradise
Is your thought and art more important than so many hungry people? Is it the time for such luxuries of which you are used to?

There is no place for discussion on sin and virtue, heaven and hell. Look, at the dawn of a new society and the fate of the new man.

Sweat is the religion for this new man and continuous labour is his god. If you can't understand this then it is your illusion.

चिन्तक, यह तेरा भ्रम है |

आठवां स्वर

समझता हूँ, लेकिन क्या करूं?

नीचे खिलते फूल और ऊपर जगमग तारे हैं,
मिट्टी और गगन मुझको तो दोनों ही प्यारे
हैं

मृति न हो तो मूल पुष्प का
किसमें करे निवास?
खिले कहाँ पर सुमन,
नहीं ऊपर हो यदि आकाश?

किन्तु, गरज उठती विपत्तियाँ
जिस दिन जनजीवन की,
कौन जानता व्यथा हाय,
उस दिन चिन्तक के मन की?

आँख फेर ले इस विपत्ति से,
ऐसा कौन कठोर ?
तन से बंधे कला, पर,
कैसे मन से नाता तोड़?

गगन भूमि में कैसे केवल
किसी एक को वरूँ ?
समझता हूँ, लेकिन क्या करूं?

कई स्वर
[समवेत]
रोटी और अभय भी दो |
तन को दो आहार अन्न का,

Eighth Voice
I do understand but what do I do?

There are flowers blooming on the ground and there are shining stars in the sky. For me, both ground and sky are lovely and beautiful.

If there is no ground, where would the roots of flower go? If there is no sky above, where would the flowers go to bloom?

However, the day the problems of the society start engulfing the humanity, the intellectual thinker's mind would be constrained to be in serious pain.

Who can be so rude and heartless to act blind to such a serious social problem? How can art and literature be associated with body and physical problems without being detached from thinking and mental process?
How can I choose only one between earth and sky?
I do understand but what do I do?

Many Voices
[Chorus]
Give us bread and give us freedom.

मन को चिंतन का अधिकार,
तन मन दोनों बढ़ें अगर तो
चमक उठे, सचमुच संसार |
बाधा मुक्त करो मानस को,
शंकारहित हृदय भी दो |

रोटी और अभय भी दो |

Let us have food for the body as well as freedom and liberty of thought. When the mind and body would be in sync then only it would be a truly blissful world. Remove all the boundaries of mind and remove the doubts from the heart.
Give us bread and give us freedom.

[करुण वाद्य संगीत]
कवि
विचारों की आँधी विकराल |
उठा रही मानस समुद्र में
चटुल ऊर्मि उताल |
हिला रही लाकर झकोर में
विश्व विटप की डाल |
टकरा रहे सपक्ष क्रुद्ध
आदर्शों से आदर्श,
चढ़ता ज्यों-ज्यों समय,
और बढ़ता जाता संघर्ष |
उड़ती हैं प्रत्येक दिशा में चिनगारियाँ कराल
|
विचारों की आँधी विकराल

[Sad Instrumental Music]
Poet
Mighty storm of thoughts and ideas. They are creating high tides in the ocean of the mental plane and are violently shaking the branches of the trees of the human world. Ideologies and beliefs are violently fighting with the counter ideologies and beliefs. These conflicts and struggle continue to increase as the time passes by and its sparks and splinters fly in all directions Mighty storm of thoughts and ideas.

[भीषण वाद्य संगीत | धमाके से युद्ध देवता के कूदने की आवाज और उसका अट्टहास|]

[Horrific instrumental music. Sound of war god jumping in with a bang and loud guffaw]

युद्ध देवता
झन झन झन झन झन झनन झनन
झन झन झन झन झन झनन झनन

War God
Jhan jhan jhan jhan jhan jhanan jhanan
Jhan jhan jhan jhan jhan jhanan jhanan

है बड़ा ज़ोर आदर्शों का
हलचल है खूब विचारों की,
चल रही रोज़ ही खोज
शांति के नए - नए आधारों की |
पर,देखें शांति महीतल पर
किस ओर क्षितिज से आती है,
मेरी कराल दंष्ट्राओं से
पृथ्वी कैसे बच पाती है ?
मेरी फुंकारो की ज्वाला,
देखें, करता है कौन शमन!
झन झन झन झन झन झनन झनन ||

There is a flurry of ideals and loud bustle of ideas.
The search for a path of peace and bliss has become an ongoing process. Oh, let me see how the peace descends on earth from horizon and how the earth is able to escape from my deadly venom.
Let me see who dares to douse the fire and venom in my hiss.
Jhan jhan jhan jhan jhan jhanan jhanan

मैं संग्रामों का देव
मही को मरघट करने आया हूँ,
नर के मन को विद्वेष,
घृणा, तृष्णा से भरने आया हूँ|
कहता हूँ, संचय करो,
लूट भी, चोरी भी अर्जन ही है,
जैसे भी पाओ विभव,
आत्मसुख का समस्त सर्जन ही है||
अपने विकास केलिए
किये जाओ समस्त भू का शोषण ||
झन झन झन झन झन झनन झनन ||

I am the god of wars and I have come down to turn the earth into a graveyard. I am here to fill the human mind with xenophobia, hatred and craving. I command to accumulate and hoard as much as possible as loot and theft, too, are all legitimate means of earning. The essence of self satisfaction is self gratification and personal interest. I command to exploit the nature to the hilt for selfish personal interest.
Jhan jhan jhan jhan jhan jhanan jhanan

मेरी शिक्षा का सार, एक
अपनेपन का सत्कार करो,
जो धर्म,जाति,कुल हो अपना,
तुम केवल उससे प्यार करो|
सबसे अच्छा विश्वास जिसे
तुमने पुरखों से पाया है,
सबसे अच्छा है धर्म वही
जिसको तुमने अपनाया है|
खुलकर विधर्मियों पर करते

The essence of my teaching is to guard the selfish personal interest. You ought to love only your own creed, caste, clan and race. The best belief is the one that you inherited and the best religion is the one that you have adopted. You must openly fight and destroy all those who do not

जाओ हालाहल का वर्षण।
झन झन झन झन झन झनन झनन ॥

तुम जिसे मानते आये हो,
उद्देश्य सभी से अच्छा है,
जन्मे हो जहाँ,जगत भर में
वह देश सभी से अच्छा है।
तुम सर्वश्रेष्ठ हो जाति,
सदा यह हठ पवित्र करते जाओ,
इस अहंकार के पालन में
मारते और मरते जाओ ।
जो नहीं मानता हो तुमको,
ठानो उस अभिमानी से रण।
झन झन झन झन झन झनन झनन ॥

मेरा संकल्प महा वसुधा को
एक नहीं होने दूंगा,
मैं विश्व देवता का भू पर
अभिषेक नहीं होने दूंगा॥
रेखाएं खींच महीतल के
सौ खंड युक्ति से काटे हैं,
देशों में अलग अलग झंडे
मैंने न व्यर्थ ही बाँटे हैं।
इन झंडों के नीचे पृथ्वी
भोगती रहे अंगच्छेदन ।
झन झन झन झन झन झनन झनन ॥

हैं कहाँ विश्व मानव? जो हैं
केवल स्वदेश के प्राणी हैं ।
मानवता नहीं, मातृभू की
महिमा के सब अभिमानी हैं ॥
जबतक ये झंडे फहर रहे,
अभिमान नहीं वह सोता है ।
देखें तो, तबतक विश्व मनुज का
जन्म कहाँ से होता है ?
मैं राष्ट्रवाद का सखा,

accept your religion and your way of life.
Jhan jhan jhan jhan jhan jhanan jhanan

The objective, goal and the cause that you have adopted is the best. The country you were born in is the best in the world.

Insist and persist on declaring your race as the most exalted and fight with those who refuse to accept you as the best and most honourable.
Jhan jhan jhan jhan jhan jhanan jhanan

I have resolved not to let the world unite. I would not let the global religion and god to incarnate on this planet. I have tactfully drawn the boundaries to divide the globe in hundreds of blocks. I have distributed separate national flags to all countries for a purpose so that the earth keeps on facing the wound of prick, cut and jab.
Jhan jhan jhan jhan jhan jhanan jhanan

Where are the global citizens? Everyone around here is a nationalist and patriot. They are all proud of their motherland but do not bother about the humanity as a whole. As long as these national flags are flying high and the pride of

कौन तोड़ेगा मेरा सम्मोहन ?
  झन झन झन झन झन झनन झनन ॥

[अट्टहास करता है | पृथ्वी के कराहने की
आवाज |]

कवि

यह प्रदाह! यह रोर भयानक!
यह वेदना अशेष!
तू भी होगा सखा युद्ध का मेरे प्यारे देश?

तृष्णा की पंकिल तरंग में
तू भी खो जायेगा?
या तेरा शुभ कलश
कमल - सा ऊपर लहरायेगा ?

पड़कर इस भीषण झकोर में
धीरज पाल सकेगा?
वसुधा को विष के विवर्त से
वीर! निकाल सकेगा?

शंकाएँ हैं बहुत, मगर,
तब भी यह बात सही है,
दुनियां तेरी ओर
किसी आशा से ताक रही है |

चन्दन के रथ पर चढ़कर आनेवाला यह
देश,
सब कहते हैं, लाया है कोई नवीन सन्देश |

nationalism is not going to ebb out, let us see from where the global citizen incarnates on this planet? I encourage the pride of nationalism and let me see who dares to break this hypnotic charm of mine?

Jhan jhan jhan jhan jhan jhanan jhanan

[Guffaws with a roar. The sound of groaning of earth]

Poet

Oh! This burning, this animosity and this endless pain! O my loving country, you too would be part of the conflicts and wars?

You, too, would lose your identity in the turbid wave of desires and cravings or would your auspicious pinnacle float above this turbid water like a lotus?

Would you be able to keep patience in this storm? O strong willed soul, would you be able to extricate this planet from the whirlpool of poison?

Despite so many ifs, buts and doubts, the fact remains that the world is looking towards you with hope and expectations.

People say that this country, the one which has come so far on the vehicle of spirituality and wisdom like the smell of sandal has brought a new message for the world.

मूक न रह, टूक बोल, हिमालय !
लोचन के पट खोल, हिमालय !
अबकी बार जगत पायेगा
मंत्र कौन अनमोल हिमालय !

जिस युग का विज्ञान वह्नि हो,
विद्या धन की दासी हो,

जिसका शिल्प मृत्यु-पूजक,
सभ्यता रुधिर की प्यासी हो।

उस युग का कल्याण कहाँ है?
दुःख से उसका त्राण कहाँ है?

मूंदे जिसने नयन धर्म से
फिर उसका उत्थान कहाँ है?

भागी जाती ज्योति,
ज्ञान करता किसकी रखवाली है?
सबकुछ पाकर भी मनुष्य क्यों
इतना खाली खाली है?

यह रहस्य बतलायेगा क्या?
शंका - तिमिर हटायेगा क्या?
उलट गया जो दीप उसे
सीधा करके दिखलायेगा क्या?

Please break up your silence and speak up Himalay!
O Himalay, please open your eyes and tell us what priceless mantra the world is going to get this time.
The era in which the technology is being used for destruction and wisdom has become subservient to commercialism where the art is oriented towards death and destruction and the culture is thirsty of blood
In such a time, what is the formula for peace and welfare? What are the tools to help such a time to come out of misery and sorrow
What is the formula for progress and prosperity of the society which has deliberately closed its eyes to the true religion?

What the wisdom is guarding as the enlightenment is fading away from human consciousness? Why is the humanity feeling so empty and lonely despite having gained and accumulated so much?
Would you please solve this mystery? Would you clear the darkness of doubt? Can you set right the source of light which has got inverted?
O Yogeshwar, why is there so much of disturbance, unrest,

योगेश्वर ! क्यों मची हुई
इतनी अशांति भारी है?
ले जाने को कहाँ जगत को
युग की तैयारी है?

[पहाड़ के फटने की आवाज]

हिमालय

(१)

लिए अंतर में व्यथा अथाह ।
हम भी तो दिन-रात
यही सोचा करते हैं मौन,
पृथ्वी पर अवतरित हुआ
आलोक नया यह कौन?
पाकर जिसे बढ़ी जाती है
और अधिक उद्भ्रान्ति,
अंधकार के साथ
दूर भागी जाती है शांति ।
चढ़ता ज्यों ज्यों समय
और बढ़ता है हाहाकार ।
बड़ी विपद में आन फंसा है,
सचमुच ही, संसार ।

(२)

दिशाओं में किरणों की धूम,
धौंकता किरणों से आकाश,
गगन के रंध्र रंध्र में बसा
नए युग का प्रज्ज्वलित प्रकाश।

जहाँ थी पहले थोड़ी छाँह,
कुञ्ज वे फूलों के भी गए,
कहीं पर भी द्वाभा का लेश
नहीं छोड़ेंगे पंडित नए ।

रहस्यों में करती विश्लेष
चली दुनिया ऐसी मग से,
महीतल से रूठी गोधुलि,
चांदनी विदा हुई जग से ।

disorder and mayhem? Where is the time preparing to lead the world to?

[The sound of bursting of the Mountain]

Himalay

(1)

Silently, I too, have been thinking of this with a deep sense of anguish and pain What kind of light and knowledge is this which has been driving the peace away from the planet along with the darkness and because of which there is more of illusion and confusion. With every passing day, the chaos and outcry has been increasing. Oh, the world has got engulfed in a deep trouble.

(2)

All the directions and every corner of the sky is shining with the rays of the brilliant light of the new era.

The flower gardens where one could get some shade to rest have been destroyed. The economic planners of the new world would not leave even an iota of the nature unblemished.

The world has adopted such a path of analysis and dissection that there is no place left for imagination, creativity and romanticism

धूप का ऐसा तना वितान,
अँधेरा कठिनाई में फँसा,
भागने को न मिली जब राह,
आदमी के भीतर जा बसा|

सघन जब हो उठता है तिमिर,
दृष्टि कुछ देख न पाती है,
ज्योति भी होकर सीमातीत
अन्धता ही उपजाती है|

एक काली होती अन्धता,
ज्योति से पलती है दूर,
एक उजली होती जो सदा
ज्ञान से ही रहती है चूर|

आज जो लगी हुई है आग,
ज्ञान के घर से आयी है,
जगत की आँखों पर रोशनी
अन्धता बनकर छाई है|

(3)

कभी सोचा भी है तुम क्या हो?
बल के अहंकार में भूले,
भरे नित्य रहते हो,
सुनता हूँ अपने को अपना
ईश्वर भी कहते हो

करते हो बन दास
यन्त्र चक्रों की नित्य गुलामी |
किन्तु प्रकृति का कहते हो
अपने को जेता-स्वामी |

The scientific knowledge is being applied in such a manner that it has cornered the darkness. When the darkness could not find a place to hide outside, it decided to run and camp inside the heart and mind of the humanity.

When the darkness is very intense and the eyes are unable to see anything, at that point of time even the endless light too leads to blindness

There is one dark blindness which is actually devoid of any light however there is another white blindness which is caused due to knowledge without wisdom and modesty.

The fire that is burning the world today has originated from the materialistic modern knowledge. The intense light of this modern knowledge has blinded the eyes of the world.

(3)

Have you ever thought of who you are?

You are perennially enjoying your ignorance under the influence of ego and false pride of your power and might. I hear that you also claim to be your own god.

You have totally enslaved yourself to the comforts made available by the machines and devices and can't live without it even for a day however you

नगरों को निर्मल रखने का
ऐसा ढंग निकाला,
नदियों को कलुषित,
समुद्र तक तो दूषित कर डाला |

जीव-जंतु को नशा ,
स्वच्छ कर डाला विपिन गहन को,
सब निचोड़ निस्तैल
किये जा रहे मही के तन को ||

लक्ष लक्ष वर्षों के संचित
खनिज लूट क्रम क्रम से,
किये जा रहे रिक्त हृदय
वसुधा का तुम निर्मम से |
धरती का अंतर खंगालना
ही अब बड़ी प्रगति है,
हरियालियाँ जला कर ही अब
करता जग उन्नति है|

यह संतुलन विनाश प्रकृति का
वृथा नहीं जायेगा,
आज दुखी है मनुज और
कल निश्चय पछतायेगा|

करते नहीं प्रहार प्रकृति पर,
गढ़ते क्लेश नया हो |

कभी सोचा भी है तुम क्या हो?

(४)
युगों में अद्भुत रूप तुम्हारा !

claim yourself to be the master of nature.

The method that you have devised to keep your cities clean has not only besmirched the rivers but has polluted even the ocean.

You have destroyed the flora and fauna and have cleaned up and cleared the dense forests.
You have been squeezing and draining the body of this earth of all its natural resources.
You have systematically been ravaging the minerals formed over millions of years. You have ruthlessly and recklessly been emptying the heart of the earth.
Exploring the inside of the earth has now become a symbol of progress and development. The current model of development is based on destruction of the greenery and environment.

Man will have to pay seriously for this destruction of the environment and imbalance in nature. The humanity is already in grief and its coming generations would repent for what their forefathers did.
You are not destroying the nature but inviting a new calamity for humanity.
Have you ever thought of who you are?

(4)

भू पर तुम सा विज्ञ मूढ़
पहले न कभी आया था,
वसुधा पर अँधा प्रकाश यह
कभी नहीं छाया था|

नहीं वंशधर तुम अतीत के,
नूतन योनि अपर हो,

जो न कभी पहले जन्मा था
वो बौद्धिक बर्बर हो|

ज्ञान तुम्हारा अन्धकार है,
किरण तुम्हारी तम है
धर्म तुम्हारा ध्वंस,
पूज्य देवता तुम्हारा यम है|

छाने तुमने अमित लोक, पर,
मन को कभी न छाना,
अगणित आविष्कार किये,
पर, अपना मर्म न जाना |

दृश्य-दृश्य रटते-रटते
कुछ ऐसे दृश्य हुए तुम,
आत्मदेवता के मंदिर में
भी अस्पृश्य हुए तुम |

छूट गयी भाषा अदृश्य की
अकथ कथा कहने की,
बकते बकते भूल गए तुम
महिमा चुप रहने की|

Never ever saw someone so weird like you.

Never before such a knowledgeable idiot like you came on earth. The earth never earlier had this kind of blind knowledge without wisdom.

You have not evolved from the past. You are a totally new and unique breed. The intellectual barbarian like the present day humanity had never earlier been born on this planet.

Your knowledge is the reason of your gloom. Your light is leading you to darkness. Destruction is your religion and the god of death has become your deity.

You have been searching the whole universe but never explored on your own mind. You have made so many inventions and discoveries but could never understand your own truth.

Because of your sustained materialistic objectivity, you yourself have become an object and as a result you have become incapable to understand the essence of your own truth and self.

You have lost the spiritual language to describe the absolute truth. You have forgotten the importance of silence as a result of your blabbering.

सततचारियों ! कभी-कभी
रुक जाने में भी सुख है,
अहंकार को भूल
कहीं झुक जाने में भी सुख है |
देख लिया नीचे पृथ्वी
ऊपर अनंत अम्बर है,
अब तो मानचित्र में खोजो,
कहाँ तुम्हारा घर है|

जान चुके, कर दौड़-धूप
कुछ और न जान सकोगे,
अब आगे का भेद
ठहरकर ही पहचान सकोगे|

बिना रुके मिलता न शांति का
शीतल कूल-किनारा |
युगों में अद्भुत रूप तुम्हारा !

You have been running continuously forgetting the pleasure of stopping and looking back. The real happiness is derived only when you forget your ego and adopt humility and modesty.

You have already searched the earth and the endless sky. Now, stop and look for your actual home on the map of the universe.

You have been running around a lot however you won't get much by continuing to run around. Further deeper mysteries of the cosmos and the spiritual realm would be revealed to you only if you stop and contemplate. Understand that you can't get peace and tranquility unless you stop and let go of your ego.

Never ever saw someone so weird like you.

(५)

कहें भी तो उससे क्या बात?
अभी भूख से ही जो प्राणी
तड़प रहा दिन-रात,
रोटी के चिंता में कटते जिसके सायं-प्रात |

दहक रहे भीषण क्षुधाग्नि से
जिसके प्राण अभागे,
निर्दय है, दर्शन परोसता
है जो उसके आगे |

(5)

What can we say to those?

Those who are cursed to live in hunger and poverty and those for whom food to sustain the body is the one and only problem to solve so that they can continue to live.

Only a cruel merciless person can talk of philosophy and ideology in front of those unfortunate people whose life and soul is burning with the flames of hunger.

रोटी दो, मत उसे गीत दो,
जिसको भूख लगी है,
भूखों में दर्शन उभारना
छल है, दगा, ठगी है।

रोटी और वसन ये जीवन
के सोपान प्रथम हैं,
नवयुग के चिंतको !
तुम्हे इसमे भी कोई भ्रम है?
व्यष्टि-समष्टि विवाद व्यर्थ है,
झगड़ा मनमाना है,

है समष्टि ही हार,
व्यक्ति तो मोती का दाना है।
बूंदे जब गिरतीं समुद्र में,
व्यथा कौन पाती हैं?
सागर से मिलकर अगाध
सागर ही बन जाती हैं।

आते सारे भाव व्यक्तियों
के समाज से छनकर,
पुनः लौट जाते समष्टि में
ही वे गायन बनकर ।

जैसे मेघ धरा से उठकर
अम्बर पर घिरता है,
और वारि बन वसुधा के
ही तन पर गिरता है।

जहाँ व्यष्टि स्वाधीन अधिक है,
नाश वहां छायेगा,
अनुशासन के बिना व्यक्ति
कुछ प्राप्त न कर पायेगा।

Provide food and not philosophy to those who are hungry. Talking of philosophy and spirituality before the hungry and poor is deceit, fraud and cheating.

Food and clothes are the basic necessities of life. O thinkers of the new era, do you have a doubt even in this fact?

The debate on individualism, capitalism and socialism is arbitrary and of no importance. The individuals are like the beads of pearl in the garland of the society.

When a drop falls in the ocean, it need not feel any pain in this process. A small drop becomes an endless ocean by falling into the ocean.

All the inputs to an individual capitalist comes from the society and all his outputs go back to the society after he adds his superior skills, efforts and knowledge in it.

It is like the clouds in a water cycle which start from the earth, rise up in the sky and then fall back on the surface of the earth in the form of rain.

Where individual capitalists are left completely free without any social accountability and responsibility for the society, that society is definitely doomed as nothing can be achieved without any discipline and rule.

झुक समष्टि के सम्मुख जिस दिन
व्यष्टि दान देती है,
तभी व्यक्ति के भीतर करुणा
विनय जन्म लेती है |

भरो विश्व-सर में करुणा के
कमल सहज अवदात |
कहें भी तो उससे क्या बात?

(६)

वृथा मत लो भारत का नाम।
मानचित्र में जो मिलता है,
नहीं देश भारत है,
भू पर नहीं, मनों में ही, बस,
कहीं शेष भारत है।

भारत एक स्वप्न,
भू को ऊपर ले जानेवाला,
भारत एक विचार,
स्वर्ग को भू पर लानेवाला।
भारत एक भाव, जिसको
पाकर मनुष्य जगता है,
भारत एक जलज, जिस पर
जल का न दाग लगता है।
भारत है संज्ञा विराग की,
उज्ज्वल आत्म उदय की,
भारत है आभा मनुष्य की
सबसे बड़ी विजय की,

भारत है भावना दाह
जग-जीवन का हरने की,
भारत है कल्पना मनुज को
राग-मुक्त करने की।

The compassion and modesty
originates in the heart and mind
of an individual when he bows
before the society and pledges to
give.
Fill the pond of human world
with the spotless and holy lotus
of compassion and voluntary
pledge to give for the poor and
deprived in the society.
What can we say to those?

(6)

Talk not of India without
knowing of it. What is found on
the map of the world is not
India. India is left only in the
minds of some people. It is not
to be found within the
geographical boundary on the
earth with the same name.

India is a dream for progress and
prosperity on earth.
India is a thought to bring the
paradise on earth.
India is a feeling which awakens
and enlightens humanity. India
is the concept of detached action
like a lotus which does not get
wet despite being in water.
India is the name of sacrifice and
active renunciation. It is the
name of self purification and self
realization. It is the aura of the
ultimate achievement and
victory of the humanity.
India is the feeling to rid the
humanity of misery and sorrow.
India is the imagination to
liberate the humanity from the
bondage of cravings and desires.

जहां कहीं एकता अखण्डित,
जहां प्रेम का स्वर है,
देश-देश में खड़ा वहां
भारत जीवित, भास्वर है।
भारत वहां जहां जीवन-
साधना नहीं है भ्रम में,
धाराओं को समाधान है
मिला हुआ संगम में।

जहां त्याग माधुर्यपूर्ण हो,
जहां भोग निष्काम,
समरस हो कामना,
वहीं भारत को करो प्रणाम।
वृथा मत लो भारत का नाम।

(७)

साधना इस व्रत की भारी।
पग पग पर हिंसा की ज्वाला
चारों ओर गरल है।
मन को बांध शांति का पालन
करना नहीं सरल है।

तब भी जो नर-वीर
असिव्रत दारुण पाल सकेंगे,
वसुधा को विष के विवर्त से
वही निकाल सकेंगे।
मना रहे क्यों, यह व्रतपाली
केवल भारत होगा?
शेष विश्व हिंसा -लिप्सा में,
इसी भांति, रत होगा?

Wherever and whenever there is complete brotherhood and love amongst the people; India is present and living in all such countries and societies

India is the place where there is no confusion about the purpose and direction of life. India is the place where diverse cultures coexist and unite to facilitate a Happy and Healthy human life.

India is where renunciation and sacrifice is with love and compassion, where enjoyment and indulgence is with a sense of detachment and where mind is in a state of equanimity. Bow to India at such a place.

Talk not of India without knowing of it.

(7)

The vow of this holy duty is a daunting task. The fire of violence is on every step and there is poison all around. It is not easy to control the mind and continue to progress on the path of peace.

Only those strong willed humans, who can voluntarily adopt painful austerity, would succeed in extricating the planet from the whirlpool of poison. Why you think that only Indians can adopt such ascetic austerity? Would the rest of the world continue to be indulged in

किसी एक को नहीं, बदलना
होगा साथ सभी को,
करना होगा ग्रहण शील
भारत का निखिल मही को|

शमित करेगा कौन वह्नि
प्रहरी का जाल बिछाकर?
रोकेगा विस्फोट विश्व को
बल से कौन दबाकर?

तब उतरेगी शांति, मनुज का
मन जब कोमल होगा,
जहाँ आज है गरल, वहाँ
शीतल गंगाजल होगा |
देश देश में जाग उठेंगे
जिस दिन सब नर-नारी
साधना इस व्रत की भारी |

(८)
धर्म को, श्रद्धा को मत त्यागो|
शील मुकुट नरता का,
सबसे बड़ी भव्यता का है,
नहीं धर्म से बढ़कर कोई मित्र सभ्यता का
है|

निरी बुद्धि के लिए
भावना का मत दलन करो रे !
जो अदृश्य प्रहरी है,
उससे भी तो कभी डरो रे !

violence, gluttony, cravings and desires?
Not a single one but everyone will have to change simultaneously. The whole world shall have to adopt the spiritual characteristics of India. No one can douse the fire by policing the whole planet. No one can prevent the blast across the globe by force.

The peace would dawn only when the global human consciousness would adopt tolerance and clemency or in other words the cool waters of Ganges would replace the poison of anger, hatred, greed, envy and desire. It will happen only when the entire humanity would awaken.
The vow of this holy duty is a daunting.

(8)
Do not let go of the faith and true religion.
Morality and ethics are the crown virtue of humanity and its greatest magnificence. There is no substitute and alternative for the true religion for the human culture
Do not stifle the feelings of heart for the mere intellectualism. Feel and sense the invisible god protecting and securing everything all around and fall in love with it. (There is

no need to fear god. God ought to be loved, not feared)

शांति चाहते हो तो पहले
सुमति शुन्य से माँगो,
नवयुग के प्राणियों!
उर्ध्वमुख जागो, जागो, जागो।
धर्म को, श्रद्धा को मत त्यागो।

If you want peace, prey for wisdom and understanding of truth from the cosmos. O humans of the new era; look upwards and wake up.

Do not let go of the faith and true religion.

ABOUT THE BOOK

"Technology for Revolution: Opportunity for a New Religion and a New Society" is a treatise on religious and social reform. It is an attempt to create a route map to a HAPPY, HEALTHY, PEACEFUL, PROGRESSIVE, PROSPEROUS, CREATIVE AND CONSTRUCTIVE world. The book advocates that ultimate social peace and individual mental bliss and freedom cannot be achieved without adopting a spiritual way of life with a sense of justice. It explores the issues with which the human society is afflicted at present and then goes on to suggest a new model of governance and administration utilizing the opportunities made available by the changes in the information and communication technology.

The author suggests that the root cause of almost all the sociopolitical issues are linked to the degeneration and corruption in the religious and spiritual values resulting in an overall degradation of the social ethics. It delves deep into the issue of corruption and degeneration of all the religious practices across the globe. It exposes how religious practices have completely abandoned Truth, God and Spirituality and has embraced blatant commercialism in the name of God and faith. It then explores the effects of this spiritual and religious degeneration in the sociopolitical and administrative arena taking examples and references mainly from the Indian society.

Having explored the problem and its root cause in detail, the book presents a comprehensive universal and global manifesto for governance and administration applicable to the humanity as a whole. It combines the concepts of social and economic justice of Karl Marx, the concepts of Ram Rajya of Mahatma Gandhi, the concepts of human equality of Mandela and Martin Luther King Jr and the concepts of universal brotherhood and global citizenship. It then blends them all with the spiritual teachings of Buddha, Socrates, Kabir and Osho Rajneesh.

The universal and global manifesto for humanity as a whole presented in this book envisions the creation of a happy, healthy, peaceful, progressive, prosperous, creative and constructive world. The ideals and optimism projected through this manifesto might initially appear to be "Utopian" in nature; however, considering the opportunities made available by the advancements in technology in general and information and communication technology in particular and after going through the detailed explanations presented with every point in the manifesto, a reader may feel compelled to add his own efforts towards the goals envisioned in this book. The innovative solutions suggested in the manifesto eliminates the need to have departments like the anti-corruption, vigilance, election observers, tax collection departments etc. in government and administration and would automatically cleanup the muck in politics and public life.

The book also has the potential to generate controversy as it has ruthlessly dissected the commercialism, irrationality and evils in almost all the major religious practices across the globe. The author is aware of the dangerous consequences as a result of his direct attack on the people running their massive business empires in the name of religion; however, he seems to be prepared to face the consequences similar to what Socrates, Meera or Mansur al Hallaj had to face. Considering what Salman Rushdie or Taslima Nasreen had to go through for much more subtle expressions, the author is likely to be inviting a serious trouble for himself despite his pious and altruistic motives behind writing whatever he has presented through this book.

हरि ॐ तत्सत्